The Pace of Modernity

Anamnesis

Anamnesis means remembrance or reminiscence, the collection and re-collection of what has been lost, forgotten, or effaced. It is therefore a matter of the very old, of what has made us who we are. But *anamnesis* is also a work that transforms its subject, always producing something new. To recollect the old, to produce the new: that is the task of *Anamnesis*.

a re.press series

The Pace of Modernity:
Reading With Blumenberg

O. Bradley Bassler

re.press Melbourne 2012

re.press

PO Box 40, Prahran, 3181, Melbourne, Australia
http://www.re-press.org

© re.press & O. Bradley Bassler 2012

The moral rights of the author are automatically asserted and recognized under Australian law (*Copyright Amendment [Moral Rights] Act 2000*)

This work is 'Open Access', published under a creative commons license which means that you are free to copy, distribute, display, and perform the work as long as you clearly attribute the work to the authors, that you do not use this work for any commercial gain in any form whatsoever and that you in no way alter, transform or build on the work outside of its use in normal academic scholarship without express permission of the author (or their executors) *and* the publisher of this volume. For any reuse or distribution, you must make clear to others the license terms of this work. For more information see the details of the creative commons licence at this website:
http://creativecommons.org/licenses/by-nc-nd/2.5/

National Library of Australia Cataloguing-in-Publication Data

Bassler, O. Bradley.
The pace of modernity : reading with Blumenberg
/ O. Bradley Bassler.

9780987268228 (pbk.)

Series: Anamnesis.
Includes bibliographical references.

Subjects: Blumenberg, Hans.
Civilization, Modern.
Philosophy, Modern.

901

Designed and Typeset by *A&R*

This book is produced sustainably using plantation timber, and printed in the destination market reducing wastage and excess transport.

Contents

Acknowledgements vii
Abbreviations ix
Introduction: Modernity's Runaway Pace 13
1. Theology and the Modern Age: Blumenberg's Reaction to A Baconian Frontispiece 35
2. At What Cost Modernity: Mental Faculties and Total Politics 61
3. The New Poetry and The Mimetic Locus 77
4. Jean Starobinski's Linguistic Modernism 93
5. Daily Rhythms 113
6. Divagation at the Crossroads: In Search of Modern Wisdom 139
7. Visionary Design: Mathematical Analogues for The Reading Of Poetry 161
8. The Outlook for Legitimacy and The Pace of Modernity 187
9. Convexity and Complexity: Trading Places With John Ashbery 205
Bibliography 217

HANS BLUMENBERG

13 July 1920 Lübeck – 28 March 1996 Altenberge

Acknowledgements

The author gratefully acknowledges a grant from the Willson Center for the Humanities at the University of Georgia.

Abbreviations

AI	Harold Bloom, *The Anxiety of Influence*
AILWL	Harold Bloom, *The Anatomy of Influence: Literature as a Way of Life*
AR	Jean Starobinski, *Action and Reaction: The Life and Adventures of a Couple*
CES	Edmund Husserl, *The Crisis of the European Sciences*
LM	Hannah Arendt, *The Life of the Mind* (2 vols.)
LMA	Hans Blumenberg, *The Legitimacy of the Modern Age*
LL	Robert Venturi et al., *Learning from Las Vegas*
LW	Hans Blumenberg, *Lebenszeit und Weltzeit*
M	Hans Blumenberg, *Matthäuspassion*
MM	Harold Bloom, *A Map of Misreading*
NTAP	Angus Fletcher, *A New Theory for American Poetry: Democracy, the Environment, and the Future of the Imagination*
OT	Hannah Arendt, *The Origins of Totalitarianism*
SPCM	John Ashbery, *Self-Portrait in a Convex Mirror*
SW	Sergei Eisenstein, *Selected Works* (3 vols.)
TP	John Ashbery, *Three Poems*
TSM	Angus Fletcher, *Time, Space and Motion in the Age of Shakespeare*
WW	Harold Bloom, *Where Shall Wisdom Be Found?*

There is nothing to be done, you must grow up, the outer rhythm more and more accelerate, past the ideal rhythm of the spheres that seemed to dictate you, that seemed the establishment of your seed and the conditions of its growing, upward, someday into leaves and fruition and final sap. For it is to be transcended... .

— John Ashbery, "The New Spirit"

Introduction:
Modernity's Runaway Pace

The inescapable attribute of our time is its runaway pace. So begins Gyorgy Kepes' 1965 introduction to a volume on "The Nature and Art of Motion."[1] Kepes' prose is exemplary of a certain attitude toward technology which dominated the era of the Cold War and, more particularly, the growingly critical reception of those trends in the art world—such as Bauhaus—which had rested on a positive valuation of technology for the future of art. Kepes continues in the vein of dystopic description laced by a strong dose of fascination for the technologically spectacular:

> Tidal waves of traffic pound us; sprawling cities and exploding populations squeeze us. Wildly erratic throbbing migrations—the daily shuttle from home to work, from work to home, the weekend surge from city to country and from country to city, the punctuations of rush-hour deadlocks—toss us in an accelerating rhythm barely within our control. Streams of speeding objects—motorcars, airplanes, intercontinental missiles, orbiting space capsules—weave a rapidly changing fabric all around us with patterns of spiraling velocities. At night, the reassuring calm of the firmament is blotted out by our cities, which are transformed into giant circuses where darting headlights, winking traffic lights, glittering, gaudy displays, and advertising signs whirl and swirl and pirouette in frantic competition for our attention.[2]

Human reality seems sucked into a giant historical updating of the vortex we find in Edgar Allen Poe's "A Descent into the Maelstrom."[3] Kepes' vocabulary emphasizes those aspects of modernity's pace—pounding, sprawling, squeezing, throbbing, shuttling, speeding, darting—which intimate the scarcely controllable energy of its forward motion. But while the tone in which Kepes depicts technological exotica may now itself feel somewhat dated, the condition he indicates is one which continues, and indeed itself *accelerates.*

---

1. Gyorgy Kepes, ed., *The Nature and Art of Motion* (New York: George Braziller, 1965), i.
2. ibid.
3. Edgar Allan Poe, *Poetry, Tales, & Selected Essays* (New York: Library of America College Edition, 1996), 432-48.

Even earlier, Paul Valéry isolated it in a more purified form in "*My Faust*" when Faust declares that

> The individual is dying. He is drowning in numbers. The accumulation of human beings is effacing all distinction. There's only a hairsbreadth of difference now between vice and virtue; the two are melted into the mass which is called "human material."[4]

The overstepping of human pace has a long modern history which can be traced back at least as far as we can trace the Faust legend, which is to say, anteceding modernity. But even though we can trace classical antecedents of the Faust myth, especially in the myth of Prometheus, so there also seems to be something peculiarly modern about Faustian overstepping: so much so that Oswald Spengler was led to speak of a Faustian epoch. What matters to me more immediately is the way in which Valéry helps us to link the phenomenon of overstepping human bounds to the tyranny of the numerical. "Humanity" is replaced by a "human material" which is fundamentally *demographic*, and in demographics it is the statistics, the numbers, which count. Paradoxically, a dynamic surplus of acceleration washes out into the static statistical tables of modern polling. But how else could we handle it? This book seeks an alternative, one that would promote tools for a dynamic "handling" of the pace of modernity.

In the face of such an arithmetization, philosophical efforts aimed at a reconstruction of the possibility of meaning or at the reacquisition of "being" will inevitably be culturally susceptible to the sorts of withering negation we find represented in the most ideological forms of advanced (or, equivalently, "post"-) modernism. The problem here is the same one we find repeatedly expressed in the political domain: everyone seems to know what the problem is, but no one knows how to fix it. Valéry, in the passage cited above, at least helps us to see why this might be so. Traditional distinctions—between virtue and vice, between being and illusion—are drowned in the very problem we would invoke them to counter. In this case, the first approach to the advanced state in which we find ourselves must be to enlist ever more powerful (because more pointedly sophisticated) vocabularies to deal with the problem of pacing, of keeping up with the numbers. The first step in redressing the pace of modernity, then, will involve the construction of a preliminary craft for the navigation of modernity's vortical dynamics, one that, like the narrator's barrel in Poe's tale, enlists the force of the vortex to accomplish our ascent from it, and the telling of the tale.[5]

---

4. Paul Valéry, "My Faust," in Paul Valéry, *Plays*, trans. David Paul and Robert Fitzgerald, Volume III of the *Collected Works of Paul Valéry* and Volume XLV in the Bollingen Series (New York: Bollingen, 1960), 38.

5. Edgar Allan Poe, "A Descent Into The Maelstrom," in *Poetry, Tales & Selected Essays*, 447. Poe invokes William of Moerbeke's translation of Archimedes' dynamics, "De Incidentibus in Fluido," Book Two. The original Greek text was first available only in

A certain empirical flexibility recommends itself in such an enterprise, to be supplied by the consideration of a variety of efforts with implications for the vocabulary of pacing. We need to begin with the rudiments of pace: forward and backward motion, linear versus circular motion, speeding up and slowing down. The chapters through the early to middle part of this volume will chart us along the trajectory from initiating (Chapter 2) to space, time, and motion (Chapter 3) through motive impact and force (Chapter 4) and into the subtler complications of motive rhythms (Chapter 5). Confronting these basic building blocks for a vocabulary of pacing already requires careful coordination in dealing with the various dimensions—literary, political, philosophical, and theological, to name a few—of the modern cultural climate. Consequently, I proceed by reading a number of efforts in the intellectual analysis of cultural, and in particular the aesthetic and philosophical, domains, all of them keyed to various problems we face in that contemporary condition I insist on continuing to refer to as modernity. There was a prominent linguistic "turn" in twentieth century philosophy, and linguistic tools will play a prominent role here. But we must equally acknowledge with full seriousness the capacity to overstress language at the expense of other, even when cooperative, forms of engagement in the world—in particular engagement through perception and action. My work will pivot upon the work of Hans Blumenberg, simply because it still presents the most advanced reflections on the set of problems we all face, and which I hope to continue facing in this book. The book is not intended as work *on*, but rather *with* Blumenberg: the goal will be to follow leads in his work, along with other figures, to establish a sense of modernity's pace.

At the heart of any attempt to account for the pace of modernity must lie the treatment of acceleration. Were this book to have a thesis, it would need to exemplify the observation that while in modern society our roads are governed by speed limits, there are no stated limits placed on *acceleration*. We know that massive acceleration cannot be sustained over a long haul without violating the limit set on speed, and we leave it at that. Road racers are still allowed to soup up their cars to make the fastest 0 to 60 mph they can. This is not merely an observation about vehicular transportation, however, nor is it one which loses any of its purchase on those who would violate the speed limit, as we all do from time to time. Our society is predicated on principles of *efficient* action, and this requires repeated acceleration to a stable speed at which we remain for some length of time. Alarm clocks are designed to wake us in *timely* fashion, meaning both: at a given time, and usually with just enough time to make it to work *on time*. An efficient society is predicated on workers accelerating to peak efficiency and remaining there as efficiently as possible.

1899, long after Poe's death. For a modern treatment, see E. J. Diksterhuis, *Archimedes* (Princeton: Princeton, 1987), 373-398.

This is the "theory," of course, and we all know that we typically operate at anything but peak efficiency. Indeed, we are often right to ask ourselves how everything works as well as it does when there is such manifest *inefficiency* in the workplace: tangles of everything from paperwork to contradictory regulations to double standards to good, old-fashioned tape. Here is where statistical principles enter in. Human nature is not by its nature efficient, and we should never expect it (thankfully) to conform rigidly to such standards. But on average there will be a higher level of efficiency if everyone is subject to the *regulations* of *regularity* (the law of law): workdays, rules and regulations, even fashions. The "law of large numbers" takes care of the rest—at the price, of course, of stripping each of us of our individuality. "I'm just following the rules," "I'm just a cog in the machine," "I'm just a number."

What about "time off"? During this period, too, the logic of unlimited acceleration and fixed velocity applies, but in a different way. In "leisure time" (the phrase has retained its ironic ring ever since Thorstein Veblen's classic early 20th work on the American "leisure class"), the speed limits go all to pieces, but only phantasmally. Our urge to unlimited acceleration is gratified not *actualiter*, but in the invocation of imaginary domains of unlimited speed, wealth and power in our mostly spectative roles: sports fan, movie-watcher, "dreamer." A garden variety conspiracy theorist could see this as off-time practice for the limited bursts of acceleration repeatedly required in reality to sustain peak efficiency during "time on": **BACK TO WORK**. The limiting problem with the contemporary conception of leisure is that unlimited phantasmal acceleration can become as boring, tedious, indeed stressful as the repeated pushes needed to "get back to work."

It will be (reasonably) objected: but many of us *like* our jobs. Here a double response is needed, divided between the paranoia of the conspiracy theorist and the requisite balance of common sense. The conspiracy theorist's response is: *of course* you like your job, that's just what "they" want. There is something to this sort of explanation, as there is, for example, to Foucault's thesis that the most powerful and efficient deployment of sexuality, particularly in the nineteenth and twentieth centuries, works through the proliferation of sexual discourse.[6] But more important, by far, is the common sense rejoinder, which deserves a paragraph of its own.

Human nature is flexible, but there are limits to this flexibility. Our nature as human beings may be understood in terms of a balancing of relatively fixed needs and our capacity to adapt to changing contexts, what I will call our capacity for assimilation. Ideally, each works to support the other. In particular, when I enter the modern workplace—as, indeed, when I enter any modern condition—my capacity to assimilate makes it possible to adapt

---

6. Michel Foucault, *The History of Sexuality, Volume One: An Introduction*, trans. Robert Hurley (New York: Vintage, 1980).

to the new needs and requirements implied by the modern opportunity for self-assertion—the capacity to assert myself and cause change in the conditions and outlook of my world. Self-assertion stands as both an opportunity and in many contexts a requirement, while efficiency seems more of a requirement than an opportunity, though it can possess the satisfying virtue of "a job well done." Yet such adaptation works only up to a point, and one that will differ from individual to individual. Our assimilation needs must be balanced against more basic, relatively fixed human needs, regardless of whether we understand these latter, fixed needs as some "essential" part of the human condition or rather simply as of longer historical standing. While we adapt ourselves to our modern environment (or any other environment) by means of the former, we adapt the environment to our needs by means of the latter. Environmental conditions are only radically unacceptable when this balancing act cannot be maintained. We are now facing the prospect that eventually (not tomorrow, or the next day, but the day after tomorrow) environmental conditions in the most literal sense (weather) will become radically unacceptable.

The largest problem in dealing with such environmental crises is not that the modern system of self-assertion and efficiency is breaking down, but indeed that it works *so well*. When a problem like global warming is produced by the very conditions of modern economic self-assertion and efficiency that govern the basic underlying dynamic of modern society—at least as far as its economic dimension is concerned—then we truly face a dilemma of massive proportions. For all the obvious "measures" that we might attempt to take to combat the problem are already governed by the underlying dynamic which is causing the problem itself. We land ourselves precisely in that condition where even if everybody recognizes the problem, nobody knows how to fix it. What is most important to underscore about this series of claims is that they are not dependent on the "conspiracy" perspective in any way: they follow directly from the premise that our culture is governed by the dynamics of human self-assertion and economic efficiency. Regulated speed limits and an unlimited number of short, accelerative bursts underwrite this dynamic.

Hans Blumenberg has provided an account of the origins of historical modernity, which he dates emblematically from the burning of Giordano Bruno at the stake by the Inquisition in 1600. Blumenberg understands the origins of modernity in terms of the introduction of a powerful legitimation of the notion of human self-assertion in the face of a crisis in late medieval culture, in which the emphasis on the radical transcendence of God in late medieval theology made the human condition progressively less psychologically supportable. This psychological escalation, documented in depth by Jean Delumeau in his volume *Sin and Fear: The Emergence of a Western Guilt*

Culture,[7] eventuated in a need to look for psychological stability not in the domain of theological justification but rather in the capacity for humans to modify their world through the exercise of their own volition. With this turn to the domain of human-self assertion, the conditions of efficient technical production—whether this be understood economically, scientifically, or in greater generality—received a new impetus which quickly transformed the dynamic conditions of society.[8] At the same time that a general cultural emphasis on efficiency made the capacity for acceleration in all technical domains a requisite, modern natural science developed a sophisticated (and efficient) account of physical force in terms of the acceleration of material bodies. Mathematics, the "language of science," became the universal calculus for "acceleration effects."

As Husserl argued in work of supreme importance for Blumenberg's own thinking, modern philosophy failed to keep up with the pace of these scientific developments, and, with portentous consequences, particularly those early modern developments in the basic science of accelerated motion. In *The Crisis of European Sciences*,[9] Husserl diagnosed an *outpacing* of the scientific enterprise relative to its philosophical foundations, which led to the philosophical predominance of skepticism in the modern period, or as Husserl put it, "nonphilosophies, which retain the word but not the task" of philosophy (CES, 15). For Husserl, such skepticism amounts to a renunciation of the Western commitment to rationality. He located the crisis in (then) contemporary culture (Europe in the 1930's) in the radical departure from traditional European values of rationality, stemming from the outpacing which this scientific endeavor implied. For Husserl, the crisis in the European sciences was to be located not in the development of a model of rational efficiency per se, but in the irrationalism of single-minded and increasingly specializing pursuit of this model, leaving behind the traditional European conception of rationality that scientific modernism de facto relinquished in opening the Pandora's box of a human self-assertion aided by the scientific calculus of accelerated effects. In so doing, the scientific enterprise abandoned, in particular, the meaning of science for human existence. "What does science have to say about reason and unreason or about us men as subjects of this freedom? The mere science of bodies clearly has nothing to say; it abstracts from everything subjective" (CES, 6). Yet this very abstraction becomes a condition for human existence in the modern age, and as such

---

7. Jean Delumeau, *Sin and Fear: The Emergence of a Western Guilt Culture 13th- 18th Centuries*, trans. Eric Nicholson (New York: St. Martin's Press, 1990).

8. Paolo Rossi, *Philosophy, Technology and the Arts in the Early Modern Era*, trans. Salvator Attanasio, ed. Benjamin Nelson (New York: Harper & Row, 1970).

9. Edmund Husserl, *The Crisis of European Sciences and Transcendental Phenomenology: An Introduction to Phenomenological Philosophy*, trans. David Carr (Evanston: Northwestern, 1970). Hereafter referred to internally to the text as *Crisis*.

may tell us something about the contemporary state of the human condition, at least. Husserl would not dispute this fact, and indeed the investigation he lays out in *The Crisis* sets itself the task of identifying just these modern constraints, which land modern man in an "existential contradiction" exemplified by the dilemma of contemporary philosophers. As exemplary in their experience of the dilemma of rationality in the modern condition, philosophers must become

> *functionaries of mankind.* The quite personal responsibility of our own true being as philosophers, our inner personal vocation, bears within itself at the same time the responsibility for the true being of mankind; the latter is, necessarily, being toward a *telos* and can only come to realization, *if at all*, through philosophy—through *us, if* we are philosophers in all seriousness. (CES, 17; see also 71, 151)

Husserl's estimation of the importance of philosophy for European humanity recalls Shelley's incompatible but no less ambitious insistence that "Poets are the unacknowledged legislators of the World."[10]

I do not share Husserl's messianic conception of the philosopher (nor Shelley's of the poet). In addition to the obvious reasons having to do with the monumental capacity such stances invite for monomaniacal self-deception, there is another, less psychological reason to part ways with Husserl here. This more philosophical reason is that Husserl *assumes* a conception of reason which, while we are not yet in a position to replace it, we can nonetheless recognize as historically inaccurate. His conception of rationality as embodying a "hidden telos" has been largely deflated by the lessons drawn from the philosophical consideration of evolutionary science (Husserl would no doubt see evolutionary theory as one of the "positive" sciences with insufficient rational grounding, but we are equally free to accuse Husserl of begging the question).[11] Either way, what Husserl's investigation in the *Crisis* volume does point out is the need for a more philosophically refined account of rationality and, by implication, the crisis which more traditional accounts of rationality face. He develops his "transcendental" conception of philosophical rationality to this end, but I suggest it fails to be sufficiently radical to meet the challenges of modern outpacing. We must look for yet more sophisticated *tools* to bolster our conception of

---

10. *Shelley's Poetry and Prose*, ed. Donald H. Reiman and Sharon B. Powers (New York: Norton, 1977), 508.

11. We should distinguish between two different senses in which we might claim that rationality is teleological. The first is that rationality is inherently goal-structured in the sense that any given rationality activity is directed toward some goal. The second is that rationality is directed toward some *overall* goal, which is the *telos* of rationality "itself." Although I would demur on both counts, it is the latter sort of claim that is particularly troublesome. For another example, see *Crisis*, 52, where Husserl speaks of "hidden reason," which knows itself *as* reason only when "it has become manifest."

human rationality—not failing to recognize the explicit reintrojection of the "essence of technology" into the "human condition" which this implies. Here the technology at issue will be conceptual technology, and in particular the tools developed by our most advanced critical practitioners of the art of reading.

For better and for worse, the most sophisticated tools for reading have predominantly been cultivated in a leading domain of the phantasmally accelerated: the domain of the literary imagination. The advantage of this condition is that here the vocabulary of acceleration is writ large in literary works which push the limits of the human condition as well as human cognition and vocabulary. While this is not a book about poetry, poetry is a privileged artifact for considering issues of pacing. Poetry presents language at its most sophisticated, and language is the basic human tool of what might be called "conceptual technology." If we are to develop a vocabulary of pacing for the modern age, we will do well to consider those critics who have articulated the construction of these most complicated of linguistic artifacts. Indeed, these critics have often recognized issues of motion and pace as integral to the excellence of these works of art.

The disadvantage of this condition is that we run the risk of mistaking the handling of the phantasmal for the handling of the real, the pace of modern art for the pace of *modernity*. To this end, I have also included, along with the consideration of critics as readers of our modern condition through the literary canon, chapters focusing on political philosophy (Arendt) and intellectual history (Starobinski). Politics and history require an acknowledgment of limits on pacing in ways which endeavors in the arts do not, and so the former enterprises present salutary cautions with respect to both the dystopic and utopic undertones of Gyorgy Kepes' characterization of "runaway pace." Most fortunately, I have been able to build on the work of three thinkers in this volume—Hans Blumenberg, Angus Fletcher, and Jean Starobinski—who balance philosophical, historical, literary and scientific concerns in an exemplary fashion. Harold Bloom, although he stands outside of the line that would balance C. P. Snow's "two cultures" of the sciences and the humanities, provides in turn a needed reminder that our ultimate experience of the human condition stretches much farther than debates about modernity, and that one of the largest problems faced by modern humanity is to find an expression of its religious convictions in a climate which often fails to do intellectual justice to these deep human needs. Once again, it is Blumenberg who seems best positioned to balance considerations of theology and the modern age, and so I allow a consideration of this agon to set the stage for what follows in the body of this volume.

Before the full-length execution of this task, which will span the entirety of this book, I want in the rest of this Introduction to provide a first sketch of the manner of proceeding by focusing on a single rhetorical figure, metaphor, indicating some of the ways I see the dynamics of pacing involved in its employment. Here, too, I will begin with Blumenberg.

In his early program-piece, *Paradigms for a Metaphorology*,[12] Blumenberg's ambitions may seem almost perversely limited, at least on the face of it. In the general arena of what some would today call non-conceptual content (and which Blumenberg later refers to as 'non-conceptuality'[13]), Blumenberg focuses on metaphor as one example among a multitude of others, not because he sees it as the most important but because it presents certain virtues of tractability—virtues which one comes to doubt soon enough while struggling to maintain the thread in his slender but difficult volume. In fact these supremely appropriate doubts are indicative not of poor choice on Blumenberg's part but of the sobriety with which Blumenberg faces challenges posed by even this single linguistic figure.

Early on in this work, Blumenberg draws a distinction between metaphor in general and what he calls *absolute metaphor*, and it is in terms of this latter that the true challenge begins, for these are metaphors for which no literal paraphrase may be substituted. An absolute metaphor, then, is the opposite of what we might call a "metaphor of convenience"—it is "irreducibly" metaphorical.[14] Lying somewhere along the middle of the spectrum from metaphor of convenience to absolute metaphor, an instance like "the laughing meadow" may be *strongly* metaphoric, but it is not irreducibly so, since we understand the idea of a countenance to be applied to a landscape analogically. Absolute metaphors are metaphors "in extremis": they qualify a term not simply by using another register, but by drawing on a register which negates the literal meaning of the anteceding terms. Although absolute metaphors may be found in a whole variety of forms and flavors, one type of absolute metaphor which Blumenberg considers interests me particularly because of the obvious relation in which it stands to the passage from Valéry cited above. This is the absolute metaphor of scale.

The obsession with scale permeates our culture at all levels from high to low: consider, for example, the recent "action thriller," *Firewall*.[15] In this film,

---

12. Hans Blumenberg, *Paradigmen zu einer Metaphorologie*, 2nd ed. (Frankfurt am Main: Suhrkamp, 1999). There is a recent English translation, *Paradigms for a Metaphorology*, trans. with an afterword [sic] by Robert Savage (Ithaca: Cornell, 2010).

13. "Prospects for a Theory of Nonconceptuality," in *Shipwreck with Spectator: Paradigm for a Metaphor of Existence*, trans. Steven Rendall (Cambridge: MIT, 1997), 81-102.

14. Caveat emptor: the treatment of Blumenberg's terminology I give here should only be taken as a sketch; as Anselm Haverkamp quite rightly remarked in a recent public lecture at the University of Georgia, Blumenberg nowhere defines these terms explicitly.

15. *Firewall* Village Broadshow Pictures DVD Video 59410. I choose this example not as a supreme instance of the genre, but simply as a recent exemplar that is intelligent enough in its pursuit of a number of American myths (under the supervision, interestingly enough, of a British director). It has the virtue, as well, that the screenplay was written in specific and declared reflection on the events of September 11, 2001, a canonical point of historical

Harrison Ford plays Jack Stanfield, a security analyst associated with a small chain of northwestern banks which is in the process of being bought out by a much larger national banking concern. In a merger meeting early in the movie, Stanfield's new boss refers to the "economies of scale" and the associated "acceptable losses" associated with scamming against a large banking operation. As the archetypal small business hero of our feature presentation, Ford's character balks at the notion that any such loss is acceptable, accruing as it does to the customers it is the business of the bank to serve. No loss is acceptable: echoes of military surveillance efforts are not difficult to hear, and the transpositions of a rhetorical figure, from "no soldier left behind" to "no child left behind" are equally easy to spin. Yet in conversation with the movie's director, Ford was insistent that in a film where the technological domain can become an unlimited invitation to special effects riffing, the *human scale of the story* must always be kept front and center. In so doing, Ford as actor recapitulates the thematic concern of the character he represents: in each case we encounter a gesture of resistance in the face of "economies of scale."

As a paradigmatic example of an absolute metaphor of scale, Blumenberg cites in *Lebenszeit und Weltzeit* (*Lifetime and Worldtime*) Husserl's creation of the term 'lifeworld'.[16] Because of the philosophical function which this term serves, its sense is irreducibly metaphorical: the world *simpliciter* is the domain of phenomenological investigation—this registers Husserl's fundamental aversion to the characterization of phenomenology as a naive form of philosophical idealism. Yet, although it is the domain in which "practically our whole life takes place" (CES, 51), the lifeworld cannot be brought *as such* to the forum of phenomenological presentation, since it is "pre-positional," "pre-thetic" in an absolute and irreducible sense: otherwise its function in preserving Husserl's insistence on an anterior justificatory source for philosophical realism would be undone. "Lifeworld" is not a reducible application of the idea of a living thing to the world, but rather a "world" which is, *phenomenologically* speaking, no world at all. All of this is encapsulated in a passage Blumenberg cites from Husserl, which also paves the way for understanding Husserl's lifeworld as an absolute metaphor of scale: "The world won an infinite breadth as soon as the actual lifeworld, the world in the "how" of its lived-givenness, was considered."[17] The world itself is *not* infinite in scale. Rather, it is paradoxically "bounded" by an indefinite horizon.

---

reference for the current American and world setting of "modernity." Any treatment of modernity worth its salt should bear on reasonably thoughtful expressions of the popular media, and so I will use this example as a check in the declared sense.

16. Hans Blumenberg, *Lebenszeit und Weltzeit*, 2nd ed. (Frankfurt am Main: Suhrkamp, 1986).

17. Translation mine. "Die Welt gewann eine unendliche Weite, sobald die wirkliche Lebenswelt, die Welt im Wie der Erlebnisgegebenheit betrachtet war," cited in Blumenberg, *Lebenszeit und Weltzeit*, 10.

The lifeworld functions as a "pure" source of "lived-givenness," and as such in itself eliminates all phenomenally bounded conditions *of* givenness. It is the "answer," we may say, that arrests a further regress of scales, landing at the level of our human being-in-the-world. It is the limiting phenomenological analogue of the narratological insistence on the human scale of "story." The world always "outpaces" the lifeworld.[18] In general, our perceptual capacities are limited by all sorts of "economies of scale": from a minimal saturation of hue to a maximal, from a minimal distance of focus to a maximal distance of what is discernible, and so on. But our *conceptual* capacities, equally, are limited: our capacity, for example, to construct large numbers. As with perceptual capacities, these conceptual capacities can be improved, but only by the interposition of the cognitive equivalent of technology. Here "non-conceptual content," so-called, plays an inherent role. Numerical notation—such as decimal notation, for example—is not *exclusively* conceptual, but depends also on marshaling the limits of our capacities for perception. The construction of large numbers depends on notational conventions which must (also) be sufficiently perceptually perspicuous, and so is not exclusively conceptual. An absolute metaphor, in this case the idea of the infinite, can help us organize the congeries of techniques for generating large numbers in terms of an inaccessible, unreachable numerical "horizon." But the infinite is not "given" any more than the lifeworld is "given." Rather, each functions as the "source," in some deeply metaphorical sense, of our capacities for givenness.[19] As Blumenberg points out in *Lebenszeit und Weltzeit*, it was in terms of the mental technology of names for numbers that Husserl first began his path toward phenomenology in his first book, the 1891 *Philosophy of Arithmetic*.[20] In *Paradigms for a Metaphorology*, Blumenberg notes a privileged source of absolute metaphors of scale in the philosophical writings of Nicholas of Cusa. Blumenberg's term, instead of a metaphorics of scale, is literally a metaphorics of "blow up" (*Sprengmetaphorik*)—the resonance with Cortazar's story and Antonioni's film is not unwelcome here. In

---

18. Blumenberg's interpretation of Husserl's lifeworld is extensive and controversial (if he is right that the term functions as an absolute metaphor, *any* interpretation will be). I have assumed it here, rather than arguing for it, in order to make points about Blumenberg's conception of absolute metaphor for general considerations of scale. For an extensive discussion, see, in particular, "Das Lebensweltmißverständnis," in *Lebenszeit und Weltzeit*, 5-68.

19. The example of the numerical infinite as metaphorical is mine; Blumenberg will refer instead to the "concept of the infinite," not arguing for its metaphorical status. See *Paradigmen*, 180. This should not be taken to imply that for Blumenberg that there is no metaphorical background for the concept of the infinite; that simply is not his focus here.

20. Blumenberg, *Lebenszeit*, 53; Edmund Husserl, *Philosophy of Arithmetic: Psychological and Logical Investigations, with supplementary texts from 1887-1901*, trans. Dallas Willard (Dordrecht: Kluwer, 2003). Blumenberg devotes a chapter to Husserl's *Philosophy of Arithmetic* in *Beschreibung des Menschen* (Frankfurt am Main: Suhrkamp, 2006), "Der Mensch zählt immer," 318-377.

these absolute metaphors Cusa considers a proto-photographic enlarging (or reducing) of a mathematical figure so that "in the limit" there will be a coincidence of opposites: we may think of a circle as an infinite-sided polygon, so that the straight sides become points on the circumference of a circle, for example, or a sphere of infinite radius becomes one "whose center is everywhere and circumference nowhere."[21] The notion of "blow up" captures simultaneously the incongruities of scale and the compressive dynamics which underlie Kepes' sense that "the inescapable attribute of our time is its runaway pace." In both ways it serves as a figure of rapid acceleration toward a horizon. In *The Legitimacy of the Modern Age*[22] Blumenberg shows how it is the functional appropriation of Cusa's metaphorics of the blow up that allows for the infinitization of the cosmos in Giordano Bruno's thought, one of the hallmarks of the modern age, as Alexandre Koyré already insisted in his book, *From the Closed World to the Infinite Universe*.[23] Such scaling metaphors serve the dual functions of providing a sense of dynamic explosion (in this case in terms of the proliferation of sides) and also of arresting this "blow up" in a paradoxical image, here a circle made out of (infinitesimal) straight lines. As such, they serve as a model in miniature for the role that a vocabulary of pacing must itself play. Such a vocabulary functions as verbal "notation" for what Angus Fletcher will suggestively refer to as a portrait of the "Zenonian trajectory," as I discuss below.

The "blow up" registers the transition from one scale to another larger one, but in the process as conceived photographically this is achieved at the expense of focusing in on a smaller canvas at greater magnification—unless, as happens in Antonioni's film (in an episode from the story line and yet also generally in the filmic presentation itself), the photographic surface itself is correspondingly enlarged. In blowing up, the tradeoff differs from the effect involved in organizing a perceptual background with respect to some orienting figure, but in both cases there is a powerful sense of underlying concentration at the same time as, and by way of, achieving a powerful sense of spatial expansiveness. Both effects are *dynamic* due to the scale-shifting involved.

These effects serve as a powerful model in miniature for the vocabulary of pacing because they model the phenomenology of cognitive assimilation in the process of reading, the constant interplay between scales which involves both the rapid accelerative burst of repeated events of recognition

---

21. For an extended discussion of Cusa's exploding metaphors see Elizabeth Brient, *The Immanence of the Infinite: Hans Blumenberg and the Threshold to Modernity* (Washington, D.C.: Catholic University, 2002), esp. 188-204.

22. Hans Blumenberg, *The Legitimacy of the Modern Age*, trans. Robert Wallace (Cambridge: MIT, 1985).

23. Alexandre Koyré, *From the Closed World to the Infinite Universe* (Baltimore: Johns Hopkins, 1957).

along with the continuous pacing of forward progress. Although this is not a book *about* reading any more than it is a book *about* poetry, the activity of reading serves as a central practical example of the underlying dynamics of pacing, and often enough reading becomes an allegorical image of pace, especially technological pace. In Antonioni's film we "read" blown up pictures alongside the protagonist. In *Firewall* Harrison Ford attaches a contraption formed out of the scanner from his fax machine and his daughter's iPod to copy the bank account numbers off a computer monitor, and later snaps a photo of the same account information off another computer screen using the cellphone of an unwitting accomplice.

Tracing back to the nineteenth century, we find a forceful model of such "imaging" in the process of momentaneous consolidation, what Heidegger, assimilating and further concentrating it, would later call "Augenblicksphilosophie," philosophy of the moment. Heidegger draws particular inspiration from Hölderlin, whose doctrine of the modulation of tones is used to describe the composition of poetry but serves also as a model for the reading of it.[24] Like Hölderlin's poetry, Kierkegaard's pseudonymous writings are organized in terms of a momentaneous consolidation governed by a variation of genre, most often between the comic and the tragic. In this respect Kierkegaard takes as his point of departure the scene at the end of Plato's *Symposium* when Socrates argues that "the same man might be capable of writing both comedy and tragedy."[25] Like Hölderlin, Kierkegaard understands the variation of genre specifically in terms of generic *crossing*, in Kierkegaard's case creating an implicit dialogue between the various pseudonymous authors. The *Symposium* which Kierkegaard includes in *Stages on Life's Way*[26] itself stages a crossing within the pseudonymous authorship in its presentation of a series of speeches by various "authors" which imitates those presented in the Platonic "original."

Kierkegaard's internalization of the competition of genres within individual works provides a precedent for models of reading in terms of the

---

24. See Lawrence J. Ryan, *Hölderlins Lehre vom Wechsel der Töne* (Stuttgart: W. Kohlhammer, 1960), and the respone of Jürg Peter Walser in *Hölderlins Archipelagus* (Zürich: Atlantis), 214-17. Hölderlin's doctrine of the modulation of tones is a privileged historical locus for investigating the relation of models of reading to models of writing, since the modulation of tones apparently governs both. A "philosophy of the moment" may be able to argue for this identification in terms of the experience of the poem which the poet and the reader *share* in the moment of recognition. With the shift from a philosophy of the moment—which still governs the enterprises of Heidegger, Arendt and even Derrida—to a philosophy in which the analysis of action is more explicitly geared to issues of pace, the distinction between writing and reading becomes more critical.

25. 223d, Michael Joyce translation.

26. "*In Vino Veritas*, a recollection related by William Afham," in Søren Kierkegaard, *Stages on Life's Way*, ed. and trans. Howard V. Hong and Edna H. Hong (Princeton: Princeton University, 1988), 7-86.

notion of *crossing*, important for the twentieth century sources I consider less in terms of the crossing of genres and more in terms of figural crossing, with metaphor as an important example. The reasons for this figural affiliation are no doubt complex, and in several authors I consider there is some passage back and forth between genre and figural criticism (Blumenberg on myth and metaphor, Fletcher on allegory and figures of threshold). The broad turn from genre to figure may be seen historically in terms of a reductive concentration on the simpler literary artifact (figure rather than literary work), and so is in line with Blumenberg's initiation of his "theory of nonconceptuality" with the consideration of metaphor. It is only after this methodological initiative that Blumenberg turns back to the much more involved case of myth.

The crossing from genre to figure can itself be figured in terms of the later figural reading of the momentaneous, as happens for example when Harold Bloom (strongly mis)reads Emily Dickinson in terms of his sixfold tropology.

> Our journey had advanced—
> Our feet were almost come
> To that odd Fork in Being's Road—
> Eternity—by Term—
> Our pace took sudden awe—
> Our feet—reluctant—led—
> Before—were Cities—but Between—
> The Forest of the Dead —
> Retreat—was out of Hope—
> Behind—a Sealed Route—
> Eternity's White Flag—Before—
> And God—at every Gate—

Bloom cites Dickinson's lyric entire in the first chapter of his volume on Wallace Stevens, and then begins his reading by locating "the crossings here, as always, in the breaks between one mode of figurative thinking and a mode sharply antithetical to that one."[27] But as the most disjunctive of poets, the crossings in Dickinson's poetry antecede the figural level, striking all the way down to the rudiments of punctuation. Dickinson's dash is the disjunctive punctuation par excellence, and here, as in many of Dickinson's poems, induces a sheerly horizontal vertigo of the threshold throughout. It is all the more dramatic, then, when she begins the second stanza with the line, "Our pace took sudden awe—". The orienting dynamic of a focal moment collocates the significant, a gathering of the tremendous. Bloom reads Dickinson's 'pace' as a trope for 'consciousness' (as according to Bloom 'feet'

---

27. Harold Bloom, *Wallace Stevens: The Poems of Our Climate* (Ithaca: Cornell University, 1977), 16.

tropes 'being') and hence juxtaposes it to the "odd fork in Being's road" of the first stanza, with 'awe' as "one of Dickinson's prime tropes for Fate or *ethos* raised to apocalyptic pitch."[28] But to speak analogically, the warrant here is not for reading Dickinson's awe in terms of Husserl's phenomenology of consciousness but rather in terms of Heidegger's phenomenology of Being. Dickinson's awe retrieves the sense of the tremendous (*to deinon*) upon which Heidegger meditates in his consideration of the famous chorus from Sophocles' *Antigone* in *An Introduction to Metaphysics*.[29] If there is a consciousness in Dickinson's poem, it is the consciousness *of* the poem: as written, and as read. The "pace of sudden awe" is a poetic invocation of the "moment" of the poem itself, sheer instantiation of being in language.

The "space" of the poem is the ominous "forest of the dead," the interzone of "absent poetic presences" which hover vestigially about the poem. It is a forest encircled by the remnants of a theological worldview: eternity "by term" and God "at every gate." A term is a unit of language but also, and more importantly, an interval of time. The "moment" is the incarnation of eternity in time "by term;" the forest a domain in which God stands upon every threshold. The dynamic is one of crossing, and Bloom is at least correct in his emphasis on the apocalyptic.

The *taking* of a sudden awe by our pace is the seizure of an acceleration, and it is in these terms, rather than in terms of the juxtaposition of Being and Consciousness, that we must understand what is most modern about the dynamics of the momentary. We might think here of the jolting of a railway carriage, that moment invoked in a thousand popular films, in which the train jerkily pulses into motion as it leaves the station, accelerating to full speed. Or, in *Firewall*, we could refer to the moment late in the movie (a last minute revision to the script insisted on by Harrison Ford) when in pursuit of his family's captors, Jack Stanfield and his secretary stop beneath an overpass to track the family pet's homing device on the secretary's laptop and trade places behind the wheel. "What are you doing?" his secretary exclaims as Ford/Stanfield, already diving back into the car, replies, "I'm going to find my dog," slamming the door and then hitting the accelerator, tires squealing as they skid back onto the road.

In Dickinson's poem there is an uncomfortable tension between the seizure of acceleration and the indefinite extension of the road ahead. In the third stanza, it feels as if the forest of the Dead will never end. Could this be the odd fork in Being's road? 'Eternity': the moment; 'by term': the element of indefinite extension? Though Dickinson proceeds in terms of more general motives, we are not so far from the pulsing circus of technology described by Gyorgy Kepes. Of the two, Dickinson's is much the stronger candidate

---

28. idem, 19.

29. Martin Heidegger, *An Introduction to Metaphysics*, trans. Ralph Manheim (New Haven: Yale University, 1959), 146-65.

for framing our technological age—in terms of what Martin Heidegger called the "Gestell." What we pursue against the far horizon is not the victory of Eternity but rather Eternity's own passive surrender. **WE** are the aggressors here.

In a first world contemporary context, this aggression has not changed, but tends to be thematized in terms of more overt fantasies of victimization. Technology, which we use, is equally that which can be used against us. A home security system, the ever dutiful son of Jack Stanfield tells his captor, keeps people out; his captor reminds him that it can also be used to keep people in. Within the Stanfield house (designed by the architect mother) the security system is a mirror reflection of the security "firewall" at the bank which Stanfield is able to violate precisely because he has built it to protect his own bank, and so his customers. In a heated exchange with his new boss, Stanfield asks him, "What, exactly, *is* my philosophy of risk, Gary?" Throughout the rest of the movie we see Ford/Stanfield forced to violate every letter of his philosophy's code as he runs a double-sided game against the bank and his captors in a heroic effort to save his family. The fantasy here is that to survive in modern society, to maintain a sense of self and personal security, we cannot play it safe, we must accelerate—at the same time that we are ideologically encouraged to put our faith in a system that "works," running constantly at peak efficiency. Here, again, we see the push-me-pull-you crux of a jolting, repeated dramatic acceleration, the constant surge beneath which the individual threatens to drown in a sea of numbers.

Although metaphor, given its capacity to figure the wrench in scale which an acceleration outward toward a horizon implies, may seem a privileged figure for considering the pace of modernity, in fact metonymy is equally critical in its capacity to figure the side-by-side, or term-by-term, stasis associated with the experience of steady, forward motion. The paradoxical pace of modernity incorporates (at least) both of these figural tendencies, and Roman Jakobson's discussion of the "bipolarity" of metaphor and metonymy, described by Vladimir Toporov in terms of a model setting metaphor along a vertical, and metonymy along a horizontal axis, is a powerful reduction of these two basic features of rhetorical figuration into a compact and efficient linguistic model.[30] The accelerated scale-shifting of metaphor along the vertical axis is "projected" down upon the horizontal distribution of metonymic terms, allowing for a stratification of the

---

30. Roman Jakobson, "Two Aspects of Language and Two Types of Aphasic Disturbances," in *Language in Literature*, ed. Krystyna Pomorska and Stephen Rudy (Cambridge: Harvard University Press, 1987), 95-114, especially Section Five, "The Metaphoric and Metonymic Poles," 109-114; Vladimir N. Toporov, "Die Ursprünge der indoeuropäischen Poetik," trans. Peter L. W. Koch (from the original Russian), *Poetica* **13** 3-4 189-251, here esp. 194ff. Toporov refers specifically to Jakobson's essay, "Linguistics and Poetics," also in *Language and Literature*, 62-94, see esp. 89-90.

linguistic artifact (and most importantly among them, the poem) into a depth (vertical) and surface (horizontal) dimension. Combining, as it does, figural representatives of these two most basic aspects of modern pacing, its discontinuous accelerative bursting and its continuous forward progression, this model may even serve as an ultimate allegorical reduction of the modern condition, but at any rate it is well geared to the most primitive dynamics of the linguistic artifact.

What this model already establishes in its rudimentary coupling of these two figures is that it would be a mistake entirely to identify "modernity" in any sense exclusively with metaphor as opposed to metonymy (or vice versa). Conversely, we can fashion a rough-and-ready chart of the biases of various attitudes towards modernity in terms of their tendency to favor metaphor or metonymy. Kepes' obsession with acceleration suggests a metaphorical leaning, and this tendency is equally evident in Derrida's identification of metaphor and modernity in Rousseau's work.[31] Such readings of modernity, like Heidegger's or Horkheimer and Adorno's, identify it with some event of "metaphysical decline" or "enlightenment" that (always) already occurred early in the mists of Western philosophical history. Fletcher's insistence on metonymy in the work of (early) Pasternak and Ashbery (taking its point of departure in an essay by Jakobson on Pasternak)[32] points in the direction of tendencies that are often enough characterized as "post-modern," but which are in fact equally central to the modern condition. (With a wicked irony thoroughly mastered, my advisor Leszek Kolakowski once offered a seminar entitled "Pascal as Prophet of Post-Modernity.") In general, Fletcher's eye is more attuned to metonymical workings in the "low Romantic" tradition stretching from Clare through Whitman to Ashbery. But eventually, his emphasis on the complex modern dynamics of scale drives him to propose a new genre, the environment-poem, that accommodates the paradoxical aspects of modern pacing by transuming the figural level. With genre criticism, the inherent danger is that the account of the genre will only amount to that of a figure "writ large," but in his early, extended battle against the notion of allegory as extended metaphor Fletcher has fortified himself against such a pitfall.[33] A new cyber-eye is needed in the face of exacerbated cultural and narrative conditions of reading. To cultivate this vision, I look

---

31. Jacques Derrida, *Of Grammatology*, trans. Gayatri Chakravorty Spivak (Baltimore: Johns Hopkins, 1976). On metaphor: "The Originary Metaphor," 270-280. On modernity and legitimation: 296. Derrida's treatment of metaphor *in extenso* is in "White Mythology," in *Margins of Philosophy*, trans. Alan Bass (Chicago: Chicago, 1982), 207-271.

32. Roman Jakobson, "Marginal Notes on the Prose of the Poet Pasternak," in *Language and Literature*, ed. Krystina Pomorska and Stephen Rudy (Cambridge: Harvard, 1987), 301-317.

33. Angus Fletcher, *Allegory: The Theory of a Symbolic Mode* (Ithaca: Cornell, 1964), 75-84. Fletcher uses 'trope' in the way that I use the term 'figure', and reserves 'figure' for a more global function, acting on "whole groups of words, on sentences, or even paragraphs" (84).

at a range of tropological models, which is to say: models of linguistic figuration, whether these be understood historically, rhetorically, dramatically, philosophically, or according to some combination of these perspectives. So far as pacing is concerned, the dramatic perspective is critical for nearly obvious reasons, but in the pacing of *modernity* the cultivation of a dynamic vocabulary will crucially rely on an integration of all these trends and more. A model of reading in terms of the crossings of figures profits from the traditions of nineteenth century historical philology (especially in Starobinski), literary criticism (Fletcher and Bloom), and the "Toposforschung" of the history of ideas (Starobinski, Blumenberg) in ways which postdate the essentially romantic, later existential, model of the momentaneous crossing (one still largely underlying, though tacitly, Arendt's philosophy of history). What is to be gained in each of these cases is a heightened *control* of the resources of language; what threatens to be lost are, on the one hand, the intensity of the romantic model and, on the other, an appreciation for the extra-linguistic dimensions of the threshold experience.

The authors upon whom I have chosen to focus—Arendt, Starobinski, Fletcher, and Bloom—minimize these disadvantages, in large part because of their sympathies for romantic and existential trends. But more significantly, what they allow us to see are the limitations of language under the most sympathetic of conditions. This will prepare us for renewed reading with Blumenberg in the penultimate chapter, and for the test case, in particular, of reading Ashbery's *Three Poems* in the final chapter. Although she antedates the other figures in this book by several decades, Arendt is placed directly after the first chapter on Blumenberg not for chronological reasons, but because she collocates the historical and intellectual conditions of pacing in a way that is exemplary for all that follows. Next we move into Fletcher's consideration of time, space and motion in the early modern period, and then aggressively into the forest of language in Starobinski's intellectual history of the terms 'action' and 'reaction'. This is followed by chapters more focused on the critical reading of poetry in the work of Fletcher and Bloom. At a turning point about two-thirds of the way along, I set a chapter squaring off Fletcher and Bloom in terms of two different mathematical models for reading, and I argue that this extension onto the mathematical figures of fraction and function can significantly improve our capacities for "guided" reading. The extensions I draw from mathematics stand in inverse relation to appeals to that religious criticism which comes to assume a more and more dominant position in the second half of Bloom's career, and which fuels his concern with wisdom literature in the work of his which is my focus in the earlier chapter.

Penultimately, I turn to a retrospective evaluation of Blumenberg and the issue of legitimation in an age of acceleration. Is it God who stands at every gate, or the edge of the world, or the end of the world in some more temporal, hence apocalyptic sense? Or do we find there instead, as I would have it, those poetic and mathematical extensions of our "ordinary language" which open our conversations onto the domains of the arts and sciences? Such questions deepen the investigation of the notion of legitimation insofar as it applies to our modern condition, and in particular requires a reconsideration of Blumenberg's notion of legitimacy. In a final chapter, I invoke our (still) most contemporary poet, John Ashbery, and look at what he might have to tell us about entering into and exiting out from those conditions in which we find ourselves.

Husserl argued for a philosophical "softening" of the accelerated pace of modernity in term of a rational reaccommodation, but this project to soften the pace of modernity is inadequate for complicated reasons I trace out along the length of this volume. For Husserl, this softening involved a revisitation of the development of early modern science as he reads it in *The Crisis*. In the drama as Husserl unfolds it, Galileo is the culprit: he becomes a model of the pursuit of science at the expense of philosophical rationality. Husserl ultimately argues for a "repacing" of modernity, a massive philosophical "tune-up," if you will, as a response to a scientific-technical mentality run amok. The resonance of this response to technological build-up with the passage from Kepes cited above should be obvious.

Like Blumenberg, I value Husserl's supreme commitment to "theory," but also like Blumenberg, I recognize that Husserl's traditional conception of philosophical rationality faces its own irrationalizing threats. Addressing the modern condition demands not just a redressing of the imbalances of the scientific-technical mentality, but a recognition that traditional conceptions of rationality are simply no longer even *pragmatically* sufficient to respond to modern conditions. Given his recognition of the unbridled force of the modern scientific-technical mentality, Husserl's supreme valuation of theory plays too easily into the hand of Heidegger's desire for a probing into the conditions of technology's "overcoming," just as Heidegger prophesies that metaphysics must be "overcome." On both sides, the problem remains that Husserl and Heidegger equally have underestimated the staying power of the modern scientific-technical attitude and what would be required to "address" it. Technology and, more specifically, its outpacings are here to stay—we must hope so, for they will be here just as long as we are.

Blumenberg's supreme virtue, to my mind, lies in the depth of his recognition of just this fact, along with the truly inspiring extent to which he develops a vocabulary for addressing it. In this book, I propose to build on the legacy Blumenberg has bequeathed us by cultivating some techniques for dealing with the issues, in particular, that beset us so far as the *pacing* of modern culture is concerned. This initiative is designed to push Blumenberg's legacy beyond questions about the *legitimacy* of the modern age toward a focus on the *pace* of modernity. Consequently I begin the book with a consideration of the way in which Blumenberg's work is grounded in questions of modernity's legitimation, and the ways in which his later work both develops these concerns and moves beyond them. At the end of the book, I revisit the issue of legitimation with a fuller appreciation of the dynamics of pacing in mind and argue that the notion of legitimating the modern condition must take a new form.

From the discussion above, I hope it is apparent that while there are ways in which we must recognize that modernity represents an "accelerated" version of culture, we also cannot simply characterize modernity in terms of an accelerated pace, nor can we redress the problems of modernity simply by slowing down. Indeed, what is largely required for addressing the pace of modernity is a cognitive vocabulary and approach which can "keep pace" with the phenomena it considers. The examples of Husserl and Heidegger serve as admirable object lessons in insufficiencies, and Blumenberg has considered both projects extensively. In short, we must not fall prey either to classical philosophical rationality or to some form of irrationalism bolstered by an appeal to classical sources. Both tacks ultimately constitute a reversion to pre-modern solutions; as Blumenberg persuasively argues, pre-modern solutions can only solve pre-modern problems. The tragic irony of Husserl's and Heidegger's projects—tragedies in a major and a minor key, respectively—is that they jointly exemplify the ironclad law that returns to classicism can only be practiced as forms of modernism—and modernisms which fail to maintain self-control precisely to the extent that they do not recognize themselves as such. It is for this basic reason that we cannot "escape" the pace of modernity simply by "slowing down." (Wittgenstein urged that philosophers should greet each other by saying, "Take your time." This registers yet another tragedy of philosophical modernism.)

Instead of the "softening" Husserl proposes, the development of a vocabulary of pacing for the modern condition follows in the tradition of Montaigne. Montaigne recognized a competition between the evacuation of our lived time in the flight toward death, which only accelerates as one grows older, and the need for an intensification of life which this speeding away of life demands.

> Especially at this moment, when I perceive that [my life] is so brief in time, I try to increase it in *weight*; I try to *arrest* the speed of its *flight* by the speed with which I *grasp* it, and to compensate for the haste of its *ebb* by my vigor in *using* it. The shorter my possession of life, the deeper and *fuller* I must make it.[34] (cited, Starobinski, 237).

---

34. Cited in Jean Starobinski, *Montaigne in Motion*, trans. Arthur Goldhammer (Chicago: Chicago, 1985), 237. The entire chapter, "«Each man in some sort exists in his work»," 214-43, may be taken as an extended gloss on this passage, which is drawn from Montaigne's last essay, "Of experience." Michel de Montaigne, *The Complete Works of Montaigne: Essays, Travel Journals, Letters*, trans. Donald Frame (Stanford: Stanford, 1958), 815-57, here 853.

Just as Arendt will recognize that the capacity to *retard* the artificial acceleration of the totalitarian condition is banked in natality, the recurring onset of new life in this world (as I discuss in Chapter Two), so Montaigne recognizes at the other end of life a complementary demand, not for retardation, but for an intensification of life which we may refer to indeed as *quickening*. This quickening, which Montaigne also identifies with weight," "arrests" the onward, horizontal flow of time only by introducing an ineliminably metaphorical "deepening" of the temporal stream. Enlisting Montaigne's suggestion requires that we transpose it from the individual context of a single life's ebb to the accelerated vanishing of horizons we face in the contemporary condition. A vocabulary of pacing will track this acceleration with a metaphorical process of quickening.

We must work, indeed, as vigorously and quickly as we can to cultivate such a vocabulary, writing and reading to promote global outlooks, and the resulting vocabulary will itself promote a "speed-up" of our capacity to address the pace of modernity. This task is intellectually demanding, yet open in its invitation to participate. Such an orientation will contribute to a softening of the modern condition only in the sense that it will provide us with an incrementally greater appreciation and fine-grained control of it, but in so doing such innovations themselves necessarily contribute to the conceptual acceleration of the contemporary condition, inviting us but also demanding of us to think with "speed and size." So far from urging fatalism about the modern condition (in a poem of ultimate concision, A. R. Ammons says that "the quickest way to change the world is to like it the way it is"[35]), I am cautioning that our images of change in the modern condition not be thematically simplified ones of phantasmally accelerated improvement, as these are part of the problem, and will effect no change at all. We almost always underestimate the complexity of the underlying dynamic, and indeed this is invited by the problem itself, but this is no counsel for thoughtlessness or inaction. We must demand thinking of a comparable sophistication to meet these sophisticated demands. Acknowledging the pace of modernity requires new forms of vigilant attention appropriate to our condition as we find it—yet in itself such care is a most traditional philosophical hallmark.

It is time to get down to the main business of this book. As is his due, I will let Husserl have the last word before setting out. At the end of his introduction to *The Crisis*, he exclaims, with only a hint of apology:

> But enough of this. I have advanced too quickly, in order to make felt the incomparable significance attaching to the clarification of the deepest motives of this crisis—a crisis which developed very early in modern philosophy and science and which extends with increasing intensity to our own day. (CES, 16)

---

35. "Old Geezer," in *Brink Road* (New York: Norton, 1996), 158; the poem is also printed on the back face of the book jacket.

I

Theology and the Modern Age: Blumenberg's Reaction to A Baconian Frontispiece

Hans Blumenberg has attempted to argue for the legitimacy of the modern age by understanding modernity as a second overcoming of Gnosticism, and in this chapter my primary concern is to show that this strategy requires that no theological appeal be made in the process of this legitimation.[36] This will serve as a first step in the larger argument of the book, in which I wish to reconsider the implications of modern dynamics of pacing for a notion of legitimating the modern condition. If legitimating the modern condition requires that we not invoke those more constant features of the human condition associated with our religious traditions, then this puts all the more emphasis on the challenges which beset human nature in its accommodation of our increasingly accelerated cultural condition. In addition, pacing is moderated in the early modern period by the residual availability of the medieval theological worldview and its early modern reworkings. As we move further into the modern period, this theological "pressure" becomes increasingly less capable of offering a "breaker" to the pace of modernity, which results in an intensified need to reconsider the issue of modernity's legitimation; we may see Blumenberg's own project in precisely this light. Yet, I will suggest, Blumenberg only initiates the project of rendering modernity's attempted self-legitimation explicit, and ultimately, a notion of legitimation more attuned to the demands of modern pacing is needed. Toward the end of this volume I will attempt to cultivate such a revised notion, taking advantage of gains made along the way in considering modes of reading our modern condition offered by Arendt, Starobinski, Fletcher, Bloom, and more incidentally by many others.

---

36. Hans Blumenberg, *The Legitimacy of the Modern Age*, trans. Robert Wallace (Cambridge: The MIT Press, 1985); hereafter cited internally in this chapter.

BLUMENBERG'S LEGITIMATION

The Christian synthesis of the Church Fathers, so Blumenberg's story goes, was a first, but unsuccessful, and specifically theological attempt at an overcoming of Gnosticism, with the consequence that the "problem of Gnosticism" surfaced once again at the end of the Middle Ages. The legitimacy of the modern age consists precisely in its succeeding where Christian theology failed. But what is the "problem of Gnosticism" that modernity seeks to overcome?

In order to answer this question, Blumenberg turns first to the way in which the medieval period "had its beginning in the conflict with late-antique and early-Christian Gnosticism," so that "the unity of its systematic intention can be understood as deriving from the task of subduing its Gnostic opponent" (LMA, 126). In particular, the Church Father's faced the problem of articulating a viable explanation for the existence of evil in a world which refused to come to an end. Here the dualism of Gnostic explanations offered itself as an obvious competitor: by understanding the world as itself an evil "prison-house," and by separating this demiurgic creation from the redemptive power of a second judging god untainted by the evil of this world, the Gnostic solution avoided any problems of theodicy associated with a monotheistic explanation in which the creative and judging powers of a single God would be yoked together. In later medieval developments, however, and specifically those associated with the rise of nominalism, the emphasis placed on the radical transcendence of God threatened to sever God from any rational connection to a cosmos which, although created by Him, need have no discernible connection to God's role as ultimate judge.

In the face of God's utter arbitrariness in the creation of this world, any defense of the cosmos as a reliable home for human existence in general and spiritual cultivation in particular threatened to collapse, and it was this potential unleashing of the world from any connection with a divine order which forced a second confrontation with the "problem of Gnosticism." It was also, however, this "aggravated circumstance" (LMA, 137) which opened the possibility of addressing this problem in a way which had been unavailable in the context of late-antiquity. In particular, "only after nominalism had executed a sufficiently radical destruction of the humanly relevant and dependable cosmos could the mechanistic philosophy of nature be adopted as the tool of self-assertion" (LMA, 151, translation corrected). The positing of self-assertion, the human capacity to change nature in conformity with its own needs, is what Blumenberg sees as the hallmark of the modern age, and specifically what distinguishes its appropriation of the atomistic tradition from the "retiring" atomism of the school of Epicurus, in which the commitment to atomism is motivated by a desire to liberate man from the purported significance of natural phenomena (LMA, 157).

All seems well enough in the trajectory of Blumenberg's explanation until it is noticed that the modern *overcoming* of Gnosticism is achieved through the hazard of modernity's extraordinarily close encounter with Gnosticism itself. Blumenberg even introduces the section of *The Legitimacy of the Modern Age* on the problem of modernity's overcoming of Gnosticism by claiming that the view of modernity as a "relapse into Gnosticism" would at least be more on target than its characterization in terms of a "relapse into paganism." He goes on to cite Eric Voegelin's claim that the modern age "would be better entitled the Gnostic age," remarking that this formulation "deserves some consideration as the most significant of these attempts [to contrast Gnosticism as a Christian heresy to the substance of Christianity], and the most instructive in its implications" (LMA, 126). Yet the nominalist view of God which effectively forces the creation of the modern age is described by Blumenberg as a position which, while it "may not be a metaphysical dualism of the Gnostic type ... is its practical equivalent *ad hominem*" (LMA, 154), and this nominalist position is overcome when "man constructs for himself a counterworld of elementary rationality and manipulability" (LMA, 173). In the process, the world created by God's arbitrary fiat is "reoccupied," and the previous focus on God's creative power is "reoccupied" by "a new concentration on man's self-interest" (LMA, 178).

Such a "reoccupation" must be rigorously distinguished from a "secularization" of the roles previously played by God's creation and His creative power. If understood in secularizing terms, the modern project would depend on what preceded it in such a way that it could in nowise be understood as a definitive "overcoming" of anything. One consequence of this need to resist a secularizing explanation is that traditional theological vocabulary, in particular, can be employed in the context of the new, modern project grounded in self-assertion, if at all, only in an ironizing and rhetorical fashion. This essentially leaves theological justification with no legitimating role to play in Blumenberg's modern age.

Such a state of affairs is questionable on at least two separate counts. First, there is the problem of whether theological justifications put forward in the modern period can uniformly be understood in such rhetorical terms—on pain, that is, of their being dismissed as "medieval residua" (LMA, 187). Second, it is questionable whether Blumenberg's own defense of modernity in terms of an overcoming of Gnostic theology (or its *ad hominem* equivalent) can remain self-consistently non-secularizing in the absence of at least some *opening* for a distinctively modern form of theological justification. What I hope to show in what follows, by focusing first on Blumenberg's reaction to the project of Francis Bacon in *The Legitimacy of the Modern Age* and then on Blumenberg's own later reaction to his earlier book, is that these two problems are in fact intimately connected. The limits of Blumenberg's legitimation of modernity are specifically those brought on by the increasing inability to counteract the growing *instability* of modern "projects" by appeal to theological pressure. In the case of an early modern figure like Bacon, such theological pressure still restricts the application of self-assertion. By Nietzsche at the latest any such theological appeal has (repeatedly) grown increasingly apocalyptic in the face of later modernity's instability on just this count.

ON THE ABSENCE OF SHIPWRECK

In order to illustrate the peculiar status of theological justification in the Baconian project I turn first to a consideration of the frontispiece to Bacon's *Novum Organum* and the theological context which Bacon generates for it. This frontispiece depicts a ship which is about to pass through the pillars of Hercules, and in the distance there is a second ship which seems sure to follow.[37] Below the depiction of the ships Bacon affixes to this frontispiece a motto from the Vulgate: *Multi pertransibunt & augebitur scientia*—"Many shall pass through and knowledge shall be increased."[38] Bacon's frontispiece thus binds a classical literary topos to a biblical passage that will ultimately lead him to reevaluate the passage through the pillars of Hercules in terms of what might be referred to paradoxically as a "providentialist eschatology."

The literary *topos* which Bacon is in the process of transforming in his frontispiece finds its classical locus in Homer; arguably the most critical revision which it received prior to Bacon was at Dante's hand in the 26th Canto of the *Inferno*. Commenting on this Dantean transformation Hans Blumenberg remarked:

> Here [in Dante] one meets not the hero of the Homeric saga who passes through the peril of the Sirens but rather the Odysseus whom Dante consistently 'further developed' and freely invented on the basis of the restlessness of his curiosity about the world, the Odysseus who does not return home to Ithaca but rather undertakes the final adventure of crossing the boundary of the known world, sails through the Pillars of Hercules, and after five months of voyaging across the ocean sights a mysterious mountain and is shipwrecked. (LMA, 338)

In Bacon, the transformation already initiated in Dante is taken to something of a logical conclusion. There is no indication of shipwreck: although the pillars of Hercules remain a significant threshold they are no longer a threshold to be *transgressed*, but rather one to be crossed over into an earthly paradise. What is announced in this frontispiece is a new attitude toward this-worldly investigation, and this attitude is conspicuously supported by biblical reference.

---

37. Francis Bacon, *Novum Organum*, trans. and ed. Peter Urbach and John Gibson (Chicago: Open Court, 1994). The frontispiece is reproduced facing the title page.

38. Bacon, *Novum Organum*, 104.

In the body of the *Novum Organon* Bacon cites from the prophet Daniel the same passage which he has taken as the motto for his frontispiece.[39] Here Bacon adapts the eschatological force of this passage to support a providential interpretation of the increase of knowledge: "this clearly implies," he asserts,

> that it lies in destiny—that is, providence—that the passage through the world (which by its many long voyages plainly seems to be accomplished or under way) and an increase in knowledge will come at the same period of time.[40]

For Bacon this providence is imminent: "Now if there were someone among us who could answer our questions concerning the operation of Nature, the discovery of all causes and sciences would be a matter of a few years."[41] Bacon self-elects himself to fulfill this role, with somewhat problematic theological consequences. The fulfillment of Daniel's prophecy will in turn legitimate the advancement of science, which is also viewed as an antidote to the Fall: "For man by the fall fell at the same time from his state of innocence and from his dominion over creation. Both of these losses however can even in this life be in some part repaired; the former by religion and faith, the latter by arts and sciences."[42] We meet here one of the central paradoxes of modernity: in an era which has registered an unprecedented burgeoning of progress, this progress is legitimated through the employment of figures of eschatological closure. For the first time, the ships which have set sail for the pillars of Hercules have *arrived*, not just in the Dantean sense of having passed through the pillars, but in the sense of having successfully *met* their intended destination. Figurally speaking, they have attained the horizon.

As mentioned above, Bacon's position requires that a special status be attributed to *his own* position as harbinger of such a final completion.[43] Bacon attempts to diffuse this personal self-elevation by insisting that he is simply the *organizer* of this enterprise, which must be viewed in terms of a *community* of investigators, insisting that his advantage over other previous investigators has been largely a matter of good fortune (*fortuna*). Nevertheless, it is hard to escape the feeling, given his characterization of the enterprise of increasing knowledge as bearing so close an association with providence, that Bacon's role is little short of filling a messianic position *despite* persistent attempts to shift his vision away from a traditionally eschatological perspective. What is at stake here is in fact a profound (further) departure from the

---

39. Bacon, *Novum Organum*, 104.

40. ibid.

41. idem, 116.

42. Francis Bacon, *The Works of Francis Bacon*, ed. James Spedding, Robert L. Ellis, and Douglas D. Heath (London: Longman, 1857-74), vol. IV, 247-48. Hereafter referred to as *Works*.

43. Bacon, *Novum Organum*, 5, and also 6 and 13.

eschatology associated with the Christian religion. In Bacon, the balance is increasingly shifted from *judgment* to *providence*, and this shift in fact intensifies the introjection of the Stoic conception of providence into Christianity. Blumenberg comments that

> ... the inclusion of the Stoics' providence in Christianity was itself already an attempt to provide some insurance for a history that eschatology no longer provided for, or at any rate no longer saw as in need of regulation: The eschatological God of the end of history cannot at the same time be the God who makes Himself known and credible in history as its caretaker. (LMA, 32)

With Bacon, the further shift in the direction of providence can thus be understood in terms of *this-worldly* realization. What is needed, paradoxically, is an understanding of closure that can be applied to an ongoing history. Here we should recall Blumenberg's presentation of absolute metaphors of scale and the associated effect I have identified above in their figural halting of the regress toward horizons.

The advent of such "self-realization" is understood by Bacon in terms of what we might call, in order to emphasize the (attempted) paradoxical overthrow of traditional eschatology, a *mute apocalypse*. Bacon identifies the increase of knowledge with *providence*—or, as he glosses this term, destiny—because it prepares for the last *judgment* "quietly":

> And the saying about spiritual things that "the kingdom of God cometh not with observation" [Luke 17:20] is found to be true in every great work of divine providence. All things glide onward calmly without commotion or sound, and the event plainly comes about before man thinks or notices that it has done so.[44]

In this regard it is interesting to note that the frontispiece depicts the passage through the pillars of Hercules *from the far side*, as is clear from the direction of the sails. The passage is not solitary, another ship closely follows, and though the pillars are surrounded with exotic flora and sealife, they do not appear menacing. There is certainly no intimation of shipwreck here. This ship is gliding on a placid sea "calmly without commotion or sound."[45] When we recognize that we view the scene from beyond the pillars, hence are already on the far side of this crossing, we are established in the position which Bacon describes: "the event plainly comes about before man thinks or notices that it has done so."[46] This has the force of shifting attention from the last Judgment, which has not happened, to an event which *has* already begun: the advent of a knowledge signaling providence. In addition to theological repercussions, this shift in emphasis has political repercussions as

---

44. Bacon, *Novum Organum*, 104.
45. ibid.
46. ibid.

well: it promotes the notion of a community organized around the pursuit of knowledge and, vitally, the improvement of the human condition. These are all aspects of what Blumenberg would take to be modernity's central project; we must now see how he would attempt to shield them from any demand for theological justification. This will then lead us directly to an inspection of Blumenberg's later reconsideration of his earlier defense of modernity in *The Legitimacy of the Modern Age*.

BLUMENBERG'S *CONFESSIO*

In examining Blumenberg's attitude toward Bacon in *The Legitimacy of the Modern Age*, I would like to begin with an anecdote Blumenberg himself considers. Situated with respect to the context of issues concerning theological justification, this anecdote and Blumenberg's consideration of it take on a rather equivocal significance:

> In the garden of the earl of Arundel, who had on display a large number of ancient statues of nude men and women, Sir Francis comes to a sudden halt and proclaims his amazement with the exclamation, 'The resurrection.' (LMA, 105-6)

Blumenberg's own interpretation of this anecdote itself has a history. According to his own later characterization (in the second edition of *The Legitimacy of the Modern Age*), Blumenberg associated (in the first edition) this anecdote with the "rhetoric of secularization" (LMA, 103-21) and its employment of figures of "renaissance," to which a critic lodged the potential objection that "perhaps what speaks here is not at all, or not only, a rhetorical daring that is conscious of its use of a frivolous equation as a technical expedient, as Blumenberg imagines, but rather genuine disconcertedness."[47] Blumenberg's response is categorical:

> Bacon's recovery of paradise is not connected with a resurrection of any kind. The identity of the hypostatized subject of science, in which individuals and generations are completely dissolved, is at the same time the identity of a mankind achieving the future perfection of domination over nature. There was no need to assure justice for those whose decease preceded that perfection. Bacon's idea of paradise is not eschatological, because it is pagan… The final times of the prophecy of Daniel have become the 'new' age ['*die Neuzeit*': the modern age] that for us is the final age—and the German translator J. H. Pfingsten renders this as the "neueste Zeiten" [newest times]… [Bacon's] concern in the application of both the biblical prophecies and the metaphor of organic growth to his own times is to make the accumulation of new discoveries and

---

47. G. Kaiser, *Pietismus und Patriotismus im literarischen Deutschland*, 2nd. ed. (Frankfurt: Athenäum, 1973), "Vorwort und Forschungsbericht zur zweiten Auflage," xvi, cited in Blumenberg, *Legitimacy*, 106.

inventions appear trustworthy and promising as symptoms of the state of the world as a whole. (LMA, 106-7)

What is at issue here is no less than the status of theology in Bacon's "modern age."

In the passage in which Blumenberg interprets Bacon's quip his contention is that there is no Christian theology which Bacon *even could* use in his defense. But Blumenberg fails to rule out the possibility of heterodox theological justification on Bacon's part, and consequently his assertion of Bacon's "paganism" remains undefended in *The Legitimacy of the Modern Age*.

It is with all the more interest, then, that I turn to a short section from Blumenberg's 1988 *St. Matthew Passion*,[48] "The Beginning of Wisdom," which is extraordinarily full of ironies concerning not only the issue of theology in the modern age, but also Blumenberg's own "theology" and its bearing, specifically, on the enterprise of his early masterwork, *The Legitimacy of the Modern Age*. This section from *St. Matthew Passion* revolves around the Solomonic saying, "The fear of the Lord is the beginning of wisdom," which, Blumenberg tells us, was to be found inscribed on the far wall of the assembly hall of his school. Here Blumenberg attended Monday devotions until 1933, and afterwards was subjected to the new Brown director's "ersatz performances, overvalued as 'speeches,' which replaced the previous Monday devotions" (M, 28).[49] Half a century later, Blumenberg recounts having encountered the "Childhood Recollections of a Lübeck Doctor" by his friend and schoolmate Ulrich Thoemmes in which, in particular, Thoemmes referred to the biblical saying on the assembly hall wall, "which naturally only could be meant to stand for the fear of the teachers, who sat there with threatening gestures in rows perpendicular to those of the schoolchildren, supporting this ritual God-fearing" (M, 28). It is with regard to this interpretation that Blumenberg confesses that it had never occurred to him to understand the saying in this way: neither to associate it with the "more or less authoritarian, exaggeratedly benevolent faces of the teachers off to one side" (M, 29), nor even to construe the saying, in terms of an objective genitive, to refer to "the *fear of the Lord* as that of those before the Lord" (M, 29). Instead, Blumenberg reports, he had always understood the biblical saying in terms of a *subjective* genitive: "the *fear of the Lord* as his before something other, the fear of which was precisely the beginning of his wisdom" (M, 29). He continues: "And with this it is already clear that the Lord's fear was directed towards humans, since he did not allow them to take part in his paradise after having made them dangerous accessories in the knowledge of good and evil" (M, 29). Blumenberg rounds out this testimony by making what he *explicitly* refers to as a "short *Confessio*": the worst of it is that "despite having long known

---

48. Hans Blumenberg, *Matthäuspassion* (Frankfurt am Main: Bibliothek Suhrkamp, 1988).
49. All translations from this work are mine.

better, my childhood interpretation of the assembly hall saying has remained the tenor of my 'theology,' insofar as it deserves this name" (M, 30).

What makes this *Confessio* particularly interesting with regard to the project of *The Legitimacy of the Modern Age* is that Blumenberg goes on to recount how, much later, he came to discover by coincidence in the Nag Hammadi manuscripts that his schoolboy interpretation of the biblical saying was in fact that given verbatim by the gnostic Justinus in a manuscript referred to as the "Hypothesis of the Archons" (M, 30). Given that in *The Legitimacy of the Modern Age* Blumenberg understands the legitimacy of modernity in terms of its definitive overcoming of Gnosticism—in contrast to the impermanent success of Christianity's attempt[50]—it is perplexing, to say the least, what to make of Blumenberg's confession that his theology "insofar as it deserves this name" (M, 30), is itself gnostic both by affiliation and, indeed, in nature.

Blumenberg's caveat is important: it ultimately becomes clear in *Matthäuspassion* that *at least the reading of the St. Matthew Passion offered there* cannot be understood as unproblematically theological (gnostic or otherwise). In fact, Blumenberg suggests that theology is a "duel" which itself seems to constitute a sort of battle to steal the concealed majesty of a withdrawn God (M, 107).[51] As such, Blumenberg suggests that theology itself becomes a function of Gnosticism, so that we might describe Blumenberg's own position as *meta*-theological. What interests Blumenberg, centrally, is the need for an "absolute realism of the commitment of divine favor to men" once "the conjunction with love, as a restraint that power places on itself, can be raised to the level of certainty."[52] Blumenberg asserts that this need arises "prior to any actual dogma of any theology whatever," and so we might also call Blumenberg's position *pre*-theological.[53]

In "The Beginning of Wisdom" Blumenberg goes on to refer to "one of his sharpest and sharpest-witted critics" (M, 32), Ulrich Wilckens, who as a

---

50. See Blumenberg, LMA, 126.

51. See also M, 103, 108.

52. Hans Blumenberg, *Work on Myth*, trans. Robert Wallace (Cambridge: MIT Press, 1985), 23; hereafter cited as *Myth*. On realism, see also Blumenberg, *Matthäuspassion*, "Caravaggios »Emmaus«," 259-61.

53. In the later chapter, "Visionary Design," below, I develop an analogous "twist" in the humanities, drawing on mathematical models which ultimately lead in the direction of recent developments in Alain Connes' non-commutative geometry. For an elementary presentation by a philosopher associated with the Vatican Observatory, see Michael Heller, "Where physics meets metaphysics," in *On Space and Time*, ed. Shahn Majid (Cambridge: Cambridge University Press, 2008), 238-277. Heller helpfully suggests that Connes' 'non-commutative geometry' be thought of as an example of what J. A. Wheeler proposed in terms of 'pregeometry', 253-257, thus making the possibility analogy with 'pre-theology' linguistically explicit. See also, in the same volume, Alain Connes, "On the fine structure of spacetime," 196-237.

professor of New Testament at the time of the publication of *The Legitimacy of the Modern Age* in 1966 was the first (Blumenberg includes himself) to speak of the book as "a very fruitful common basis for the conversation he (i.e. Blumenberg) seeks and provokes with theologians" (cited, M, 32). In 1988, his response to this sharp and sharp-witted critic was to declare: "I hope that I have not disappointed him or am not now in the act of doing so" (M, 32).[54] Such a declaration certainly provides us with a warrant from Blumenberg himself for taking seriously the problem of theology in the modern age in a way that his characterization of the Baconian enterprise in *The Legitimacy of the Modern Age* might have led us to foreclose. But it should also leave us profoundly uncertain of the status of the previous enterprise of *The Legitimacy of the Modern Age* itself: how are we to understand a defense of modernity as an overcoming of Gnosticism if the defense is itself delivered to us by a gnostic theologian?!

Blumenberg makes what may count as a tacit acknowledgment of this quandary in the final page of this short section on "The Beginning of Wisdom." For he goes on to declare that it would be insufficient reason to bring up Wilckens "had he not provided something like the *coincidentia oppositorum* for the concordances and discordances already discussed" (M, 32). Blumenberg's reference to the medieval notion of the coincidence of opposites in this context is itself already fraught with irony, given that Blumenberg's legitimation of the modern age depends on his reading Bruno as providing a *non-theological* reconfiguration of the Cusan's system, while the latter takes the notion of the coincidence of opposites as a central element. However this may be, *what*, we may ask, is the coincidence of opposites (or something like it) which Wilckens provides? Significantly, the reconciliation is provided by a historical account of the difficult position in which the Greek translators of this biblical saying were put: according to Wilckens, the conjunction of the concepts of fear and wisdom remained foreign to their ears. That is, they remained in a position of discordant *incomprehension*, but generated a concordance through the acceptance of a canonical translation. The concordance does not *resolve* the incomprehension so much as it overcomes it by (productively) leaving it behind. Similarly, the concluding sentence of "The Beginning of Wisdom" may be read as implying that Blumenberg's own "theology" was itself born of an analogous *modern* incomprehension on Blumenberg's part: "What the 'Septuagint' did not want to succeed in doing failed two thousand years later through the completely grammatically unrefined confusion of a genitive" (M, 32). Although this concluding sentence is not yet in itself enough to ascribe *modernistic*

---

54. Blumenberg's *Matthäuspassion* may be seen, in part, as an extension of remarks Blumenberg makes in Chapter 3 of Part II of *The Legitimacy of the Modern Age*, "A Systematic Comparison of the Epochal Crisis of Antiquity to That of the Middle Ages;" see, in particular, LMA, 170-9.

incomprehension to the (nonetheless precocious) schoolboy, Blumenberg's previous declaration that his theology *retained* the tenor of this interpretation despite his "better knowledge" (M, 30) may allow us finally so to understand it.

In light of Blumenberg's own belated confession regarding the theological tenor of his own thought, I return now to Bacon with specific suggestions concerning the theological tenor of *his* thought and the problems this poses for *The Legitimacy of the Modern Age*. What I will suggest here, in advance, is that Blumenberg's recourse to gnostic theology in *St. Matthew Passion* serves the function of *promoting* (as opposed to specifically *legitimating*) modernity in a *structurally* analogous way to that in which theological justification functions in the Baconian enterprise. I will attempt to make a case for this structural analogy in the final section of this chapter.

THE BATTLE OF THE GODS AND THE GIANTS

What we might call the "theological volatility" of the Baconian enterprise is a consequence of the need to circumscribe the tremendous new power that Bacon is in the process of unleashing, a power that we may identify with his pursuit of science and the technology associated with it. No passage from Bacon makes the problem clearer than his declaration that in providing charitable inventions, "man is a god to man."[55] The theological dangers of such an assertion are obvious, and the technological consequences are quick to follow. To the extent that a theological context is lacking for containing these technological consequences, the challenges of a radical anthropology are posed which must lead us to ask, along with John Briggs, whether "human beings [can] fuse [human knowledge and human power] without reducing knowledge to power, wisdom to willful force?"[56] What sort of context do we have within which the paradigm of human self-assertion which Bacon is in the process of developing can situate itself?

Whether or not we can find a "Baconian theology" within which this central equation of knowledge and power can be absorbed, it is impossible to come to an understanding of this equation without recognizing the theological *context* which it renders problematic. It is for this reason that the picture Blumenberg gives us in *The Legitimacy of the Modern Age* is ultimately too one-sided, for in the conception of legitimacy around which Blumenberg's early masterpiece is oriented he must imply that modernity achieves a quasi-stable state ultimately independent of any *positive* contribution from the "drag" which is exercised by what can only seem to be the "pre-modern" demands of theology, and that consequently modernity must be legitimized without any such positive intrinsic appeal to historical context. But, in fact,

---

55. Bacon, *Novum Organum*, 130.
56. Briggs, "Bacon's Science and Religion," 183.

to the extent that "pre-modern" theological demands fade, modernity faces the new problem of an unbridled equation of knowledge and power resulting in the threat of a radical anthropology with Nietzschean consequences, and hence it is not clear that once this later context is taken into account Blumenberg has provided any legitimation of modernity whatsoever. It is arguably just this dilemma which will later lead to Blumenberg's growing interest in philosophical anthropology.[57]

Although Blumenberg does not ever give a distinct, explicit characterization of what would count, for him, as a legitimation of modernity, it is clear from his critique of the secularization thesis that modernity cannot be indebted to Christianity in any large *positive* way. This is apparent, for example, from Blumenberg's remark that "the continuous self-confirmation of its autonomy and authenticity by science and technology is brought into question by the thesis that 'the modern world owes its uncanny success to a great extent to its Christian background'" (LMA, 116, citing Carl Friedrich von Weisäcker). On the other hand, it is abundantly clear that the modern re-occupation is to be understood as the defense of a positive *revaluation* of a position which was in evidence but negatively stigmatized within the worldview of late medieval nominalism. Thus Blumenberg says that

> the absolute certainty founded on human thought itself, which Descartes seeks, is not the 'secularization' of the certainty of salvation, which is supposed to be guaranteed in faith and its *nuda fiducia* [naked trust], but rather its necessary counter-position, which is theologically demanded and (unexpectedly) legitimized by Luther's thesis. Theological absolutism has its own indispensable atheism and anthropotheism. It postulates as complementary to itself a position that does not want to be postulated in *this* way, that denies itself *this* legitimation, of being what is 'natural'—in the sense of ungraced by God—and not what is rational and humanly necessary, grounding itself in itself." (LMA, 179)

The legitimation then consists in a defense of this revaluation.

This does not solve the problem, however, for what it shows is only that Blumenberg and Bacon are *joined* in their need to defend, for example, the positive valuation of natural scientific investigation. But whereas Bacon's defense is at least partly theological, it is a consequence of Blumenberg's position that we cannot take this theology "seriously," i.e. as anything other than rhetorical in its force. I would suggest that we cannot expect Bacon's defense (or ultimately, for that matter, Blumenberg's) to be successful in the sense of being ultimately consistent, and that in such circumstances we are best off recognizing both Bacon's appeal to theology and the ultimate unorthodoxy

---

57. See, in particular, the posthumously published *Beschreibung des Menschen* (Frankfurt am Main: Suhrkamp, 2006). Editor Manfred Sommer suggests that the published work, *Lebenszeit und Weltzeit* (1986), may be read as the third part of a project of which *Beschreibung des Menschen* would constitute the first two parts ("Nachwort des Herausgebers," 901).

of his theological position. Blumenberg's *Confessio* suggests that Blumenberg himself is in an analogous position.

It is just this dilemma of "legitimation crisis" which his earlier project faces to which Blumenberg indirectly responds in "The Beginning of Wisdom." Reflecting on his childhood interpretation of the Solomonic saying, Blumenberg states: "It only became clear to me much later that the 'Fear of the Lord' must extend very far if the 'death of God' was the last threat of mankind in his self-elevation to 'overman'" (M, 30).[58] The antagonism of the gods and the giants which is embodied (and ultimately dismembered) in such a Nietzschean "revaluation" indicates the extent to which theological disputes have not been settled by the modern notion of self-assertion, but in fact have if anything only been aggravated. To aggravate matters even further, the *coincidentia oppositorum* which Blumenberg suggests would "reconcile" modern humanism with gnostic theology is an attitude toward history which stresses the inevitable *incomprehension* with which one "age" faces another. To be sure, this is already an element of the account which Blumenberg provides in *The Legitimacy of the Modern Age*, but in such later writings as "The Beginning of Wisdom" Blumenberg probes the subtle ironies which are implied with much greater sensitivity.

At issue, then, is the understanding of Bacon's central equation of knowledge and power and its problematic relation to the possibility of any theological justification or even "contextualization." In this regard it is important to note that Bacon's earliest explicit equation of knowledge and power occurs in a theological context, in the early *Meditationes sacrae*.[59] Here Bacon refers in a thoroughly unoriginal way to the convergence of the knowledge and power of God, which is beyond understanding. Two decades later, however, in the *Great Instauration*, it is to the justification for the *human* equation of knowledge and power that Bacon has turned. From the perspective of theological concerns, what is most important in Bacon's formulation is that in this realm of enquiry Nature has become man's "new Lord":

> For man is only the servant and interpreter of Nature and he only does and understands so much as he shall have observed, in fact or in thought, of the course of Nature; more than this he neither knows, nor can do. No force whatever can unfasten or break the chain of causes, and Nature is only overcome by obeying her. So it is that those two objects of mankind, *Knowledge* and *Power*, come in fact to the same thing; and the failure of works derives mostly from Ignorance of causes.[60]

From the perspective of *The Legitimacy of the Modern Age*, Blumenberg would stress that we should understand Nature as "re-occupying" the position

---

58. See also M, 297-307.
59. Briggs, "Bacon's science and religion," 183.
60. Bacon, *Novum Organum*, 29.

previously held by the Christian God, and not as a "secularization" of a previous theological content. More precisely, Blumenberg sees the infinite universe (of Bruno) as occupying "the very position that the intratrinitarian generation of the second Person occupied in theology" (LMA, 564). Blumenberg asks, however, whether this reoccupation was one which Bruno did not see how to make entirely explicit. But he also asserts that

> if one proceeds from the assumption that human autonomy can henceforth articulate its positive character only outside the Middle Ages, then it becomes clear that only two fundamental positions remain open to it, if it wants to throw off its supposedly 'natural' role: hypothetical atheism, which poses the question of man's potential under the condition that the answer should hold 'even if there is no God'; and rational deism, which employs the 'most perfect being' to guarantee this human potential—the 'most perfect being' that is functionalized by Descartes as the principle of the deduction of the dependability of the world and of our knowledge of it. The double face of the Enlightenment, on the one hand its renewal of a teleological optimism and on the other hand its inclination to atheism, loses its contradictory character if one places it in the context of the unity of the onset of human self-assertion and the rejection of its late-medieval systematic role. (LMA, 129)

From Blumenberg's perspective in *The Legitimacy of the Modern Age* we might attempt to understand Bacon's shift as one from a Christian theology incompatible with the Baconian project to a compatible "natural" theology. What Blumenberg does not explicitly remark is that, given the existence and functional equivalence of the two "options" of hypothetical atheism and rational deism, there is in his scheme not only no theological legitimation of the modern age, but in fact not even any *legitimation of theology* in the modern age.

THE WISDOM OF SOLOMON

In fact Bacon's theology is *not* accurately described as natural (and certainly not deistic), although from the perspective of *The Legitimacy of the Modern Age* it is difficult to see why it should not be. Having foreclosed the possibility that we could understand Bacon's appeal to resurrection as anything other than figurative, Blumenberg, as we have seen, is led to declare Bacon's characterization of providence to be pagan. In addition he understands Bacon's position as standing in much closer proximity to medieval traditions of magic than to any contribution of Christian theology. It would be more accurate, however, to say that Bacon's position cannot be understood as either consistently Christian *or* pagan. Understanding Bacon's "theology" (insofar as it deserves the name) is in fact much more a matter of understanding the *limits* of Bacon's equation of knowledge and power in the face of theological pressures militating against its unrestricted extension.⁶¹ Here we find a situation which is in fact much more appropriately described in those terms which Blumenberg's later writings make central: a situation in which there is a demand to *translate* the traditional theological requirements as the result of a need which renders their traditional *formulation* incomprehensible. For Blumenberg, the difficulties involved here ultimately lie in the need to make unselfevident decisions against a background of indecision and incomprehension.⁶² The difficulty which accrues to Blumenberg's stress on such "retranslation" is that it is hard to see what criteria could be provided for a successful or even a legitimate translation in such circumstances. Indeed, in *The Legitimacy of the Modern Age* Blumenberg speaks of Christianity as a "translation" (his scare quotes) of Gnosticism (LMA, 136).

We can highlight such a translation in action by comparing the Baconian justification for the equation of knowledge and power, and the system of intellectual pursuit which it supports, with the Calvinistic doctrine of double-predestination. John Briggs notes two ways in which Bacon defends his inquiry.⁶³ First, and perhaps somewhat surprisingly if we take into consideration only his equation of knowledge and power, Bacon asserts that contemplation takes precedence over the active life. Taking King Solomon as his model, Bacon remarks that he is most to be praised "for his detection of concealed laws of nature, not for the fruits he brought forth with them."⁶⁴ Here Bacon makes recourse to biblical precedent, but even more significantly he is in the process of justifying his enterprise through the development of a doctrine of works as signs: "works themselves are of greater value as pledges of truth than as comforts of life."⁶⁵ Secondly, however, we also find Bacon justifying inquiry by its fruits: "Wherefore, as in religion we are warned to show our faith by works, so in philosophy by the same rule the system should be judged of by its fruits."⁶⁶ Briggs sees these two justifications as at odds,⁶⁷ but whether they ultimately are or not, the tension which they express is analogous to that of the Calvinists in their discussion of works within the context of double predestination. Briggs himself goes on to describe the tension in Bacon admirably:

---

61. I thank Elizabeth Brient for insisting on this point. For an extended discussion, see Briggs, "Bacon's science and religion."

62. See Blumenberg, M, 211. It must be pointed out that the recognition of this condition need not serve as a warrant for methodological decisionism.

63. Briggs, "Bacon's science and religion," 182. For a more ambitious (and questionable) treatment at length of Bacon's defense of his enterprise, see John Briggs, *Francis Bacon and the Rhetoric of Nature* (Cambridge: Harvard University Press, 1989); hereafter cited as *Bacon*.

64. Bacon, *Works*, vol. IV, 114.

65. Bacon, *Novum Organum*, 126.

66. Bacon, *Works*, vol. IV, 74.

67. Briggs, "Bacon's science and religion, 182.

> Elsewhere Bacon explains that the charitable deeds of the new sciences serve as 'the seal which prints and determines the contemplative counterpart'[68] ... the practical applications of knowledge not only reveal the laws of natural operation; works justify and determine wisdom. This paradoxical relationship between contemplation and action must be embraced faithfully so that it does not cultivate new forms of vanity.[69]

Vanity is here a threat to be counteracted just as it is for Calvinism: the performance of good works should not be done with the *intention* of gain for oneself *or even for others*. It is for this reason that "contemplation" (or in the Calvinist case "grace") must take precedence. If we take Bacon's theology seriously, then as for Calvin good works are not allowed to exhaust themselves in their *this-worldly* purport. But this makes the Baconian alignment between contemplation and the otherworldly all the more important.

What such passages require is that we reject the traditional interpretation of Bacon's enterprise advancing in terms of a strict separation of the concerns of theology from those of natural philosophy. Briggs has also rejected such an absolute division, but still argues that the study of divinity itself, though occupying a place within the Baconian project, must be carefully separated from Bacon's own work. He understands this division of labor in terms of the dual function of reason, which, on the one hand works "in the conception and apprehension of the mysteries of God to us revealed,"[70] and on the other, in "the inferring and deriving of doctrine and direction thereupon."[71] In the first case reason does *not* inquire, but only grasps and illustrates revelation: it "piously interprets the scripturally revealed meaning of God's inscrutable *will*."[72] In its latter use, however, reason "inquires into the world as God's manifestation of his *glory* or power."[73] This distinction then takes over the function that was previously assigned to the distinction between the book of scripture and the book of nature. Yet there is a hierarchical distinction to be made as well: the scripturally revealed meaning of God's inscrutable will is in no way dependent on the inquiry into the world as God's manifestation of his glory. In the *Advancement of Learning* Bacon asks:

> How then is it that man is said to have by the light and law of nature some notions and conceits of virtue and vice, justice and wrong, good and evil? Thus; because the light of nature is used in two several senses; the one, that which springeth from reason, sense, induction, argument, according to the laws of heaven and earth; the other, that which is imprinted upon the spirit of man by an inward instinct, according to the

---

68. Bacon, *Works*, vol. IV, 121.
69. Briggs, "Bacon's science and religion," 183.
70. Bacon, *Works*, vol. III, 479.
71. ibid.
72. Briggs, "Bacon's science and religion," 173.
73. ibid.

law of conscience, which is a sparkle of the purity of his first estate."[74]

Here Bacon distinguishes between reason and intuition in a way which will be preserved in much the same form by Locke, who speaks of reason as a *natural Revelation*.[75]

In spite of the division between the two senses of the light of nature, Briggs points out that nonetheless Bacon uses the vocabulary of *wisdom* when describing the procedure of inquiry, and this suggests that although, as with the distinction between contemplation and works, we are dealing with two distinct "senses," nonetheless Bacon will understand the one as a "pledge" of the other. He thus asks God to "graciously grant to us to write an apocalypse or true vision of the footsteps of the Creator imprinted on his creatures."[76] Rather than understanding Bacon's "mute apocalypse" as a rhetorical figure employed to dramatic effect, we should instead understand it as indicative of the theological pressures which generate a genuinely paradoxical formulation of the Baconian enterprise. Recognizing the positive function of (heterodox) theological justification for Bacon thus requires that we go beyond Briggs' recognition of the division of theology and natural philosophy to a stronger recognition of the *coordinated* function of these two components of the Baconian enterprise.

With Bacon's equation of apocalypse and true vision we have returned to the thematic identification of the contemplative with the otherworldly. Drawing once again on an analogy to Solomon, Bacon is intent upon "laying a foundation in the human understanding for a holy temple after the model of the world."[77] From the perspective of *The Legitimacy of the Modern Age* Blumenberg would perhaps explain this by saying that because God's will is inscrutable, we transfer—not secularize—the energy devoted to "building a temple to God" to "laying a foundation in the human understanding."[78] This would require that we understand Bacon's notion of a "true apocalypse" as a mere figure. But by understanding Bacon's "apocalypse" in merely rhetorical terms we prevent ourselves from understanding precisely that regard in which Bacon's position *cannot* be understood as theologically naturalistic: Bacon's theology of the mute apocalypse is what guarantees safe passage from the "worldly" model to other-worldly contemplation and back again, and so prevents the equation of knowledge and power from obtaining unbounded application. Like later deism, the foundations for Bacon's holy temple in the human understanding are laid *in God's creation*, which, so far from being a gnostic prison-house, is in fact our guide for the acquisition of

---

74. Bacon, *Works*, vol. III, 479.

75. John Locke, *An essay concerning human understanding*, ed. Peter H. Nidditch (Oxford: Clarendon Press, 1979), 698; hereafter cited as Locke, *An essay*.

76. Bacon, *Works*, vol. IV, 33.

77. Bacon, *Works*, vol. IV, 107.

78. ibid.

wisdom. But the pressure to find the key to inquiry in God's creation, which Bacon uses to provide a theological justification of this-worldly investigation, is coupled to a theological pressure to tie this "naturalistic" impulse back into an eschatological scheme that finds no (overt) place in the tradition of rational deism. Bacon's theology of the mute apocalypse is no more deism than Calvinism is Feuerbachian anthropology, and without such theological pressure Bacon's enterprise would indeed degenerate into the (covertly) materialistic and nominalistic enterprise it has been taken by so many (including Blumenberg) to be.[79] Yet it is just his unorthodox theological attitude which prevents Bacon's project from being traditionally Christian as well: unlike Solomon's temple built to house the Ark of the Covenant, Bacon's temple is, paradoxically, *otherworldly*. And yet this "temple" has as end a "'sabbath' attained not by scientific labor alone, but by that labor for the sake of providing mankind with rest from hardship."[80] In both regards Bacon's attitude registers a diametrical inversion of the earliest Christian attitude, which was one of worshiping an otherworldly God in a world which is devalued by virtue of its imminent demise. In this sense Bacon's position is as much a "logical conclusion" of the revision of the Christian tradition which was initiated through the inclusion of a Stoic conception of providence as his setting sail through the pillars of Hercules is a logical conclusion of Dante's revision of Homer.

ANXIETY AND MYTH

In *The Legitimacy of the Modern Age* Blumenberg offers his own interpretation of the Baconian frontispiece:

> The pillars of Hercules, which are presented on the title page of the *Instauratio Magna* as already being transcended by shipping traffic, are indeed a fateful boundary (*columnae fatales*)—but rather than representing a divine warning against hubris they represent the discouragement of desire and hope by myth. (LMA, 384)

Part of Blumenberg's support for such an interpretation of Bacon's frontispiece is drawn from Bacon's own identification of the pillars of Hercules with traditional literature in the dedicatory preface to *De dignitate et augmentis scientiarum*.[81] Blumenberg also refers to a passage in the preface to the

---

79. Instead, Bacon's philosophical position is profoundly realist in orientation, although in the tradition of the "maker's knowledge tradition;" see Antonio Pérez-Ramos, "Bacon's forms and the maker's knowledge tradition," in *Cambridge Companion*, 99-120, and Antonio Pérez-Ramos, *Francis Bacon's Idea of Science and the Maker's Knowledge Tradition* (Oxford: Oxford University Press, 1988). Blumenberg's position in *The Legitimacy of the Modern Age*, on the contrary, is that modernity is founded on the *rejection of any appeal to realism*. He supports this position by making an explicit appeal to Nietzsche: see *Legitimacy*, 141-42.

80. Briggs, "Bacon's science and religion," 182.

81. Bacon, *Works*, vol. I, 485, cited by Blumenberg, *Legitimacy*, 636 n. 26.

Instauratio Magna in which "man's false assessment of himself appears as embodied in the Pillars of Hercules" (LMA, 636 n. 26). Yet neither of these passages has a direct bearing on Blumenberg's insistence that here desire and hope are discouraged by *myth*; in order to understand Blumenberg's specific appeal to myth we must turn to his own concerns with, and understanding of, the mythical. The significance of myth is, of course, the central theme of Blumenberg's *Work on Myth*, his third major work, which first appeared in 1979.[82] But rather than confront this monumental work head on, I will address Blumenberg's interpretation of Bacon's frontispiece indirectly by turning to a much shorter pendant to *Work on Myth* which appeared at the same time, the long essay or short book, *Shipwreck with Spectator*. These two works are related in several regards, perhaps the most obvious of which is that while *Work on Myth* focuses on the myth of Prometheus as a locus of the concern with self-assertion and its punishment or sanction, *Shipwreck with Spectator* focuses on the metaphorics of foundering and the response of onlookers to this crisis in man's ability to govern his own destiny.

At issue in particular is the reception of the passage at the beginning of the Proem to Book II of Lucretius' *De Rerum Natura* in which Lucretius declares:

> Sweet it is, when on the great sea the winds are buffeting the waters, to gaze from the land on another's great struggles; not because it is pleasure or joy that any one should be distressed, but because it is sweet to perceive from what misfortune you yourself are free.[83]

Blumenberg shows how this passage was first used to develop a model of philosophical remove from the circumstances of life, only later to be transformed into a problematic metaphor for a transcendental reflection which would nevertheless not signal a withdrawal from the world. In this regard, the difficulty in the modern transformation of this metaphor bears significant analogy to the difficulty Bacon faces in his account of contemplation: in both cases a role must be found for reflection which neither disjoins it from, nor reduces it to, this-worldly engagement.[84] Here, I would suggest, Blumenberg is more successful in addressing the central dilemma confronting modern conceptions of subjectivity than he could be in *The Legitimacy of the Modern Age*, given the strategy for *legitimating* modernity that is employed there.

The difficulties which are involved in the modern transformation of the shipwreck metaphor may be indicated by considering two examples, drawn from Blumenberg's essay, which focus on the problem which modernity faces,

---

82. Blumenberg deals with the interrelated themes of this section—anxiety and myth—in the first chapter of *Work on Myth*, "After the Absolutism of Reality," 3-32.

83. Lucretius, *Lucretius on the Nature of Things*, trans. Cyril Bailey (Oxford: Clarendon Press, 1910), 65.

84. Blumenberg, *Shipwreck*, 61.

not with the metaphorics of shipwreck *per se*, but rather with the problem of the *calm sea*. Blumenberg points to Voltaire's novel *Zadig*, in which the passions are described as "the wind that fills the sail of a ship, which, although it sometimes capsizes the ship, is also responsible for its moving at all."[85] In the face of such a modern recognition, Blumenberg asserts, "Montaigne's advice not to leave the harbor for the sea is no longer feasible."[86] In this regard, we might point out that Bacon, too, rejects Montaigne's advice, but at a pivotal moment in the history of the seafaring metaphor at which he is burdened neither by the ancient insistence on shipwreck nor by the modern anxiety of the doldrums.

With regard to the latter of these two concerns, an anecdote about Nietzsche which Blumenberg discusses in *Shipwreck* is particularly illuminating. During the course of a four day voyage as the sole passenger on a steam freighter traveling from Genoa to Messina, Nietzsche "believed he had understood the Greek Epicurus."[87] In contrast to the Lucretian spectator, whose distanced observation of an emergency Nietzsche "wholly neglects,"[88] Nietzsche describes the happiness of the Epicurean spectator, the "happiness of eyes that have seen the sea of existence become calm."[89] As Blumenberg points out, here

> it is not the sea's calm and serenity that gratify the spectator, by way of his eyes; rather, wholly in the style of the idealistic subject, it is the power of the sufferer, the happiness of his eyes, before which a metaphorical "sea of existence" has *become calm*. The metaphor is a projection, a mastering anthropomorphizing of nature in the service of the subject, who is reflected in it. Here Nietzsche has brought the Greek completely under his power.[90]

Although the calm sea of Bacon's frontispiece is absent from *Shipwreck*, what Blumenberg discusses here may be read (inverting my previous characterization with an eye now to the "progeny" rather than the "prehistory" of Bacon's frontispiece) as the logical culmination of what Bacon has initiated. What Blumenberg points out with regard to Nietzsche is already nascent in the case of Bacon: the *power* of the "sufferer" (as, for Bacon, we must "suffer" nature, i.e. obey her) obtained by the metaphoric projection of an anthropomorphic conception of power onto a vision of natural tranquillity. This is the humanistic equivalent of Bacon's theology of the "mute apocalypse" and the "providentializing" of eschatology which it implies, as is made clear

---

85. idem., 34.
86. ibid.
87. Blumenberg, *Shipwreck*, 22.
88. idem, 23.
89. Friedrich Nietzsche, *The Gay Science*, trans. Walter Kaufmann (New York: Vintage, 1974), 180-1; cited by Blumenberg, *Shipwreck*, 23.
90. Blumenberg, *Shipwreck*, 23.

by the interpretation of sailing on the calm sea which Bacon provides. For Bacon, too, this maneuver signifies a "bringing under his power" of the ancients: we may say that Bacon has aspired to master Solomon in the way Nietzsche has attempted to master Epicurus. And it is only in such terms that it first becomes apparent what Blumenberg could intend by saying that the pillars of Hercules in Bacon's frontispiece represent the discouragement of hope and desire by myth: that the calmness of the sea which permits the passage beyond the pillars of Hercules is itself the metaphorical projection of man's overcoming of ancient myth *through its metaphorical introjection.*[91] In both cases, what we have is a distinctly *figurative* employment of an ancient topos. This is, in fact, what must ultimately lie behind Blumenberg's insistence in *The Legitimacy* that Bacon's employment of motifs of resurrection be understood as figurative. Yet the impact of a figure depends on its context, and what is dramatically missing in the Nietzschean context is the sort of theological pressure which Bacon faced. Although it is equally true in the cases of Bacon and Nietzsche that, as Blumenberg puts it, "the metaphor is a projection, a mastering anthropomorphizing of nature in the service of the subject, who is reflected in it,"[92] from Bacon to Nietzsche the limits within which it is permissible for such a metaphor to be employed are dramatically broadened. With Nietzsche's liberation of the will from its Baconian servitude to nature, the "mastering anthropomorphizing of nature"[93] is elevated to the role of an expansive metaphysical explanation in the vacuum supplied by the death of God and, more specifically, the absence of theology. We are left in the paradoxical position that the very metaphor which attempts to provide a picture of our mastery over *nature* becomes equally a picture of our *inability* to master *ourselves*. Nietzsche's attempt to introject the picture of the calm sea into the "happiness of eyes that have seen the sea of existence become calm"[94] is in fact self-refuting because (to speak figuratively) it is a figure which can no longer make any reference to a ground. Here, to borrow a description from Blumenberg, will has replaced *sophia* as "the last ground of all fear that could befall an earthly being" (M, 31), so that "anxiety becomes the last place-holder of the will or later of Dasein."[95] Will cannot be self-mastered: the attempt to gain mastery through *self*-mastery of the will culminates in the diaspora of anxiety. Nietzsche's mastery is successful only to the extent that he can understand it as a bringing of another, Epicurus, "completely under his power."[96]

---

91. Compare *Legitimacy*, 127ff.
92. Blumenberg, *Shipwreck*, 23.
93. ibid.
94. Nietzsche, *The Gay Science*, 180-1.
95. ibid.
96. Blumenberg, *Shipwreck*, 23. It is important to note that this characterization is Blumenberg's, not Nietzsche's.

To the extent that such mastery remains a human desideratum, we remain faced, to borrow a phrase from Leszek Kolakowski, with the presence of myth.[97] And to the extent that Blumenberg's defense of modernity cannot be accepted as demonstrating the "definitive" overcoming of Gnosticism, modernity remains, to appeal to Kolakowski once again, on endless trial.[98]

SPECIALIZATION AND THE THREAT OF FALSE IDOLS

Having discussed both the theological pressures on the Baconian enterprise and the consequences of Bacon's equation of knowledge and power in the eventual absence of such pressures, I will return briefly to the pressures of the *Baconian* enterprise upon theology, its "theological volatility." This will put me in a position to compare the role of theological justification as it enters into Bacon's project and as it belatedly surfaces in Blumenberg's *St. Matthew Passion*, which will in turn allow me to draw some morals about the notion of a legitimation of modernity that Blumenberg proposed earlier in *The Legitimacy of the Modern Age*.

So far as Bacon's enterprise is concerned, what must be mentioned are the difficulties it would face should it attempt to usurp the traditional position of theology. What is at issue in Bacon is not the *secularization* of Christian theology but rather the impossibility for the Baconian enterprise to satisfy such a demand. In *The Legitimacy of the Modern Age* Blumenberg insisted on the impossibility of understanding the modern project as a secularization of Christian theology; his "confession" in "The Beginning of Wisdom" now invites us to reflect upon the "theological insufficiency" of this same modern project, as he understands it. The type of scientific investigation which Bacon begins to promote cannot replace the Christian theological worldview, in the first place, because of the inaccessibility of scientific knowledge to the populace at large. As Bacon acknowledges, "the things I am introducing will not be very suitable for such purposes [i.e. being accepted and used by common consent], since they cannot be brought down to the common man's comprehension, except through their effects and works."[99] The need to rely on the "effects and works" of scientific knowledge leads to the cultural characterization of our age not as the age of science but rather as the age of technology.

With the advance of technology new areas of anxiety, and the need to master them, are exposed. At the beginning of *Shipwreck With Spectator*, Blumenberg states that "among the elementary realities we confront as

---

97. Leszek Kolakowski, *The Presence of Myth*, trans. Adam Czerniawski (Chicago: University of Chicago Press, 1989).

98. Leszek Kolakowski, *Modernity on Endless Trial* (Chicago: University of Chicago Press, 1990).

99. Bacon, *Novum Organum*, 129.

human beings, the one with which we are least at ease is the sea—with the possible exception of the air, conquered later on."[100] It was, of course, the later conquest of the air which led to our greater dis-ease with it in the first place. And our dis-ease with the air is in fact succeeded by our dis-ease with space at large, which Blumenberg addressed by the increasing attention devoted to "astronoetics" in his later writing.[101] No matter how quotidian the products of technology become, since the causes of nature remain outside the bounds of common comprehension, the products of science must appear miraculous (how does a radio work?). Thus, although science may be put in the *service* of the populace, its organization must be *protected* from the populace for science's own good. Here we have an eminently political problem that accrues to the democratic application of science.[102]

But ultimately the problem is of a specifically theological nature. We are led back, in particular, to the problem of false idols. How are we, without previously acquiring the scientific knowledge we would desire to evaluate, to distinguish between charlatans and true possessors of knowledge? As is most intensely the case within an apocalyptic context, we must separate the false from the true prophets. And this further parallel forces us to take seriously Bacon's "re-formation" of the notion of apocalypse as true vision: this is precisely what the true inquirer into scientific knowledge, as opposed to the charlatan, possesses. Yet the Baconian enterprise leaves us in the position of distinguishing true from false without any traditionally theological understanding of the idols we face. While Bacon's itinerary of idols "besetting human minds"[103] in the *Novum Organon* is *modeled* on the traditional theological enterprise of distinguishing false idols and clearing them away in preparation for the reception of truth, by virtue of the *scientific* goal of this tour the list cannot receive a traditionally theological treatment. A new approach to vision is required.

Blumenberg's account of Bacon has only told one side of the story: that Bacon's position cannot be construed as unproblematically theological. It in fact seems likely that the lack of an entirely satisfactory resolution of the theological problem of false idols in an enterprise such as Bacon's has served as a tacit warrant for an entire tradition (of which Blumenberg is himself a member) to refuse to recognize the full force of the problem of theological justification in its modern context. But although Bacon's position, in particular, remains "theologically unresolved," neither can it extricate itself entirely from theological pressures, and it is in fact *only* such theological pressures which block the Baconian enterprise from an extension of the equation of

---

100. Blumenberg, *Shipwreck*, 7.

101. See in particular Hans Blumenberg, *Die Vollzähligkeit der Sterne* (Frankfurt am Main: Suhrkamp Verlag, 1997).

102. See Bacon, *Novum Organum*, 9.

103. Bacon, *Novum Organum*, 53.

knowledge and power which would culminate, as in the case of Nietzsche, in its own self-refutation. Here the contrast between Bacon's enterprise and Nietzsche's may be characterized in terms of their respective appeals to myth: unlike Nietzsche's exploding myth of the eternal recurrence of the same, Bacon's passage through the pillars of Hercules remains precariously perched atop a paradoxical appeal to theology.

In the retrospective light cast by his *Confessio* in *St. Matthew Passion*, Blumenberg's own project ultimately remains equally precariously poised, albeit for different and ultimately more complicated reasons. Blumenberg suggests that modernity rests just as much on a fact of "uncomprehending translation" as did the Gnosticism of Justinian in his reception of that Solomonic passage joining fear to wisdom. Once again, modernity is here brought into intimate proximity with Gnosticism. Yet what ties Blumenberg's belated stance toward modernity most closely to Bacon's justification of his project in terms of a "mute apocalypse" is the paradoxical, if not indeed contradictory, status that any appeal to *legitimacy* must possess in such a context. In both cases it is not just the inapplicability of traditional theological categories of justification which must be recognized, but the equally lethal consequences of ignoring the theological context within which Bacon's (and Blumenberg's) "incomprehensible" translations occur. The most ironic aspect of Blumenberg's enterprise, as witnessed by his discussion of theological issues in *St. Matthew Passion*, may well be that it most effectively *promotes* modernity precisely by resuscitating that (pre-modern) context within which modernity first achieved expression. As Blumenberg puts it toward the beginning of *The Legitimacy of the Modern Age*:

> There are entirely harmless formulations of the secularization theorem, of a type that can hardly be contradicted. One of these plausible turns of phrase is 'unthinkable without.' The chief thesis then, roughly put, would be that the modern age is unthinkable without Christianity. That is so fundamentally correct that the second part of this book is aimed at demonstrating this fact—with the difference, however, that this thesis gains a definable meaning only through a critique of the foreground appearance—or better: the apparent background presence—of secularization. (LMA, 30)

Just as modernity could be mistaken for a return of Gnosticism but is "correctly" seen as its overcoming, so the historical accounting for modernity could mistakenly be presented as a secularization of medieval categories but is only "correctly" presented in terms of the overcoming of this secularization narrative.

Although these contexts are already resuscitated in the process of attempting the legitimation Blumenberg seeks in his earlier project, their problematic *status*, I have argued, is something indirectly indicated by Blumenberg in later reflections. Moreover, the question of this status is not one of small consequence: to the extent that we *cannot* see modernity as a successful and final overcoming of Gnosticism and other heterodox theological positions, we cannot speak of a *legitimation* of modernity on Blumenberg's terms at all, but at best of a *promotion* of it. Even if the claim to legitimation has been relinquished, Blumenberg's work continues to offer us such a promotion of modernity, but one which persistently forces us to reassess the terms in which Blumenberg has attempted to deliver it. Ultimately, Blumenberg's work is such a conspicuous laboratory for investigating issues surrounding "the promotion of modernity" for reasons which are structurally analogous to Bacon's own successful promotion of its "inauguration." Just as Bacon's work perspicuously illuminates the problems theological justification faces in the context of promoting this-worldly investigation, so Blumenberg's work perspicuously illuminates the problems faced by an attempt to provide a historical promotion of the project inaugurated, in all its problematic glory, by figures such as Francis Bacon.

In this chapter, we have traversed the modern terrain with a Blumenbergian eye directed toward the issue of theology's problematic status in the modern age. In the next chapter, I take up the issue of political modernity through the lens of Hannah Arendt's diagnosis of limiting political conditions in the modern age. In the absence of a theological "breaker" to the pace of modernity, Arendt looks to the limits on modern pacing imposed by the natural life cycle of humans, and in particular the need to regenerate the human community regularly through the birth and death of human generations. She thus locates a key regulator to the pace of modernity in what she calls *natality*: the repeated introduction of new human life into the larger historical and social condition of modernity. Such a natural feature of the human condition puts much weaker limits on human self-assertion than traditional theology, and hence Arendt and other secular theorists find themselves in the position of needing to supply a new metaphorology of the human to meet the legitimation needs associated with the modern condition. 'Man' will shift from a referential to a metaphorical marker in a dramatic attempt to find both the legitimacy of and limits to pacing in the modern age.

2

At What Cost Modernity: Mental Faculties and Total Politics

ENDINGS, BEGINNINGS

On Thursday evening 4 December 1975, Hannah Arendt died suddenly while entertaining friends. As her editor and literary executor, Mary McCarthy, reported, Arendt had just completed the second of the projected three volumes of her last work, *The Life of the Mind*; after her death the first manuscript page of the third volume, *Judging*, was found in Arendt's typewriter.[104] Although it is unclear exactly how the third volume would have filled out *The Life of the Mind*, Arendt's Kantian affiliations in the domain of judgment are already evident in the first two volumes, and there exist lectures on Kant's political philosophy, some excerpts of which are provided in the one volume edition of Arendt's unfinished work as a rounding out, and which were subsequently published separately.[105] The second volume of *The Life of the Mind—Willing*, following a first volume, *Thinking*—still required heavy editing, which was undertaken by McCarthy, and the two extant volumes end on an unsettled note, to put it mildly. In the last two pages of the second volume, Arendt states as her conclusion that "[i]n its original integrity, freedom survived in political theory—i.e., theory conceived for the purpose of political action—only in utopian and unfounded promises of a final 'realm of freedom' that, in its Marxian version at any rate, would indeed spell 'the end of all things,' a sempiternal peace in which all specifically human activities would wither away" (LM II, 216). Arendt acknowledges the

---

104. Hannah Arendt, *The Life of the Mind* (San Diego: Harcourt, 1978), II, 241.
105. Hannah Arendt, *Lectures on Kant's Political Philosophy*, ed. with an interpretative essay, Ronald Beiner (Chicago: University of Chicago, 1992).

"frustrating" nature of this conclusion, and the sense we are left with at the end of the second volume is that a problem has been much more articulated than a solution found. Indeed, in the final line of the work as published, Arendt tells us that the enigma of freedom as we find it in the political realm in particular "cannot be opened or solved except by an appeal to another mental faculty, no less mysterious than the faculty of beginning, the faculty of Judgment, an analysis of which at least may tell us what is involved in our pleasures and displeasures" (LM II, 217).

It is enticing to attempt to reconstruct what sort of solution Arendt would find in the domain of judgment, but I believe any *solution* in Arendt's third volume would have inevitably been less satisfying than her articulation of the *problem* in this second volume. In any case, we do not have it. As far as the problem of freedom is concerned, what is most striking is that *Willing* ends, like Arendt's earlier *The Origins of Totalitarianism*,[106] with a veritable paean to beginnings, what Arendt refers to specifically as "natality." It is the confluence of these two endings along the lines of such a celebration of birth which will exercise me here in an effort to begin constructing an account of the contribution of initiating to the dynamics of pacing. How much can be expected, and how much can be promised, in Arendt's appeals to natality? Ultimately, I will insist that answers to these questions must cede to the consideration of a more modest question: what must the modern condition be like, as Arendt receives it, that such an appeal would be required for its recuperation? In seeking a response to this question, we may at least begin to understand how the dynamic phenomenon of repeated initiation, as expressed both by the repeated birth of new human beings and of new human initiatives, contributes to the underlying rhythm of human self-assertion in the modern age.

In the case of philosophical modernity, where conceptually speaking the problem of freedom has been posed in the most extreme terms, there has been an incapacity for our traditional conceptions of human mental faculties to keep pace with the philosophical problem of freedom as it finds itself articulated in the modern tradition and the modern condition. The problem of the philosophical status of the human, and particularly human freedom, has radically outpaced our vocabulary for dealing with it. This is not just a case of philosophical questions outstripping our capacity to provide answers for them, which in itself is far from a new phenomenon, but rather the case of such a rapid acceleration in the human condition that there has been an inability even for philosophical *questions* to keep pace. As such, the issue is not so much a philosophical one *per se* as it is an issue of the place of philosophy in modern culture. But given that philosophical developments are implicated in central ways in this modern development, the problem presents

---

106. Hannah Arendt, *The Origins of Totalitarianism*, new edition with added prefaces (San Diego: Harvest, 1968).

a tangle that is not easily unraveled, or even adequately characterized. This leads directly on to the second, political problem of freedom. Here the pacing of modern developments, particularly in the rise of totalitarianism, outstripped the capacity for the protection of political freedoms. This, too, is in itself nothing new: what distinguishes the modern situation as Arendt diagnoses it in *The Origins of Totalitarianism* is the way that modern conceptions of political freedom and the rights of man themselves contributed to just those political accelerations which led to a radical breakdown in the political fabric. We need some schematic sense of these two outpacings in order to identify the functional role of Arendt's appeal to natality, both as a fundamental political fact and as a model for the initiating of action.

A first piece of documentary evidence for considering all of these questions lies in Arendt's own intellectual trajectory, from the study of philosophy through the domain of politics and political theory and ultimately back, at the end of her life, to an ambitious project on the life of the mind. In this regard, it is not merely intriguing but indeed critical to notice that the two published volumes of Arendt's final project, while dealing exclusively with the philosophical tradition's reflections on the mental faculties of thinking and willing respectively, are nonetheless framed at either end by reflections on politics. In the second volume, after detailed analyses of the faculty of willing in Paul, Epictetus, Augustine, Aquinas, Duns Scotus, Nietzsche and Heidegger among others, Arendt turns at the end of the volume to the tradition of what is nowadays called "political philosophy," represented by such thinkers as Montesquieu, Adams, and Jefferson. The discussion centers on a detailed consideration of Virgil's *Aeneid* as founding narrative and the turn of the American founding fathers to the Romans for inspiration in representing the founding of their New Republic. This part, too, of Arendt's conclusion is moderate, if not disappointing: "The abyss of pure spontaneity, which in the foundation legends is bridged by the hiatus between liberation and the constitution of freedom, was covered up by the device, typical of the Occidental tradition (the only tradition where freedom has always been the *raison d'être* of all politics) of understanding the *new* as an improved re-statement of the old" (LM II, 216). In particular, such a self-representation is insufficient (though not necessarily incompatible) if we wish to recognize the legitimacy of human self-assertion as a founding condition for the modern age.

Only in the domain of the purely philosophical has the new been thought "on its own terms," and in this regard Arendt singles out Augustine, upon whose conception of love, closely linked to his own interest in beginnings, Arendt wrote her doctoral dissertation under the direction of Karl Jaspers. Effectively, her account of willing is framed, philosophically at least, by Augustine's pioneering insights into this faculty at one end of the historical spectrum,[107] and, at the other end, by Heidegger's claim that "solitary thinking in itself constitutes the only relevant action in the factual record of history" (LM II, 181), arguing for the cultivation of *Gelassenheit*, which Arendt glosses as a "will-not-to-will." But, continuing her line of caveats and apologies, Arendt acknowledges that

> the argument even in the Augustinian version is somehow opaque, that it seems to tell us no more than that we are *doomed* to be free by virtue of being born, no matter whether we like freedom or abhor its arbitrariness, are "pleased" with it or prefer to escape its awesome responsibility by electing some form of fatalism. (LM II, 217)

It is faced with this impasse that she turns to the faculty of judging, "an analysis of which at least may tell us what is involved in our pleasures and displeasures" (LM II, 217). So ends the extant portion of Arendt's *The Life of the Mind*.

The appeal to a politics of judgment, based on the Kantian accounts of teleological and aesthetic judgment, is appealing for various reasons, not least for the sense of relevance it would offer to those humanists who are, or believe themselves to be, schooled in the fine art of distinguished sensibilities. But this is at least insufficient, and at worst irrelevant, for reasons Arendt herself recognizes—but which are difficult enough to retain in focus. Targeting Jaspers and Buber in particular, Arendt asserts that "[a]n error rather prevalent among modern philosophers who insist on the importance of communication as a guarantee of truth ... is to believe that the intimacy of the dialogue ... can become paradigmatic for the political sphere" (LM II, 200). Indeed, it is just such reconstitutions of the domain of political philosophy around the Aristotelian ideal of the friend—whether for or against—which lead most directly to those countermodern trends from which modernity's discontents are able to draw powerful ideological solace, either in the security of a popular political stance pitched as a fight against an evil empire or a war on terror, or in the more intellectual formulations of political theory as debates around the status of the friend and the enemy as constitutive political categories. For these reasons as well, we should be hesitant to attempt a reconstruction of Arendt's proposed politics of judgment. Baldly put, the faculty of discriminating taste has been most fully developed in the aesthetic realm, and, contrary to much opinion in the humanities, as social phenomena art and politics are as far from each other as they could possibly be. In addition, judgment is identified by Arendt as the most recent and least well-developed of the mental faculties she considers. By all counts, we should proceed with caution, if only as a first step in restoring to the

---

107. According to Arendt, the Greeks did not possess a faculty of willing in the relevant sense. Aristotelian *proairesis*, which Arendt calls "the forerunner of the Will" (LM II, 55), involves only the capacity to select among means to a specified end, and as such does not count as willing in the full-blown philosophical sense. See LM II, 55ff.

pursuit of theory some of the intellectual credibility upon which it has massively defaulted in recent times.

Even so, or just by virtue of such circumspection, we are left with problems both of crucial significance and broad implication. Here I consider only an example in terms of the way in which Arendt's diagnosis of limits of the modern condition—once in terms of the development of an account of mental faculties, once in accounting for the political condition of the rise of totalitarianism—ends on both philosophical and political counts in an appeal to natality. The key element which binds these two accounts together is clearly the cultivation, and specifically the modern cultivation, of freedom: freedom of thought, and freedom of action. Indeed, Arendt characterizes her second volume as "devoted to the faculty of the Will and, by implication, to the problem of freedom, which as Bergson said, 'has been to the moderns what the paradoxes of the Eleatics were to the ancients'" (LM II, 3). Arendt's first volume, *Thinking*, is heavily weighted toward the consideration of ancient philosophy, the second toward the medieval development, but ending in the final section with specifically modern political predicaments surrounding the protection of political freedoms. Given Arendt's declaration that "Kant was the first, and has remained the last, of the great philosophers to deal with judgment as one of the basic mental activities" (LM I, 95),[108] we may assume that the third volume would have been weighted toward the modern period, if only because of Kant's location in it.

Arendt's discussion of human freedom is organized around the root phenomenon of natality as the most basic human experience of new beginnings, and hence also as the most basic symbol of it. The place of Arendt's discussion of natality is easier to discern in *The Life of the Mind*: in a work on "the faculty of beginnings," in particular, there are more clues. But the various aspects of Arendt's discussion do not obviously cohere until we recognize the relation between natality and the category of the person which runs through Arendt's account. With the advent of modern philosophical optimism, specifically as embodied in the notion of progress, a need arises to find a category against which progress can be measured. Since the finite, human lifespan is too short to serve as a reference point against which progress may be measured, ultimate recourse must be to an ideal human perspective which outstrips the span of any given finite, human life.

> The notion that each subsequent generation would necessarily know more than its predecessor and that this progressing would never be completed—a conviction that only in our time has found challengers—was important enough; but for our context, even more important is the simple, matter-of-fact perception that "scientific knowledge" has been and

---

108. Husserl's extraordinarily acute cultivation of the notion of judgment is not ackneowledged by Arendt, perhaps because his discussion is most trenchant in the sphere of "theoretical" judgment.

can be attained only "step by step through contributions of *generations* of explorers building upon and gradually amending the findings of their predecessors."[109] (LM II, 152)

While Blumenberg investigates this issue of a "time" against which scientific progress, and the scientific enterprise, may be measured in his book *Lebenszeit und Weltzeit* (*Lifetime and Worldtime*), for Arendt's purposes the basic fact which needs to be recognized is that it is the rhythm of the recurrence of new humans being born which marks off the tempo of the human life cycle and so establishes a natural limit for the extension of the subject as agent. In each new generation human subjects cede their places to new and younger human subjects, and these new subjects guarantee the replenishment of human agency.[110] Arendt's celebration of natality is a historical echo of the early modern optimism which made the notion of progress possible, but its differences must equally be stressed. In particular, it is not specifically *invested* in a notion of modern technological progress, about which Arendt remains understandably dubious. Rather, it finds itself to be a limiting biological condition on the philosophical notion of any acceptable account of the willing faculty at all.

Arendt locates a perspicuous development of the need for an ideal human observer in Pascal's remarks on the notion of progress: "all men together progress continually while the universe grows older ... so that the whole succession of men throughout the centuries should be *considered as one and the same man who lives forever* and continually learns" (cited, with italics added by Arendt, LM II, 153). As Arendt puts it, Pascal appeals to a personification, *man*,

> of a 'subject' that could serve as a noun for all kinds of activities expressed in verbs. This concept was not a metaphor, properly speaking; it was a full-fledged *personification* such as we find in the allegories of Renaissance narratives. (LM II, 153)

This personification is an instance of what Angus Fletcher has taught us to recognize as *daemonic agency*—here a very special one, given that its name is 'Mankind'—, and in philosophy it finds perhaps its quintessential expression in the Hegelian philosophy of history.[111] That this allegorical "man" is not a secularization of any concept of the divine is made manifest, as Arendt recognizes, by the fact that "we find the personification of Mankind in Pascal, who would certainly have been the last to desire a secular replacement for God as the true ruler of the world" (LM II, 154).

Kant, too, explicitly recognizes the need to appeal to Mankind in a passage from the *Ideas for a Universal History from a Cosmopolitan Point of View* (1784)

---

109. Quoting Edgar Zilsel, "The Genesis of the Concept of Scientific Progress," in *Journal of the History of Ideas*, 1945, vol. VI, 3.

110. Here see also Arendt's essay, "The Crisis in Education," in *Between Past and Future* (New York: Penguin, 1977, originally Viking, 1961), 173-196.

111. Angus Fletcher, *Allegory: The Theory of a Symbolic Mode* (Ithaca: Cornell, 1964), 25-69.

when he writes: "It will always remain bewildering that the earlier generations seem to carry on their burdensome business only for the sake of the later ... and that only the last should have the good fortune to dwell in the [completed] building" (cited LM II, 155.) In the context of Kant's political philosophy, Arendt will recognize the conflict between the value of the individual person and the need for a general human "subject" as a "contradiction" between the particular and the general (LM II, 272). This contradiction can be related back to the tension in Kant's reception of the French Revolution, which he approves from the position of the spectator but must disapprove from that of the actor. Given that Arendt recognizes a contradiction between the vantages of the particular and the general in Kant's political philosophy, it seems clear that she would attempt to overcome this problem. But can this contradiction not be traced back to the grounding of a political philosophy of judgment in an ideal of communication (and its relation to the *sensis communis*, in particular as regards aesthetic discrimination)? If so, then it is unclear how Arendt could appeal to the faculty of judgment in establishing her own political philosophical position.[112]

EXCURSUS: BLUMENBERG ON UNIVERSAL MAN

Hans Blumenberg provides a parallel account of the modern cultivation of the metaphor of universal man in his work *Lebenszeit und Weltzeit* (*Lifetime and Worldtime*). He, too, centers his discussion on Pascal, looking back briefly at Descartes, then touching on Laplace, historicism, and an epistolary exchange between Goethe and Schiller. In the chapter "Universal Man and World Reason in Time-Relation," Blumenberg is exercised in particular by the homogenization of time which the institutionalization of science enforced upon human experience. From the perspective of scientific methodology the birth and death of generations goes unremarked, with the implication that no account of the life-bearings of individual humans can be supplied therein. Here Blumenberg sees the origin of Pascal's "horror of infinite space"—even if, as he remarks, this famous expression is to be attributed to the voice of the atheist opponent in Pascal's *Pensées*, intended as an "apology for the Christian religion." "The success of the scientific impulse is bound to the renunciation of meaning (*Sinnverzicht*)" (LW, 173).[113] Those continuities—and indeed, discontinuities—of human generations guaranteed by their lifeworldly interaction are renounced by the scientific enterprise in

---

112. On the role of communication in Kant's theory of judgment, particularly as it applies to political philosophy, see LM II, 267ff. On the contradiction in Kant's political philosophy insofar as the individual is valuable as particular but the conception of progress requires an appeal to a "general" subject, see LM II, 272.

113. All translations mine. Much of the unquoted material presented in this section is closely paraphrased from Blumenberg's chapter, since it is not available to English speakers.

favor of a "non-affiliation" of the scientific enterprise with the individual experience of the subject.

Appropriating the classical figure of the Ages of Man, Pascal takes the Renaissance ideal of universality as an educational characteristic of the individual and transfers it to the figure of the *homme universel*, universal man, now no longer understood as an individual (ideal or otherwise), but as a capacity relative to the *dimension of time*. In so doing, the temporal scale is shifted from "lifetime" to "worldtime," in a transformation which applies the dynamics of scale-shifting I have discussed in the Introduction directly to the dimension of time itself. Education is no longer understood on the scale of an individual human life, but rather with respect to "universal man," or as we might now put it, with respect to the human species. Blumenberg notes that as a consequence we move from a closed ideal of individual human cultivation to an open-ended and ongoing process of cultivation. "For this, criteria of maturity and completion, of satisfaction and satiation cannot be given" (LW, 174).

In the prefatory fragment to his 1647 "Treatise on the Void," Pascal declares that man "is only produced for infinity," yet Blumenberg notes that the medieval understanding of this assertion in terms of an enjoyment of the *actu infinitum* and the immortality requisite for this enjoyment must be linked to an account of the infinite as indefinite in Pascal's physics. According to Blumenberg, this unending infinite becomes a lesser form of the actual infinite, one which in its incompleteness stimulates dissatisfaction, and thus can be enlisted as a motor, in particular, for scientific investigation. The ultimate "compatibility" of this-worldly and other-worldly ends in medieval theology is a function of the finitude of time: "with a finite time, nothing qualitative[ly new] could be initiated," and so transcendence faces little resistant force from this-worldly investigation (LW, 175). All this changes with Descartes.

Descartes sees in the eventual *completion* of physical investigation a double dividend in medicine and morality. Each of these latter domains will be improved as an application of the growth of this-worldly knowledge, with the result that mankind will "win time," even if any given individual will not yet win out or will win out only insufficiently. This has as its most important consequence that the pressure of time slackens and a precipitancy in forming judgment no longer remains a fundamental trait of the human intellect: "the logical possibility of refraining from judgment (*epoché*) can become institutional" (LW, 175). Such are the consequences of the renunciation of the educational model of individual completion.

On the one hand, Pascal's program offers a scientific alternative to the classical conception of this-worldly investigation; on the other, it offers an alternative to Bruno's embrace of the frightening cosmological infinite, which can only be thought to completion in Bruno's pantheism. Even if his biographer Morris Bishop goes too far in depicting Pascal as having observed humanity not as one human among others but rather as a godlike visitor, nonetheless Blumenberg finds this characterization germane for Pascal's attitude toward history. For Pascal, the historically contemporary find themselves in the same situation in which the ancient philosophers would have found themselves if they could have lived up until the present. Pascal could even have embraced Friedrich Schlegel's "blasphemous" formulation, "to philosophize is collectively to seek omniscience," since such a seeking allows itself to be made a not-finding. The succession of future generations can be seen in terms of "one same man, who always subsists and continually learns" (Pascal, cited LW 177).

In this way, the speed of intellectual progress attains a bearable and even conducive relation to the life span of the individual. A first dissonance in this orientation is registered in the program of Diderot's encyclopedia, which was planned for reading, but which in its execution came to be more and more organized for consultation. Only at the end of the eighteenth century, in Laplace's lectures and philosophical essay on probability, is the idea of the integration of the knowing subject taken over by the ideal of a causal extrapolation from the instantaneous analysis of a natural system—the famous ideal of the "Laplace demon." Blumenberg emphasizes the emergence of this ideal specifically in the context of an analysis of probabilities, quoting Laplace: "All efforts in the search for truth are directed to bringing the human mind nearer to this intelligence, which will yet always remain at an infinite distance from it ... The calculus of probabilities concerns on the one hand this ignorance and on the other our knowledge" (Laplace, cited LW, 178).[114]

Standing in contrast we find the attitude of historicism, which is simply irksome to any such ideal of ultimate accounting. For historicism, time is the least indifferent of all, and while the scientific spirit makes the identity of the individual subject superfluous, historicism puts the identity of the individual subject back into question. Without the provision of some further account, the individual subject's past experience can not be attributed to it as "its own" at all. The accumulation of experience is understood no longer simply in terms of the passage of time, but rather over uncertain paths of making-known which understand themselves as "understanding." Modernizing somewhat, Blumenberg suggests we might indicate them in terms of the "communication difficulties" of humanity in the temporal dimension (perhaps with an ambivalent nod in the direction of Habermas, who is otherwise conspicuously absent from Blumenberg's work). The trend of historicism ultimately leads to the demolition of Pascal's ideal of universal man: "the divergence of lifetime and worldtime takes on the specific form

---

114. Translated from Blumenberg's German.

of the difference between lifetime and historical time," and "the idea of the unity of the subject sinks from the status of a postulate grounded in the nature of man back to that of a pure fiction, a rhetorical figure, a demagogical simplification: since an *acting* Oversubject is needed in order to place confidence in history, one must be assumed which *experiences* it" (LW, 179). I hope my translation has captured some of the menacing tone of Blumenberg's original German.

Blumenberg ends his chapter on "Universal Man and World Reason in Time Relation" on an anecdotal note, looking back to his beloved Goethe and, in this case, an exchange of correspondence with Schiller. At almost the same time Laplace and Schlegel formulated their ideals of all-knowing, Goethe writes of nature in a letter to Schiller on 21 February 1798 that "the whole of mankind could well grasp it," but under an unfulfillable condition, since they are "never gathered together" (cited, LW, 179). This is just what allows nature to hide from men. It is the constitutive lack of historical identity, Blumenberg notes, which makes nature an unreachable secret, and language is but an expression of this lack. Schiller's response registers this lacuna when he remarks in language a "tendency entirely directed against individuality." In a typically dialectical summation, Blumenberg concludes the chapter: "what is won in intuition does not pass into the medium of language, will not be transportable for history, does not constitute the Oversubject adequate to nature. The just won ideas of totality also already condition the pain of the withdrawal of experience." It is in terms of the ideals of universal man that the withdrawal of experience in the modern age is first understood; Husserl's absolute metaphor of "lifeworld" will eventually seek to redress this withdrawal. We thus possess, in brief outline, a sketch of the way in which a classical figure (the Ages of Man) will be transformed into an early modern ideal (Universal Man), in turn reduced to a mere "demagogic figure" by the historicism's resurgent emphasis on individual human experience, and will finally be replaced by an ultimate locus of metaphorical insolubility ("lifeworld") in Husserl's philosophical enterprise.

So far as the pace of modernity is concerned, the primary fact which both Blumenberg's and Arendt's analyses reveal is that in the transition to the scientific mentality a significant shifting of scale is attempted with respect to the perspective of 'man'. Whereas the classical figure of the Ages of Man was not intended as a conception of the human at all, but rather as an analogical application of the phases of human life to the totality of history (LW, 174), the proposal of the ideal perspective of universal Man (which, for my own purposes, I will henceforth capitalize) transports the conception of the human from one temporal dimension (experiential, "lived" time) to another (objective, "world" time). The mechanism of scale-shifting which this embodies perfectly parallels Blumenberg's metaphorics of scale as I have discussed above in the Introduction, and for purposes of convenience, I will refer to this particular scale-shifting in terms of the displacement: 'man → Man'. In the absence of anything analogous to the theological pressure which limited the early modern application of the scientific ideal, the man → Man transition quickly succumbs to the repeated demand for an acknowledgment of the scale level of individual human experience.

Husserl's philosophy proposes a mixed strategy in response to this demand. On the one hand, Husserl will introduce into his late philosophy the central metaphor of the lifeworld in an attempt to "open up" the domain of individual, pre-positional (and in particular, pre-*judgmental*) experience to phenomenological investigation. On the other hand, he will insist on a transcendental *epochê*, a suspending of the attitude of judging in the "natural attitude," as a prerequisite for phenomenological philosophy. In so doing, he inherits the withholding of judgment which served as an institutional underwriting of the scientific endeavor. (In such a light, it should seem anything *but* a coincidence that Husserl would be preoccupied with a "crisis in the European sciences.") The philosopher delivers a "minority report" in a culture largely constituted of non-philosophers, but must stand as the "functionary of humanity" insofar as he or she serves as a repository for that purified conception of judgment which, according to Husserl, underwrites our basic commitment to European culture. In the absence of a general transition from 'man' to 'Man', for Husserl the philosopher must serve as the cultural guarantor of a transcendental perspective, and in particular a transcendental perspective on history.

JUDGMENT, ONCE AGAIN

Returning to Arendt, there is a final point to make about the faculty of judgment. Even if it is ultimately unsuccessful in addressing the political issues of utmost concern, it is important to see the historical concurrence of this faculty's development and the *extent* to which it promotes a certain model for understanding politics. The vision of politics which results from a cultivation of judgment generates a regulative ideal of undistorted intersubjective communication as a guide for overcoming those "difficulties of communication" mentioned by Blumenberg. One finds such a model at the heart of Habermas's work, but one also finds it, albeit in a more limited way, in the work of John Rawls. Habermas' insistence on communication and Rawls' emphasis on deliberation ultimately qualify the significance of judgment in Kant's political philosophy in ways which tailor it to post-historicist hermeneutics and the modern theory of rational (economic) deliberation respectively, but both programs are inheritors of a broadly Kantian tradition, and Kant's innovative insistence on the faculty of judgment descends to each of them in indirect but powerful ways. Habermas' account of political modernity, in particular, is shaped by this context, which also helps to indicate the ultimate limitations of his account.

For Arendt, in any case, with German idealism the appeal to a personified concept of Mankind

> began to proliferate to an incredible degree. The activities of men, whether thinking or acting, were all transformed into activities of personified concepts—which made philosophy both infinitely more difficult (the chief difficulty in Hegel's philosophy is its abstractness, its only occasional hints at the actual data and phenomena he has in mind) and incredibly more alive. (LM II, 156)

Schelling, in particular, identifies Will as "primordial Being," and Arendt argues that, in so doing, traditional ontology is replaced by what we might call a philosophical allegory of the Will. The later responses of Nietzsche and Heidegger to the philosophical tradition are then seen as thoughtful attempts to work through this reversal. In his "turn" (*Kehre*) Heidegger reverses this reversal in turn: "the *false* 'opinion [easily] arises that the human will is the origin of the will-to-will, while on the contrary, man is being willed by the Will-to-will without even experiencing the essence of such willing.'"[115]

WILLING, MOTION AND MODERN POLITICS

The peculiar dilemma which faces modernity is that its legitimacy must be established by arguing for a newness that is situated not at the personal level of individual humans but rather at the transpersonal level of "Mankind." Even in Blumenberg's account of the legitimacy of the modern age, acts of self-assertion are legitimated not *individually* but rather *coordinatively* in their contribution to the larger transformation of humanity's condition in the world. At the end of the volume on willing, Arendt considers this need in the context of providing a *foundation* for the new political order of modernity as exemplified by the English, French and American Revolutions. What is lacking is in each case of a linguistic nature: the capacity to deliver this legitimation in terms of the category of human freedom. And so the founding fathers revert to a quasi-religious vocabulary:

> This seems to be why men who were much too "enlightened" to still believe in the Hebrew-Christian Creator-God turned with rare unanimity to pseudo-religious language when they had to deal with the problem of foundation as the beginning of a "new order of the ages." We have the "appeal to God in Heaven," deemed necessary by Locke for all who embarked on the novelty of a community emerging from "the state of nature"; we have Jefferson's "laws of nature and nature's God," John Adams' "great Legislator of the Universe," Robespierre's "immortal Legislator," his cult of a "Supreme Being." (LM II, 208)

---

115. Quoted from *Vorträge und Aufsätze*, LM II, 156.

Here the dilemma is that there is no single will to which we can refer this beginning. And so the founding fathers return to some sense of Divine creation, however abstract. But in the absence of any such appeal, we know the underlying requisite for the type of historical change that concerns Arendt: it is that new people are born. As Arendt herself admits, in a passage quoted above, Augustine's injection of natality in terms of his philosophical cultivation of the concept of Will remains insufficient here: it makes us seem as if we are *consigned* to freedom. The modern, mechanistic world-picture is even less helpful: as generations of philosophers who have attempted to take scientific modernity seriously have demonstrated, not by their work but by their example, there is little resource here for understanding the human faculty of initiating. Even in the domain of quantum theory, where it is often philosophically fashionable to appeal to an introjection of human will into science by way of the act of measurement, this human act is almost always registered as a "boundary condition" in terms of which the quantum-mechanical probabilities are calculated. It does not penetrate the exterior of the scientific enterprise. Although professional philosophers' hesitancy to see any help for the philosophy of the will in the development of quantum mechanics is no doubt sociologically driven by various academically disreputable attempts (among both laymen and professional physicists) to align quantum theory with new-age or Eastern philosophy, even in the absence of these prejudices the structure of quantum theory would require wholesale revaluation before it could be brought to bear on these issues.[116]

In the case of political philosophy, the theory of the will has fared little better, though for different reasons, which are best considered in the context of Arendt's account of the rise of totalitarianism. Here, Arendt understands totalitarianism as the ultimate historical outcome of what she calls the politics of motion. Given that she traces its lineage back to the political philosophy of Thomas Hobbes, whose overall philosophical venture is grounded in his treatise on motion, *De Motu*, Arendt's claim should not be understood entirely metaphorically. Hobbes' *Leviathan* is the political equivalent of the New Science, for it grounds the state directly in the motion of its human participants. In Hobbes' case we need not speak of human actions, at least in Arendt's sense, for "a free Subject, a free Will ... [are] words ... without

---

116. To my mind, the most interesting attempts to accomplish this are those of David Bohm and David Finkelstein. It is not coincidental that Bohm has developed a new age philosophy of "implicate order" while Finkelstein has affiliated himself with the Buddhist tradition. In the latter case, which interests me most, the revaluation requires the development of a notion of particle's acting on analogy to human action. This allows the sense of activity to "penetrate" into the core of the quantum project, but the status of this analogical move requires further philosophical investigation. See David Finkelstein, *Quantum Relativity: A Synthesis of the Ideas of Einstein and Heisenberg* (Berlin: Springer, 1997); D. Bohm and B.J. Hiley, *The Undivided Universe: An ontological interpretation of quantum theory* (London: Routledge, 1993).

meaning; that is to say; Absurd" (cited, OT, 139). The fundamental force, or better, passion in Hobbes' political philosophy is the desire for power: "[i]t regulates the relations between individual and society, and all other ambitions as well, for riches, knowledge, and honor follow from it" (OT, 139).

But by grounding the state in man's desire for power (not, as Arendt recognizes, a descriptive grounding, but rather a normative condition for participating in the bourgeoisie), Hobbes makes the state depend on what is essentially a condition of instability. Hobbes' Commonwealth includes in its conception "its own dissolution," depending on "an instability that is all the more striking as Hobbes's primary and frequently repeated aim was to secure a maximum of safety and stability" (OT, 140). But since "power is essentially only a means to an end[,] a community based solely on power must decay in the calm of order and stability; its complete security reveals that it is built on sand" (OT, 142). This gives rise to the demand of what we might call a *metastability* of the political community which is grounded instead in the constant *expansion* of power, and this political economy of expansion is the social equivalent of the scientific ideal of progress.[117] Given its analogous structure, the political community faces the same tension between man and Mankind as does the scientific enterprise.

> Not the naïve delusion of a limitless growth of property, but the realization that power accumulation was the only guarantee for the stability of so-called economic laws, made progress irresistible. The eighteenth century notion of progress, as conceived in pre-revolutionary France, intended criticism of the past to be a means of mastering the present and controlling the future; progress culminated in the emancipation of man (OT, 142).

Such was the visionary stance, predicated on a successful man → Man(kind) transition. What we find, instead, is a vicious unmasking of the ambiguity involved in the phrase 'emancipation of man', for "this notion had little to do with the endless progress of bourgeois society, which not only did not want the liberty and autonomy of man, but was ready to sacrifice everything and everybody to supposedly superhuman laws" (OT, 142). Instead of the liberty and autonomy of man, man is "emancipated" in the perverted sense that the economic progress of "Mankind" is substituted for the betterment of individual men. Invoking the philosophical distinction between sense and reference, we are dealing here not with an emancipation of man, but an emancipation of the term 'man'. What we see is a historical viciousness underwritten by the man → Man transition analogous to that which Blumenberg diagnosed in the wake of historicism.

The principle condition for belonging to the bourgeoisie, of which Hobbes' *Leviathan* constitutes the prescient philosophical expression, is not

---

117. See also Arendt's essay, "Rosa Luxembourg: 1871-1919 in *Men in Dark Times* (San Diego: Harcourt Brace Jovanovich, 1968), 33-56.

ownership but rather commitment to the principle of the accumulation of wealth, yet this perspicuous characterization of the essence of the bourgeoisie isolates the underlying contradiction in the formation of the bourgeois state at its most concentrated: "[p]roperty owners who do not consume but strive to enlarge their holdings continually find one very inconvenient limitation, the unfortunate fact that men must die" (OT, 145) Here, too, the solution is to transfer the underlying principle from the private domain of individual men to the public domain of "men": "[b]y transcending the limits of human life in planning for an automatic continuous growth of wealth beyond all personal needs and possibilities of consumption, individual property is made a public affair and taken out of the sphere of mere private life" (OT, 145). But "the whole thing is a delusion," and "the most radical and the only secure form of possession is destruction, for only what we have destroyed is safely and forever ours" (OT, 145). "Hobbes was the true, though never fully recognized, philosopher of the bourgeoisie because he realized that acquisition of wealth conceived as a never-ending process can be guaranteed only by the seizure of political power, for the accumulating process must sooner or later force open all existing territorial limits" (OT, 146), and "[i]f the last victorious Commonwealth cannot proceed to 'annex the planets' [Cecil Rhodes], it can only proceed to destroy itself in order to begin anew the never-ending process of power generation" (OT, 146-47).

The radical nature of Arendt's approach must be recognized in the fact that structurally, all the principles of the totalitarian state are already implied in such a reading of Hobbes' bourgeois commonwealth. All that is required for the rise of the totalitarian state are the historical conditions which Arendt goes on to diagnose. This puts Arendt's reading of the origins of totalitarianism very close to the question of the legitimation of the modern age. In the absence of any breaker which might be supplied by a principled appeal to the political status of individual humans, totalitarianism is the historical reality of the acceleration of political movement, modernity's quintessential "outpacing," which Hobbes unwittingly forecasts. Lacking any such principled appeal, the frenzy of totalitarianism can only be braked by the residual *existence* of individual humans. Hence the functional organization of the totalitarian state can be read in terms of its multifarious attempts to eliminate the humanity of its subjects. The limit of this political capacity to reduce the existence of humanity lies, once again, in the fact of new humans being born:

> Total terror, the essence of totalitarian government, exists neither for nor against men. It is supposed to provide the forces of nature or history with an incomparable instrument to accelerate their movement. This movement, proceeding according to its own law, cannot in the long run be hindered; eventually its force will always prove more powerful than the most powerful forces engendered by the actions and the will of men.

> But it can be slowed down and is slowed down almost inevitably by the freedom of man, which even totalitarian rulers cannot deny, for this freedom—irrelevant and arbitrary as they may deem it—is identical with the fact that men are being born and that therefore each of them *is* a new beginning, begins, in a sense, the world anew. From the totalitarian point of view, the fact that men are born and die can be only regarded as an annoying interference with higher forces. (OT, 466)

Again Arendt recognizes natality as a limiting condition on the *pace* of (here political) modernity, a breaker on any "transhuman" law of accelerated movement.

The conception of freedom which Arendt is able to find implied simply by the fact of human natality is still a very thin one, and so the recognition of this ultimate "breaker" can only provide a first, and tentative, step. In her own project, apparently, this overly general conception of human freedom was to be bolstered by an appeal to the standards of human judgment. What is needed, instead, is a global comprehension of the dynamics of acceleration and retardation in the movement of modernity. Arendt's investigations into the mental faculties and the historical development of political modernity are only examples among others. In the chapters to follow I propose to look at a cross-section of such examples and attempt to extract some general tools for dealing with the pace of modernity. These chapters will also remain tentative steps, but they do lay out a number of extended "experiments in reading." Cumulatively, they indicate a scaffolding upon which such a global understanding of the dynamics of modernity may be built. As in Louis Zukofsky's "Gas Age," a disclaimer is in order here: "They'll tell me it's difficult."[118] But in an Age of Acceleration we should expect no less.

After Arendt's lesson on beginnings, we enter, then, into the modern labyrinth of pacing. Angus Fletcher helps us to see the way in which *motion* becomes a constitutive category for the modern literary enterprise in the age of Shakespeare. Jean Starobinski will focus on the couple 'action'/'reaction' as a linguistic guide—with roots in physics, physiology and psychology—to the organization of the pacing of initiative and impact in the modern age. A chapter on Fletcher's American poetics extends his account of motion in the early modern period to a vision of the complex rhythms which pace daily experience in our contemporary condition, as expressed in American poetry from Whitman to Ashbery, and with roots in the English tradition stretching back to James Thomson and John Clare. And Harold Bloom's search for wisdom will be seen as a latter day Guide for the Perplexed, squarely facing the crossroads of ultimate life decisions in the modern age. Only after considering such exemplary enterprises at length will I venture my own vision of modern orientation and pacing in the final three chapters of this volume.

---

118. Louis Zukofsky, "Welcome to the Gas Age," in *Prepositions: The Collected Critical Essays of Louis Zukofsky*, expanded edition (Berkeley: University of California, 1981), 172.

3

The New Poetry and The Mimetic Locus

If, as Hannah Arendt asserts, totalitarianism is the ultimate historical outcome of the politics of motion in the modern age, then a first requisite for understanding the development of political modernity in greater detail will be a thorough comprehension of the status of the category of motion in early modern thought. In fact, such a requisite will contribute much to an understanding of the development of modern politics along the lines sketched by Arendt, but more generally still it serves as a *pre*requisite for understanding the dynamics of pacing in the modern age. In his most recent book, *Time, Space and Motion in the Age of Shakespeare*,[119] Angus Fletcher has attempted to understand the status of the categories of time, space and motion in their contribution to the development of a distinctively modern literature in the age of Shakespeare.

Fletcher takes as his particular point of departure a consideration of the impact of the "New Science" on the culture of renaissance English poetry. In looking to the New Science for inspiration, poetry turned away from the more traditional, medieval appeal to a theological frame. With the growing cultural prominence of The New Science there was a relative decentering of the religious tradition without any obvious substitution of cultural function: "the Copernican Revolution and the "New Philosophy" … were so clearly *not religious in character* that few believers could find in them an equivalent replacement for the theology of the Passion of Christ" (TSM, 2). It is out of a twinned sense of cultural destabilization and aspiration that Fletcher's portrait of the "New Poetry" emerges, set against the probing backdrop posed in the question "whether the human yearning for fixed cynosures is not the *actual* source of long term instability" (TSM, 4). In terms of this

---

119. Angus Fletcher, *Time, Space and Motion in the Age of Shakespeare* (Cambridge: Harvard, 2007).

paradoxical dialectic of stability and instability Fletcher traces the drama that the New Poetry itself plays out upon the stage of early modern literary history. Perhaps the most powerful formulation of this paradoxical dialectic is one that Fletcher gives later in the book: "Somehow the correct view of the mysterious must emerge from a clear view of a demystified nature, which brings us to the question of a radically new rethinking of the old theories of the occult." (TSM, 106) The mysteries Fletcher has in mind here are clearly pagan in nature, and it is this pagan mystery which is adapted onto the dramatic stage:

> Instability of mind in picturing the universe [as promoted by science] is necessarily compensated by an enhanced professional use of the drives, the motives that make for good acting. The fact is that acting demands hysteria, for acting is mimetic, which as Freud observed, implies creative cultural "parody" of what in psychoanalysis is called a "conversion symptom." ... We ask then what differentiates dramatic impersonation from the rhetorical figure of personification. Usually the answer will point to the dependence of the latter figure upon what used to be called "personified ideas," as when a poet said that "Terror bore the misbegotten children of desire"—a patent mixture of abstract ideas and physical embodiment. In all figurations like this there is a primitive element of the dramatic ... (TSM, 124)

This is a fundamentally *human* mystery, not one which sets the human in relation to the gods. Along these lines, Fletcher will insist that human *action* precedes character, and also that the notion of material action cannot be *derived* from human action. With these preliminary pieces in place, we may turn to the task of mapping out the architectonic structure of Fletcher's argument, designed to establish space, time and motion as fundamental categories for the New Poetry. In so doing, Fletcher's argument provides a significant embodiment of early modern pacing.

ACTION PRECEDES CHARACTER

The locus of drama is in human action, and so the consideration of the dramatic dimension of poetry must begin here. Fletcher maps out a fourfold plan according to which the science of motion may be transformed for poetic purposes suitable to dramatic action.

> *First*, the physical concept of the movement of objects, of the kind a natural philosopher would study in astronomy or on earth, is translated into its human equivalent, activity and action, such as one might see on the stage or find in a narrative. *Second*, we find that action in this humanized sphere creates what we call character, what Aristotle called *ethos*, to be distinguished from the dramatic part of a role acted by a specific player. *Third*, this characterizing action is a motion that is generated in and

through language. *Fourth*, the drama gives the moving action its embodiment, as on a stage, acted by the *dramatis personae*. (TSM, 38)

Locke traced our understanding of material causality back to our experience of human volition, hence our understanding of the collision of bodies back to our experience of their resisting and impacting our own bodies. Fletcher is interested in the reverse translation: how are we to take our understanding of physical motion and use it as a template for the consideration of human interaction? It is this paradoxical, "reverse" movement which fuels the particular aesthetic of the poetry Fletcher considers, and what enables it to achieve a locus capable of deepening both mimetic representation and the representation of mimesis. For mimesis is quintessentially human action, but action as it is given in the world of time, space and motion. It is *inter*action, conditioned not only by the imitation of other human actions but also by the environment in which human action finds itself situated. A general vocabulary of natural motion will serve as a powerful semantic tool for mimetic expression.

More specifically, the early modern natural philosophers developed a counter-language set against the traditional Aristotelian description of natural motion. In this latter Aristotelian vocabulary, as Fletcher puts it, "things had to act like persons" (TSM, 108). The point of the reverse translation Fletcher identifies in The New Poetry is not to make persons act like things—it will not be until much later that we explicitly meet a work like La Mettrie's *L'homme machine*. Rather, this reversal makes possible a precedence of human actions over human character. If the qualitative description of nature which Aristotle promotes is transferred to the dramatic domain, then we will find "that dramatic events occur as they do only because each person acts according to his or her own character, which is an inward and inherent quality of that person's nature" (TSM, 107). Abandoning the recourse to such a qualitative explanation along with the Aristotelian theory of the four causes which supports it,

> it seems that early modern science must rethink the whole idea of human individuality, of what makes a person rare and his relationships rarefied, in order to establish the soul's independence. This is an old fashioned way of expressing the poet's new task, since persons, like objects in nature as now understood, are only to be looked at *from the outside*. (TSM, 108)

What wears itself on its external sleeve, so to speak, are precisely human actions. It is for just this reason that action must precede character in the historical context of the New Science.

In opting for the precedence of action over character, Fletcher departs from the characterological analysis which A.C. Bradley standardized in his influential discussions of Shakespeare. Fletcher does not recommend a wholesale rejection of such character-based reading since "so much in literature depends upon legitimate concerns with character" (TSM, 107). Fletcher finds much in Bradley that is still of use, but in the last analysis, a redressing of the balance is required. Characterological analysis is circular, much in the way Fletcher suspects Aristotelian explanations, perhaps all essentialist explanations, of being. Character is understood in terms of actions, which are themselves in turn explained by an appeal back to character, forging at best a hermeneutic circle, at worst a vacuous non-explanation. As Hannah Arendt insisted drawing on the work of Adolf Portmann, we are only able to understand humans and other biological creatures by way of their presentational surface[120] (it is this and not functional similarity, as John Searle has argued, that is required for the embodiment of mind). In place of essentialist appeals, Fletcher will emphasize "the role of probable causes among prime movers of both Shakespearean plots and Galilean motion" (TSM, 44).

This leads us back to the fourfold typology of action by which Fletcher effectively replaces the appeal to the four Aristotelian causes. In a recent essay Fletcher has identified Aristotle's four causes as the ambient source for the fourfold typology of traditional allegory, and so we may effectively view Fletcher's dramatic typology as a replacement of allegorical typology as well.[121] So far we have considered Fletcher's first two points: the translation of motion into the register of human activity and the grounding of character in human action. The latter two points move specifically into the realm of embodied representation, where actions are taken up into words and then redoubled in the dramatic re-presentation of action, leaning heavily on the theatrical sense of 'drama'.

In the elaboration of his third point, that "characterizing action is a motion that is generated in and through language," Fletcher focuses intensively on the metrical structure of poetic language: how it simultaneously conveys quantitative rhythm and emotional expression. In this respect, it is the twin of music. Motion is taken up into language at a nearly presemantic level, but one which stands in intimate proximity to what, following Fletcher, we might call "semantic crossover." Most interesting are those cases (as Fletcher seems to imply, if not stating directly) like Donne's and Shakespeare's, where the metrical structure of poetic expression is loosened from strict metrical devices but in a way which not only preserves but in fact intensifies the musicality of language. Fletcher transposes the point into a modern context: "Poets like Auden and Hollander, and their poetic siblings and more important, those they admire who may differ stylistically from them, continue to remind us that poetry would be prose, if it did not deploy all the forces of a controlled and "numbered" motion" (TSM, 46). Yet this control is

---

120. Arendt, *The Life of the Mind*, I, 27-28.
121. Angus Fletcher, "Allegory Without Ideas," *boundary 2* **33** 1 (2006), 77-98, here 81-82.

at full throttle in the poetry of Stevens and Ashbery rather than the more mannered Auden and Hollander.[122] "For not keeping of accent," Ben Jonson would convict Donne of "deserving of hanging," but in fact it is the "turbulence" (TSM, 52) which Donne's deviant rhythms express which carries the ultimate power of motive, and emotive, language. Fletcher laments the "prosiness" of today's poetry, and it is certainly this predominant fault of the world of contemporary poetry which induces him to soft-peddle the less common fault of a rigid metrical constraint.

The need for a wresting of metrical rhythm from all Procrustean beds leads directly on to Fletcher's fourth point, that "the drama gives the moving action its embodiment." To convey the dramatic, in particular, action must outstrip commentary. There is a critical issue of tempo in the dramatic presentation of action, for *in reality* we act "on the fly," with niceties of comprehension traveling in action's wake. It is just this pacing of dramatic action which saves it from the threat of rigidity always faced by allegory, and which makes possible the dynamic sense of forward motion which is needed for plausible embodiment. In contradistinction to allegory, this provides a dynamic conception of pacing, but one still strongly tied to the scale of individual human action. As Donne remarks in a passage Fletcher cites, there is never "[t]ime enough to have beene Interpreter / To Babells bricklayers" (cited, TSM, 52), as is reflected particularly in the " rapid verbal transport" of the then raging pamphlet wars. Fletcher cites also Anthony Nutall's diagnosis of the rhythms of *Timon of Athens* in "the curious way in which Shakespeare's mind continually races ahead of itself" (cited, TSM, 53-54), and we might remark that it is such racing which makes possible the capacity Shakespeare's characters have to overhear themselves which Bloom identifies throughout the Shakespearean corpus. No doubt this explains in part Bloom's particular fondness for Macbeth's "proleptic imagination," which Fletcher glosses in terms of "an insane drive to accumulate and annihilate the traces of his past, whipping them into his future, before he has time to think" (TSM, 54). It is the *overloading* of dramatic action which expresses the strange non-traditional "essence" of the New Poetry's drama, just as, we might hazard, it is proliferation which expresses the non-essence "essence" of technology.

THE MIMETIC LOCUS

Let us return, briefly, to the two formulations of the "paradoxical dynamic" which frame Fletcher's enterprise: first, asking whether "the human

---

122. Hollander, for example, is at his best in a collection such as *Powers of Thirteen*, in which the formal mechanisms of poetic production become the theme of the poetry itself. Auden declared that we should be grateful for any poetic contrivance—such as rhyme—which encourages a deemphasis of the self.

yearning for fixed cynosures is not the *actual* source of long term instability" (TSM, 4), and second, the demand that "the correct view of the mysterious must emerge from a clear view of a demystified nature ..." (TSM, 106). I suggest the function of the latter demand is to take the paradoxical demand reflected in the first question to a new and higher level. The demystification of nature requires a setting aside of human terms for nature's description, as we have seen above in the transition from an Aristotelian, anthropomorphizing description of nature's causes in favor of a description of nature which restricts itself to a non-essentializing account of bodily motion. In so doing, the "human yearning for fixed cynosures" is thrown back upon the physical world: all intrinsically human sources of fixity—including the human yearning for fixity—are thereby (apparently) bracketed. Such a frustration of the human yearning for fixity generates the conditions for a general descriptive hysteria, we might say, which makes possible a revolutionary development in the capacity for dramatic representation of action. The emphasis on natural description will extend the dynamic account of action in dramatic terms out from the human domain into the larger arena of the natural world. The key to understanding this dramatic transition from man to nature lies in the nature of human action as mimetic.

As early as 1964, Fletcher's account of mimesis was already grounded in the Freudian appeal to hysteria as a neurotic analogue of the mimetic function in art. According to Freud, the hysteric acts out desires for sexual contact by "conversion," that is, by a mimetic gesturing. As Fletcher put it then,

> Hysteria must be understood in its *outgoing*, extroverted character: the hysteric, in normal conditions, is a markedly outgoing person who seeks intimate contact—one might say, erotic contact—with others. It is this impulse to come into intimate knowledge and contact which characterizes the mimetic mode also, the mode which Freud equated with "art." The chief ground for making art the analogue of hysteria is therefore the common fact of *identification*. To make his dramas and fictions the poet "identifies" with other real or imaginary people, imitating their actions and passions. In hysteria identification "enables patients to express in their symptoms not only their own experiences but also those of a large number of other people…. and to act all the parts in a play singlehanded."[123]

What renders the mimetic locus, the locus of identification, so powerful in the age of Shakespeare is that such identification must now pass through the *division* of the human from the physical. This naturally intensifies the hysteria required for such identification. An almost Faustian "pact" is required for such identification: as Fletcher puts it,

---

123. Angus Fletcher, *Allegory: The Theory of a Symbolic Mode* (Ithaca: Cornell University Press, 1964), 283; the cited passage is from Freud's *The Interpretation of Dreams*.

> The Galilean approach is dedicated to a mathematical cleansing of physics and astronomy, so that we should say that his separating science gives a new permission to the prior Aristotelian science—which is now, as it were, allowed to inspire the poet's work with interior knowledge, on the condition that the four causes are no longer believed to represent physical fact. Galilean thought manages the new permission by letting the older science move to the inside of psychological knowledge, if need be, by resolutely staying outside of the psyche and its desires... What results is that the new drama parallels the new science in balancing objective externality against subjective internal psychic states, by fully accepting the psychological implications of the problem of change. This predominantly secular drama acquires new techniques of participation and mimesis. (TSM, 92-93)

First and foremost among these new techniques is the development of the dramatic soliloquy, which in sectoring the actor off from the drama allows the actor to represent an entire world of refracted voices. It is here that the technique which Bloom identifies as "overhearing" reaches its acme. This mimetic representation is achieved only at the pitch of a radical hysteria, best exemplified in this period in the dramatic soliloquies of Hamlet, leading on eventually to the mad scenes of nineteenth century opera. It is just this hysterical production which makes the drama objectionable to many Elizabethans, and especially the Puritans (TSM, 93).

But perhaps we should say that its moral hysteria is the flashpoint around which the Puritan objection to the drama configures itself. For as Fletcher himself recognizes,

> With no religious sanction, the theater fills a gap left by the loss of religious authority. What is required is that a central subject and aim of science assume something like the position of common and unanalyzed authority once held by religious beliefs. Specifically, theater participates in the larger cultural extension of the idea and the problem of mobility in all spheres of life and thought. The merely physical implications of this problem can no longer be contained behind a narrowly scientific wall, but must now become part of generalized cultural beliefs, in effect a new basis on which ordinary intelligent people judge the foundations of their world. (TSM, 31).

Science, and the authority it courts, cannot in any way be seen as a secularization of religion and its antecedent authority, and in the absence of such a translation, the secular, or more accurately *pagan*, drama steps in to assume the functional role previously played by the appeal to religious faith. In Blumenberg's terms, we are dealing not with a secularization of religious faith but rather with a *reoccupation* of its cultural position.[124]

---

124. Herman Melville, "The Two Temples," in *Pierre, Israel Potter, The Piazza Tales, The Confidence Man, Uncollected Prose, Billy Budd, Sailor* (New York: The Library of America,

In accepting the full "psychological implications of the problem of change," in assuming, that is, the psychological analogue of the New Science's account of motive change as its primary condition, the new drama orients itself around the problem of depicting ongoing psychological transition. In so doing, "this predominantly secular drama acquires new techniques of participation and mimesis. It enhances the role of the actor." (TSM, 93). The core of this actor's new role is to *embody* the dramatic progression, and the dramatic soliloquy is the pinnacle of such embodiment. Here there is no "incarnation" of "the" Word, but rather a continuous play back and forth between interior emotional state and external action. Rather than an embodiment of the Word, we have an embodiment of action *by way of words*: this embodied integration of language and action is a necessary condition for overcoming a linguistic decisionism in which the ontotheological position of the Word is reoccupied by the dramatic position of human action. This obligation leads directly on to the dynamic requirements of pacing and rhythm, discussed above, associated with the need for the drama to give moving action its embodiment. The mimetic locus explodes traditional ontotheology in demanding the technical skills of the new drama. The powder-keg which ignites this explosion is the intensity of hysterical conversion, a new, psychologically heightened form of Pan-ic pagan rituals.

FAUSTIAN THEMES

Although not the most eminent, Marlowe is the exemplary New Poet, standing to the literary domain as Giordano Bruno to the philosophical, each poised on the threshold of modernity. We do not find equivalent intellectual intensities again until Rimbaud, on the one hand, and Nietzsche on the other. Whether Marlowe and Bruno ever met, it is likely that they were involved in common circles of espionage.[125] The joint connection to spying is provocative, even were it to prove fortuitous, which I believe it is not. Spies are "readers." Later, Leibniz would die in poverty and disregard, suspected of a complicated game of double agency, and many of the best early recruits to the CIA were from the literary stock of Harvard and (especially) Yale.[126] *harlot's ghost*, Norman Mailer's massive tale of mid-twentieth century espionage, is an attempt at the great American novel by that writer who was earlier deputized to supply us with 'One small step for man, one giant step for mankind' when Neil Armstrong descended, left foot first, onto the moon.[127]

1984), 1242-1256.

125. On Bruno: John Bossy, *Giordano Bruno and the Embassy Affair* (New Haven: Yale, 1991).

126. Eliot Weinberger, "James Jesus Angleton 1917-1987," in *Outside Stories: Essays by Eliot Weinberger* (New York: New Directions), 51-55; Burton Hersh, *The Old Boys: The American Elite and the Origins of the CIA* (New York: Charles Scribner's Sons, 1992).

127. Norman Mailer, *harlot's ghost* (New York: Random House, 1991). Guy Davenport,

In Fletcher's reading of *Doctor Faustus*, "Marlowe Invents the Deadline," the focus is on the more basic sense of spying: the ever focal line-of-sight which pierces through Marlowe's play: "Faustus has thrown away all inwardness of meditation and deep theological pondering and metaphysical study. He has chosen 'lines, circles, schemes, letters and characters'—all of them visual signs inscribed, to be read, to be seen as the talismans of alchemy." (TSM, 64-65) But the curious "alchemical task" which Faustus proposes is, on Fletcher's reading, to see "the disappearance of the moment" (TSM, 64), that is: to see time itself in its pure diaphaneity. If this is alchemy, it is in a new and distinctively modern spirit, akin to Pascal's application of the man → Man transition directly to the temporal dimension. Although "time begins to seem such a riddle that to have it at one's command is tantamount to possessing divinity" (TSM, 67), Faust's contract "makes it ruthlessly clear that even the famed magician cannot escape being human, which in this changing world of magic skills seems to him to require rivalry with God, which in turn gives a unique importance to human time" (TSM, 69).[128]

In conversation, Fletcher has suggested that in the early modern turn, the role of the alchemist is handed over to the experimentalist; if so, the role of the mystic, we might say, is handed over to the natural philosopher. Marlowe's Faustus stands at the intersection of both trends. His desire to see time directly is redolent of Brouwer's early twentieth century temporal mysticism, and is better understood as proto-phenomenological than alchemical:

> *Consciousness* in its deepest home seems to oscillate slowly, will-lessly, and reversibly between stillness and sensation. And it seems that only the status of sensation allows the initial phenomenon of the said transition. This initial phenomenon is a *move of time*. By a move of time a present sensation gives way to another present sensation in such a way that consciousness retains the former one as a past sensation, and moreover, through the distinction between present and past, recedes from both and from stillness, and becomes *mind*.[129]

Brouwer's account of the "phases consciousness has to pass through in its transition from its deepest home to the exterior world in which we cooperate and seek mutual understanding"[130] runs parallel to Faustus' exit from the cave of his study into the world of "deadlines." In this centrifugal passage, emphasis moves from the flow of time to its sectioning off into measurable intervals, from a "move of time" to a cut in the temporal continuum. By quantifying time, time is possessed, and if Faustus "is to own his own time for twenty-four years, as his contract states, the story must explore the

---

"The Dawn in Erewhon," in *Tatlin!* (New York: Charles Scribner's Sons, 1974), 261.
   128. See Blumenberg's *Work on Myth*, Part IV: "Against a God, Only a God."
   129. L.E.J. Brouwer, *Collected Works* (Amsterdam: North Holland, 1975), I, 480.
   130. ibid.

tragic emptiness of an ever more perfectly invisible medium—a dimension for measuring motion, as the scientist would have it" (TSM, 67). The scientist measures time by dividing it, cutting it up, paradoxically divesting time of its flow in order to supply a dimension for the measurement of motion. But the motion of what? For science the answer is clearly, "the motion of bodies," but what for Faustus? What will Faustus measure by cutting time into twenty-four years of life?

What Faustus measures with this "temporal hoard" is what he can buy, according to the modern dictum that "time is money." And what can he buy? "Fame perhaps, 'that last infirmity of noble mind'; or material comfort and things 'of rare price'; health perhaps, if one could find the right doctor; the chance to be restlessly active and inventive, perhaps" (TSM, 63). Perhaps, according to one seventeenth century physician of souls this purchase is instead the cause and symptom rather than the instrument for the avoidance of melancholy. One dimension of the "dreaming alternative" supplied by the dramatic "world of magic shows, where appearance *is* reality" (TSM, 64) which Fletcher does not suggest is the possibility that "in reality" Faustus never leaves his study, his books, his cave at all, just sitting instead, as Robert Burton did, writing a long digression on the misery of scholars.[131]

But in any case, the most powerful answer to the question what Faustus buys is surely Fletcher's, that Faustus buys *acceleration*, a faster ascent to the outer horizon. The emphasis on vision is an intensification of the power, hence rate, of perception (what, not coincidentally, makes the computer simulation of vision so challenging and costly). "Whenever humans try to hold back the flux of change, the fixed image always disappears. Faustus therefore tries to define his power as an accelerated perfection of seeing, glimpsing the momentary appearances so quickly as to make them permanent" (TSM, 64). This is an early, more powerful, and more purely modern version of Wordsworth's later spots of time, or the momentaneous consolidation of the *Augenblick* which Kierkegaard takes over from Plato, leading on as Fletcher points out to Husserl's "internal time consciousness," with Brouwer's deepest home of consciousness in the primordial intuition of time somewhere close by. Later, in the chapter on Ben Jonson, Fletcher associates alchemy with the acceleration of time "in that it seeks to speed up the *effects* of the passing of time" (TSM, 98), seeing modern technology as "the implementation of the alchemist's desire to control time so radically as to *eliminate* all slow natural processes" (TSM, 101). Hence we arrive at the fundamental paradox: in cutting time, arresting it by imposing a deadline, we free time from its natural "scale." This is the "cold heart" of science, written in the "language" of mathematics, that fuels the modern culture of The New Poetry, and its canonical scientific author is Galileo, whose aim in the

---

131. Robert Burton, *The Anatomy of Melancholy*, ed. Floyd Dell and Paul Jordan-Smith (New York: Tudor Publishing, 1927), 259-82.

Two New Sciences is to "investigate and demonstrate some of the properties of accelerated motion (whatever the cause of this acceleration may be)" (cited, TSM, 106). Here Fletcher identifies a condition of the *pacing* of the modern scientific enterprise, and by extension the modern enterprise more generally, which goes beyond the first step indicated earlier in terms of the man → Man transition. Drama provides a privileged locus for this investigation, for it is here that the literary representation of the lifeworld will find its most dynamic expression in terms of the exacting modern demands placed on time.

Might we poetically suggest that the ultimate cause of this acceleration is Brunonian heroic frenzy? Not, of course, in the sense that all physical motion literally has a human source, but that the source of the *analysis* of motion lies in the human desire to unmask Diana and thereby accelerate time. This would shift the balance from a Cartesian/Pascalian/Husserlian avoidance of pantheism onto a more radical cosmological terrain. For Bruno, banking on Plato and also the tradition of Lucretius, it is impossible to see the sun, "but very possible to see its shadow, its Diana, the world, the universe, the nature which is in things, the light shining through the obscurity of matter and so resplendent in the darkness."[132] In so unmasking nature, the hunter becomes the hunted, transformed into a deer, free and living "like a god under the protection of the woods in the unpretentious rooms of the cavernous mountains ..."[133] Devoured by his dogs he is "freed from the senses and the fleshly prison of matter, so that he no longer sees his Diana as through a glass or a window, but having thrown down the earthly walls, he sees a complete view of the whole horizon."[134] Marlowe stands by Galileo as joint inheritor of this ecstatic Brunonian legacy, so that Galileo "is spiritually closer to Doctor Faustus than one might think ..." (TSM, 139).

Because Marlowe's presentation is dramatic, the emphasis on seeing must ultimately be directed at the most powerful locus of dramatic expression, the face. "Is this the face that launched a thousand ships?," perhaps Marlowe's most famous line, transcends the level of rhetorical conceit by virtue of the fact that "all throughout *Doctor Faustus* there is a play upon the magic visage and epiphanic beauty of a mythic Helen" (TSM, 55). The quickening of time in Marlowe (and for Faustus) is an intrinsically dramatic quickening, so that the pressure of mounting time is sedimented in facial feature and expression. Faustus' "vision of Helen is a dramatic expansion of that magic moment in *Hero and Leander*: 'Who ever lov'd that lov'd not at first sight'" (TSM, 64). The sense of pure temporal extension builds out from the consolidation of a dramatic crux, magically fusing the flow of time with its possession. The only competitor for the mystical model of a retreat into the

---

132. Giordano Bruno, *The Heroic Frenzies*, trans. Paul Eugene Memmo (Chapel Hill: University of North Carolina, 1964), 225.

133. ibid.

134. idem, 226.

homeland of consciousness is the bracing of a dramatic encounter. By reducing time to its pure dimensionality, Faustus has boiled this encounter down to its formal condition, leaving us with the mystery of time, "a mystery far transcending anything our religions customarily present to us by means of personifying figures and narrative parables" (TSM, 68). If there is a positive appeal to the alchemical in this modern dramatic context, it is to the form, rather than the content or goal, of alchemy. *Doctor Faustus* is the form of drama itself in its modern manifestation, beginning and ending in the fantasy of an overthrow of everything bookish.[135]

ASTRONOETICS

At the end of The New Poetry's age, Marlowe and Galileo converge in Milton's astronoetic line, displacing theological controversy in a new acceleration of vision. In *Die Vollzähligkeit der Sterne* (*The Full Complement of the Stars*), Blumenberg ends with a short section entitled, "What is Astronoetics?" In it, he paints a picture of an interdisciplinary group of scholars in which he participated at the Christina Albert University in Kiel, gathered together in close quarters across the long winter season when sailing was no longer an option. In this northern *Societas litterarum* "almost everyone knew almost everything about almost everyone," and that was risky if one hadn't something to announce. Political pressures mounted as in 1957 the first "false comet" (*falsche Komet*), the "chirruping artificial moon" (*piepende Kunstmond*) Sputnik orbited the earth. On all sides came the question, "And what do we have that is comparable?" The brain-scientist Wolfgang Bargmann's ironic answer was astronoetics, which would investigate such experimentally inaccessible issues as the geography of the far side of the moon through pure thought.[136]

Blumenberg points out that no one thought about the fact that it was only a matter of time until the far side of the moon *would* be investigated with the same astronautical instruments (as late as the early 1950's Wittgenstein had asked how he could be wrong in his assumption that he had never been to the moon).[137] In *Die Vollzähligkeit der Sterne* Blumenberg

---

135. In *Architecture and the Text: The (S)crypts of Joyce and Piranesi* (New Haven: Yale, 1993), Jennifer Bloomer refers to a letter from Guy Davenport, in which he summarizes John Gordon's book on *Finnegans Wake* as follows: "The whole book [i.e., *Finnegans Wake*] happens in a room in Chapelizod. The guided tour of the Museyroom is an inventory of the room, based on a mnemonic device of sharpening your memory by rehearsing all the objects in a room you know well" (cited, 170). Davenport refers to John Gordon, *Finnegans Wake: A Plot Summary* (Syracuse: Syracuse University Press, 1986). Bloomer argues that the Museyroom is constructed on the model of Sir John Soane's House and Museum, 135-146.

136. Hans Blumenberg, *Die Vollzähligkeit der Sterne* (Frankfurt am Main: Suhrkamp, 1997), 547-49.

137. Ludwig Wittgenstein, *On Certainty*, ed. G.E.M. Anscombe and G.H. von Wright

assembled texts from over three decades circumscribing the notion of theory as a function of instrumental impotence and the disappearance of the spectacular.

It might seem oddly retrospective to frame Milton's fusion of Marlowe and Galileo, The New Poetry and The New Science, in such belated terms, but in fact we may see Milton, and before him John Donne and Cyrano de Bergerac, as anticipating the enterprise of astronoetics, for the time of literature's assimilation of scientific progress is always out of joint, yoking theological and mythological imagery to outstrippings even of what science itself is capable. It exemplifies the situation in which we, as humans, stand to science: always in cognitive arrears, failing to understand the epistemic reach of the enterprise, yet always in imaginative anticipation, producing fantasy images in advance of science's current state. *Paradise Lost*

> sustains a massive inquiry into mysteries of our world. Yet nature remains obscure to the poet, beckoning his thought toward deep space, as if somehow he could understand the ratios and relations between all things and all events. (TSM, 151)

Milton is drawn *into the realm of astronoetics*, preparing the way for that popularization of science which would find its foremost exemplar some one hundred years later in Fontenelle's *Discourses on the Plurality of Worlds*.[138] As I write this paragraph, it has only been several months since the discovery of a planet 1.5 times the size of the earth orbiting a "nearby" red dwarf star.

The force of the Miltonic line is to accelerate us into just this deep space, providing the blast-power needed for liftoff. Galileo's presentation of the relativity of motion transfers the emphasis from absolute motion to motive acceleration, and Newton's consequent gravitational theory generalizes the theological notion of The Fall into a multiplicity of "lateral" falls in which bodies are pulled toward each other. "Already in Spenser and the medieval Romance tradition, this lateral principle had been understood, so that the Myth of the Lateral Fall was given expression in stories not of descent, but of errant sidewise wandering in ethical and spiritual digression" (TSM, 147). In Milton, this lateral fall takes hold in the individual poetic line, sailing in verbal acceleration out towards the horizon.

> In *Paradise Lost*, the primary aesthetic effect of such relativizing is that we are more aware of acceleration, and what Aristotle called "violent motion," than of any constant movement, and it is hard not to believe that once again the poet has anticipated later science, since the effulgent light of the Divine Creator traverses the universe with the greatest possible velocity. (TSM, 146)

(New York: Harper Torchbooks, 1972), 87 (§661).

138. Bernard le Bovier de Fontenelle, *Conversations on the Plurality of Worlds*, trans. H.A. Hargreaves (Berkeley: University of California, 1990).

I am inclined to see what Fletcher points to here as a privileged example of the "disjointedness" of the literary, enlisting traditional descriptive registers in ways that outstrip scientific theory, which is bounded by speeds less than the "speed of thought."

The underlying literary mechanism for astronoetic acceleration lies in the figural presentation of scale-shifting, that feeling of liftoff we have been tracing since the beginning of this volume. Fletcher follows these mechanics through the complications of Milton's Galilean figures, first of Satan's shield, then later Satan's "space-travel," and finally in the celebration of the telescope. In the first, "all possible questions of scale and scale-differences confront the reader, producing an effect at once both intricate and impressive" (TSM, 137), hence well beyond synopsis here. The effect, in any case, is one which warps not only space *but also time*, automatically we might say, by bringing Satan into proximity with Galileo's telescope: there is a "zoom forward" into temporal relevance, into "timeliness."

But most important, since it lies at the heart of Milton's power to generate figural *concentration*, is the capacity for scale change to complicate figure by an intermixing of the cognitive and the perceptual:

> In effect, the mixing of learning and immediate sensations forces the poet to change the scale of his vision, from moment to moment, thus making the reader constantly aware of scale changes. These perspectival shifts are precisely what the complex Miltonic similes create; and when the similes are extruded by association, the effect of the whole becomes sublime. An ancient rhetorician would have called this procedure "transumptive" or "metaleptic." (TSM, 140-41)

What Marlowe thematizes in Faustus' compilation of perception upon perception, Milton is able to achieve at the considerably more sophisticated level of figural proliferation. Although the mechanism lies in scale-shifting, the effect is ultimately that of a shifting of level on the scale of figure itself: from simple simile or metaphor to the hypercomplications of transumption and metalepsis, a trope-consuming trope that paradoxically inflates poetic rhetoric by ostensibly quashing it.

Fletcher's invocation of transumption and metalepsis hearkens to Harold Bloom's filling out of the four traditional rhetorical figures into six by the addition of hyperbole and metalepsis, and so Fletcher perhaps explains why Bloom would see Milton (rather than Shakespeare) as the ultimate source for modern lyric poetry. It is here that The New Poetry first historically achieves its full figural repository and responsiveness, in Milton's "Galilean line," eminently readerly. In writing a history of the emergence of the New Poetry, Fletcher has set his sights on the dramatic core of the English poetic tradition in the modern age. Here we see a literary parallel to the Scientific Revolution which culminates in an invitation to the post-Miltonic lyric.

SHAKESPEARE, MILTON AND MONTAGE

Many of the points which Fletcher makes about space, time and, in particular, motion assume only a growing significance as we push forward toward the contemporary condition in aesthetics, culminating in the dominance of the "movie" as a popular art form in the last century and this one. It is therefore most welcome, but not ultimately surprising, to find many of Fletcher's points anticipated in the analyses of cinema's most intellectual visionary, Sergei Eisenstein.[139] Eisenstein's theory of montage, which extends beyond the boundary of film to provide a synoptic view of aesthetic technique, while having as its means the juxtaposition of images, takes as its particular goal the production of images of *movement*. In this central task, Eisenstein traces the early pedigree of montage technique in a line with roots in Homer, Shakespeare and Milton. In his last completed work, the autobiographical memoirs, *Immoral Memories*, Eisenstein identifies Pushkin as a canonical example of montage technique in the Russian technique, and "when an example is needed in the English language, John Milton also."[140] As becomes clear elsewhere in his writings, Eisenstein has in mind especially Milton's battle scenes in *Paradise Lost*.[141] In the depiction of battle Milton faces the challenge of aligning massive forces through selective descriptive representation, and it is in such contexts that montage technique functions most powerfully and transparently.

But it is rather in Shakespeare that we find Eisenstein identifying the core of the montage technique in the image of movement. Analyzing the presentation of the human body as an image of the state in *King Lear, King John*, and *Henry VIII*, Eisenstein sees Shakespeare's depiction of the body going beyond a concerted juxtaposition of images to the coordinated presentation of bodily phases in transition, conveying a powerful image of movement. Thus Shakespeare progresses "beyond the stage of phasal perception, beyond the aesthetics of phase, and into the region of compositional dynamics which flows from the relationship *between* phases, from the combination of phases, from phases which converge into an image of movement, from the interrelation of montage sequences, in fact" (SW II, 189). In this way Shakespeare is able to present *"sequentially changing* positions in the context not of a body torn apart *in itself* but of a body that is breaking up the static configuration of its parts as it moves from phase to phase of a movement"

---

139. Fletcher acknowledges Eisenstein in his own work on Milton, *The Transcendental Masque: An Essay on Milton's* Comus (Ithaca: Cornell, 1971), in a section on "Montage and Perspectivism," 136-140.

140. Sergei M. Eisenstein, *Immoral Memories, An Autobiography* (Boston: Houghton Mifflin, 1983), 230.

141. Sergei M. Eisenstein, "The Problems of the Soviet Historical Film," in Sergei M. Eisenstein, *Selected Works*, Volume III, ed. Richard Taylor, trans. William Powell (London: British Film Institute, 1996), 126-141, here 139.

(SW II, 189). Indeed, Shakespeare is "inclined toward the very *Urphänomen* of cinema itself ... *movement*. And more precisely: not so much movement as such but the *image of movement* ..." (SW II, 192). In this way, Eisenstein arrives at a position consonant with Fletcher's more extended analysis.

The fact, however, that Eisenstein identifies Shakespeare's treatment of the motive body serving as an image of the state has yet further significance. In the political domain we find a need for a body → Body transition analogous to the man → Man transition considered above. Yet Shakespeare's strength is manifested in his command of this transition in a *motive* form which is altogether lacking in Pascal's application of the man → Man transition. For Pascal, the transition is applied *with respect to* the dimension of time, but it does not embody the motive force implied by this dimension. In Shakespeare's bodily imagery we find a more sophisticated appropriation of the motive dimension, internalizing it in the representative power of the body → Body transition. In Shakespeare's treatment of the body, we should speak not simply of a metaphor of scale but of a metaphor of *mobilization*, as the issue is not just one of *dimension*, but an integrally dynamic one of *pace*.

Eisenstein, aided by his ambient concern with the quintessentially *motive* aesthetic genre, helps us to see that Fletcher's analysis of time, space and motion leads us beyond the dimensional considerations natural to Blumenberg's orientation into a more dynamic attitude for which pacing becomes an unavoidable issue. Although I will ultimately insist that Fletcher's project does not extend nearly far enough, his work assumes a central position for the larger project of this book because it is here that the significance of motion for the dynamics of pacing first becomes explicit.

4

Jean Starobinski's Linguistic Modernism

FROM MOTION TO ACTION

The "prime mover" in Starobinski's modern canon is not Shakespeare but Montaigne, to whom Starobinski devotes one of his seminal works, *Montaigne in Motion*.[142] But since I have already looked at Fletcher's treatment of motion in the early modern period in the previous chapter, I choose to focus instead on a later point along the trajectory of Starobinski's work, when he investigates the linguistic status of action and reaction, taking as one physical point of departure the science of motive impact in the early modern period. Starobinski's magisterial work, *Action and Reaction: The Life and Adventures of a Couple*,[143] spans the intellectual history of the seventeenth to late twentieth centuries, and so provides a dynamic overview of the language of "force" in the modern European intellectual tradition.

In the "Preface to the American Edition" Jean Starobinski identifies this book as the one among his (considerable) corpus which constitutes the

---

142. Jean Starobinski, *Montaigne in Motion*, trans. Arthur Goldhammer (Chicago: University of Chicago, 1985). The title of Starobinski's original French volume would be literally translated, "Montaigne in Movement." The seminal chapter of this work is the penultimate, "«Each man in some sort exists in his work»," 214-43. Starobinski's chapter on Montaigne's "movement" could be profitably, and extensively, compared with Fletcher's account of time, space and motion in what I have called The New Poetry. The two are largely complementary: Starobinski focuses on Montaigne's reception of the skeptical tradition whereas Fletcher focuses on what we might call the dramatic proto-history of the New Science in literature. The two investigations illuminate complementary, though not always compatible, sources for early modern ideas of motion. The project of Starobinski's *Action and Reaction* is anticipated in the last chapter of *Montaigne in Motion*, see esp. 291-93.

143. Jean Starobinski, *Action and Reaction: The Life and Adventures of a Couple*, trans. Sophie Hawkes (New York: Zone, 2003).

clearest proof of his experience attending meetings of the History of Ideas Club during his three year tenure at Johns Hopkins University early on in his career. Indeed, this work by Starobinski attests not just to the influence of traditions in "history of ideas, semantic and philological history, literary history, the history of medicine and biological sciences" (AR, 11) represented at Johns Hopkins at that time, but also to the burgeoning of a structuralist and post-structuralist approach to language which also found its American reception in considerable part through the conference on Structuralism and the Human Sciences held at Johns Hopkins in 1966.[144] These two currents intersect in Starobinski's semantic history of the terms 'action' and 'reaction' as he traces the adventures of this couple from their early modern advent through usage in contemporary culture.

I take Starobinski's volume as a model of reading modernity that would ground itself in linguistic evidence, and in this regard it bears much in common with the "metaphorological" enterprise of Blumenberg, at least as Blumenberg identifies his project in the early *Paradigms for a Metaphorology*. In the later addendum, "Prospects for a Theory of Nonconceptuality," which serves as a qualification of the earlier conception of his project, Blumenberg remarks that his metaphorology, while originally intended as being "directed mainly toward the constitution of conceptuality" should now be seen in terms of its direction back toward "the connections with the life-world as the constant motivating support (though one that cannot be constantly kept in view) of all theory."[145] This later reformulation indicates a greater skepticism about the extent to which the world of experience can be "taken up" into language. Yet even in Blumenberg's earlier characterization of his enterprise, the emphasis is on concepts and concept-formation, whereas Starobinski is, or at least claims to be, interested in the history of *terms*, with conceptual innovation playing only a secondary role. Starobinski's methodological nominalism—his focus on terms, and their history—is connected to the broader version of methodological decisionism which is a primary target of attack in Blumenberg's attempted legitimation of modernity. By 'decisionism' I understood an orientation which posits rationally indefensible volitional acts as ultimate grounds delimiting the field of all rational accounting. Late medieval theological nominalism found such an ultimate ground in the acts of God's will, and as Blumenberg has persuasively argued, it is in terms of the overcoming of such decisionism that modernity is able to assert its legitimacy. Declining an equivalent legitimation in the methodological sphere, Starobinski fails to keep pace with the history he seeks to investigate. Looking at Starobinski will serve

---

144. Richard Macksey and Eugene Donato, eds., *The Languages of Criticism and the Sciences of Man: The Structuralist Controversy* (Baltimore: Johns Hopkins, 1970), ix.

145. Hans Blumenberg, *Shipwreck with Spectator: Paradigms for a Metaphor of Existence*, trans. Stephen Rendall (Cambridge: MIT, 1997), 81.

in part to tell a cautionary tale about the consequences of an over-reliance on linguistic history.

A LINGUISTIC COUPLE

Starobinski takes as a sort of motto a passage from the correspondence of Erich Auerbach, which serves even better as a motto for his work than for Auerbach's own masterwork, *Mimesis: The Representation of Reality in Western Literature*:[146]

> I would be very happy ... if in your working method you began not with a general problem but with a singular phenomenon, carefully and decisively chosen, something like the history of a word or the interpretation of a passage. This singular phenomenon could never be too small or too concrete and should never be a concept introduced by us or by other scholars, but rather something suggested by the object itself. (cited, AR, 13)

Whereas in *Mimesis* Auerbach chose to focus on the problem of the linguistic depiction of reality, Starobinski focuses even more narrowly on the historical use to which the single pair of terms 'action' and 'reaction' have been put in a panoply of modern contexts encompassing physics (or "natural philosophy"), chemistry, biology, medicine, psychiatry, literature, and the discourses of the social and political spheres. Of particular interest to Starobinski is the way this pair of terms allows him to focus on the "lexical traces" left in the wake of the revolution inaugurated by the classical mechanics of Newton (AR, 10). In the process of this study we see the way in which "the couple 'action/reaction' could successively pertain to the material universe—in its totality or in the intimacy of its particles—the living body, the events of history, and psychological behavior" (AR, 18), eventually integrating itself into the common usages of political discourse and the discourse of everyday life.

The title of Starobinski's volume, and indirectly even the choice of focus itself, derive from a passage in Balzac's novel *Louis Lambert*, which receives an extensive analysis in the course of Starobinski's history.[147] In the passage upon which the title of Starobinski's volume draws, Balzac's hero apotheosizes the historical study of words:

> Often have I made the most delightful voyage, floating on a word down the abyss of the past, like an insect embarked on a blade of grass tossing on the ripples of a stream. Starting from Greece, I would get to Rome, and traverse the whole extent of modern ages. What a fine book might be written of the life and adventures of a word! ... But is it not so with every root-word? They all are stamped with a living power

---

146. Erich Auerbach, *Mimesis: The Representation of Reality in Western Literature*, trans. Willard Trask (Princeton: Princeton, 1953).

147. Compare Eisenstein, SW II, 168.

that comes from the soul, and which they restore to the soul through the mysterious and wonderful action and reaction between thought and speech. (cited, AR, 13)

In this passage we espy our crucial couple, but the passage from Balzac also points to a critical reflexivity that will run throughout Starobinski's account. For it is just this couple 'action'/'reaction', which Balzac uses to describe the relation between thought and speech, which Starobinski will in turn take as the example internal to speech itself (or, more generally, language) upon which to focus. Even if Lambert declares that any "root-word" might be chosen, Starobinski's particular choice connects to the modern intensification of the concern with freedom and determinism, and allows him to focus on the way in which the relation between thought and language is articulated within the domain of language itself.

NIGHT FANTASIES

So far as the history of his own research is concerned, Starobinski tells us that "my initial questions concerned the adoption of the word 'reaction' by Enlightenment thinkers, and then by the medical sciences, psychiatry in particular" (AR, 9). It is the term 'reaction' which is novel in that modern context in which action is opposed to reaction, and so throughout the book it is the changes in the usage of this later term which most obviously indicate the historical trajectory of the opposition reflected by the couple. Starobinski asserts, although he is not able to document, that the Latin term *reactio* "was introduced gradually into narrative Latin in the early Middle Ages;" but in any case, "between the twelfth and the thirteenth century, *reagere* and *reactio* appeared in scholarly Latin and never left it" (AR, 23). These were technical terms introduced into the natural sciences: Starobinski's first example is taken from the philosopher Albertus Magnus. Here the medieval philosopher uses the verb 'react' to characterize the response of an agent which, in acting, is acted upon: "The more distant any natural agent is from its beginnings, the more continuous its operation, the more it weakens and tends to fail, since the agent, in the realm of nature, must in turn be acted upon when it acts, and in being acted upon, it reacts, as the Philosopher [i.e. Aristotle] says" (cited, AR, 27). In the context Albertus Magnus considers, this reaction is used to explain the "slackening" or "remission" of seminal fluid which is responsible for the weakening of inherited resemblance, including the formation of daughters and monsters, as a function of the resistivity of the feminine material substratum. Specifically, these effects occur in the case of less energetic seminal emission being met by the resistance of this medium.

In several important regards, seminal emission serves as a privileged locus for the semantic development of the couple 'action'/'reaction'. In the second chapter, on Diderot and chemistry, Starobinski considers Diderot's frequent linkage of agitation and fermentation in this context (AR, 85). It is "at the culmination of *D'Alembert's Dream,* d'Alembert's ecstatic tirade, which Diderot makes coincide with the dreamer's seminal emission" (AR, 71), that the dreamer's body is illuminated by a vision of "an infinite succession of little animals inside the fermenting atom" and life is seen "as a series of actions and reactions" (cited, AR, 71-2). Here, too, we have a reflexive production of the imagery of action and reaction which is itself understood to be occasioned by physiological processes of action and reaction. In particular, if in the dream "the image should appear initially at the center of the bundle of fibers, then the reaction in the voluptuary fibers will take the form of tension, erection and emission of seminal fluid" (AR, 74). Diderot characterizes this as a "descending" dream, as opposed to an "ascending" one in which, conversely, sexual excitation produces images. Starobinski notes that D'Alembert's dream follows first an ascending, then a descending, course, from an initial living point, which then rises "ecstatically to the spectacle of Saturn, the universe, and millions of centuries; and closes by returning to this last 'point' found in 'all of nature,' a synthesis of the whole and the infinitesimal element" (AR, 73). The scope of the process of fermentation as action and reaction is extended from the animalcule to the universe and back again, and the descent corresponds to the slackening after the dreamer's nocturnal emission.

Diderot views fermentation as the source of all life, and by transposition the inspirations of the "somber and melancholic" are attributed to a "periodic derangement of the machine" in which,

> [d]rawn from this lethargy by the tumult suffered by the humors rising in them, they imagined that it was the divinity descending, visiting them, working them; that the divine breath, with which they had been first animated, had suddenly come alive again and revived a portion of its ancient and original energy; they formulated precepts for artificially attaining this state of orgasm and drunkenness, in which they found themselves exalted and which they missed ... (cited, AR, 83).

Starobinski points out that the term 'orgasm' "was not restricted to the single banal erotic meaning it has today," but rather "[i]n the eighteenth century, the word 'orgasm' retained a pathological meaning from the medical tradition, completely forgotten today," which combined the senses of agitation and fermentation and was, according to Bartolomeo Castelli's medical dictionary, "the name of the abnormal movement [*pravus*] of the humors and their expulsion through the excretory stimulus [*impetus cum stimulo excretionis*]" (AR, 85).

Starobinski revisits this locus in the context of early nineteenth century medical science, in particular the memoirs of Pierre-Jean-George Cabanis, who writes of the phenomenon of nocturnal emission among "[m]en of letters, thinkers, artists, in a word all the men whose nerves and brains receive many impressions or combine many ideas" (cited, AR, 159). Starobinski cites an extended passage from Cabanis' reports which he invites us to compare with *D'Alembert's Dream* or with the work of Freud, who mentions Cabanis in passing in *The Interpretation of Dreams*. Cabanis views the phenomenon of nocturnal emission as a function, in part, of the lack of external stimuli during the period of sleep, and in part as a transference of the activity of the imagination to other bodily organs, in this case those of generation. He relies on the hydraulic imagery of fluid transmission which one still finds in Freud's work, and he synthesizes this register with an appeal to the notion of shock as engendering the reactive response of one body to the impression of another. In this way Cabanis is able, as Starobinski points out, to develop a vocabulary in which sympathy may be understood in terms of the transformative power of imitation and in which he is able to discuss "the means by which the moral influences the physical, as well as the educational therapeutic effects that can result from these means" (AR, 160).

In these examples the couple 'action' / 'reaction' serves as an integral component in the vocabulary which links the realm of physical bodies to the realm of biological and moral beings by bridging the discursive gap between the physical process of seminal emission, understood in terms of the mechanical model of colliding bodies, and the biological and moral realms in which such a phenomenon finds its cultural insertion. Just as Locke linked our understanding of the phenomenon of bodily resistance to our perception of resistance through the sense of touch, so the figure of seminal emission provides an experiential locus for the description of a range of actions and reactions of explosive type and a coordination of vocabularies which, while joining the various dimensions of this explosive power, equally subject it to the control provided by the regulation of multiple vocabularies. That these vocabularies are transient and "metaphorical" is no criticism of them, but integral to their functioning. As Starobinski puts it, we must recognize that "a vocabulary's semantic *variation* is itself a signifier, and by referring back to successive 'states of language,' it allows us to see more clearly the changes undergone by various 'states of culture'" (AR, 15). In this way, attempts to describe variation in the world "induce" variation in language.

Yet it is not only such descriptive variation that induces variation in semantic register. Starobinski suggests further that as vocabularies become ensconced there is an inherent tendency toward the neutralization of their novel charge, in considerable part simply by virtue of dissemination, so that for purposes of retaining their cultural force new semantic innovation is required. In his discussion of Freud, Starobinski focuses in particular on the development of the term 'abreaction' to just this end: whereas in the examples considered above the vocabulary of action and reaction was sufficient to accommodate the violent expulsion associated with the phenomenon of seminal emission, in Freud a "quasi-synonomy" is established between the terms 'evacuation', 'catharsis' and 'abreaction' which collectively "accumulate a sense of deviation, elimination, discharge, with an obvious connotation of intestinal expulsion" (AR, 181). "In adding the Latin-Germanic *ab*-," Starobinski asserts, "Breuer and Freud doubled the prefix and reactivated, for a very well defined use, a term that had become exhausted through too many different meanings. 'Reaction' needed to be specified by a determining adjunct term or by forming a compound in German" (AR, 179). Once again, Starobinski quietly indicates the way in which the linguistic maneuver, "reactivation," itself enlists the very process which it seeks to renew.

Starobinski views the semantic innovation associated with the joint phenomena of prefixing and compounding as so important for the development of psychoanalysis that he is willing to assert that "[t]he deployment of the prefixal possibilities of German accompanied (or guided) the rise of psychoanalysis." With implicit reference to the later development of psychoanalysis in France by Lacan and others such as Laplanche and Pontalis, whom he has just cited, Starobinski continues: "it is primarily not the unconscious but psychoanalysis that is constituted as a language. Later it would be easy to find in the unconscious what had been attributed to it when it was first conceived" (AR, 183).

Abreaction functions in Freud's works, up to 1909, as a "master word" (AR, 196) which indicates the process whereby an excess charge, which has accumulated as the result of reflex action, can itself be discharged in turn. Freud provides a canonical example in his description of the process whereby a paralysis only setting in several weeks after a traumatic event is identified as the reflexive response to the victim's thought at the time of the event that "My arm is paralyzed." This paralysis is combated in turn through the engagement of a second "reflex arc ... in which the favorable stimulus will be the suggestive voice of the physician" (AR, 186), leading to an "abreaction" of the excess stimulus. Freud's approach is explicitly, and intrinsically, psychological in its endowment of the patient with intentional and volitional capacities. Thus, Starobinski insists, "[t]he *ab*- in 'abreaction' is not merely a distancing spatial prefix; it indicates an intentional externalization. As early as Breuer's and Freud's first writings, it found an equivalent in the *aus*- of *ausdrücken*, analogous to the *ex*- in "expression" (AR, 188). Starobinski's point recalls a remark made by the narrator in Musil's *The Man Without Qualities*: "There was also something known as Expressionism. Nobody could say just what it was, but the word suggests some kind of squeezing-out ..."[148]

In 1909, a new master word takes the place of abreaction: transference. Yet here once again the notion of reaction is focal, and in fact Starobinski directs us to the way in which this transformation of the Freudian vocabulary,

---

148. Robert Musil, *The Man Without Qualities*, trans. Sophie Wilkins and Burton Pike (New York: Alfred A. Knopf, 1995), 493.

and hence enterprise, harks back to a sense of reaction which emphasizes images of fermentation. Referring to an idea of Sándor Ferenczi, Freud describes transference as a process in which the physician "plays the part of a catalytic ferment, which temporarily attracts to itself the affects liberated in the process" (cited, AR, 196). As Starobinski notes, the singular advantage of the idea of transference was that it eliminated the need to retrieve the historically distant cause of the precipitated emotion, substituting for this search "an approach based on a present reaction to a present emotion" (AR, 196). In this way, psychoanalyst and patient "establish themselves on a terrain that is both safer and more dangerous—that of a relationship" (AR, 197). We will have occasion to return below to such "relationships" in the discussion of the political use of the 'action' / 'reaction' couple and the potential banalization of this vocabulary in the contemporary political context.

NOSTALGIA

In the same year, Karl Jaspers concluded his thesis in psychiatry with a final chapter on the problem of "Nostalgia and Crime," dealing with the most extreme consequences resulting from the forced separation of adolescents or young servants from their families, including "intentionally setting fires, murdering the children entrusted to their care, and so on" (AR, 205). This situation puts the psychiatrist in the uncomfortable position of being required to assess the moral responsibility of the youths who have committed such criminal actions. Jaspers views these actions, in fact, as behavioral *re*actions comparable to "prison psychosis," and rather than presenting a typology in terms of the diagnosis of various clinical conditions, he asserts that here there are only "personality types or types of reaction to external influences" (cited, AR, 205). The problem of behavioral taxonomy is thus translated into one of providing a taxonomy of reactions. As Jaspers extends this reactive typology into his *General Psychopathology*, which Starobinski calls "the only true 'monument' of twentieth-century psychiatry" (AR, 205), the classification bridges between explanations which would provide a cause and those which would increase understanding, straddling a gap at the heart of the problem of assessing moral responsibility.

We find a literary precedent in Balzac's *Louis Lambert*: in this novel we have a study in which

> the schism between the actional being and the reactional being is closely tied, as we will see, to the madness of Balzac's hero, who, at the end of the story, presents some symptoms of what today is called schizophrenia. This schism is a *schizis*, in the sense of the word used in 1911 by Eugen Bleuler, who coined the term "schizophrenia." (AR, 237)

Here again, as in his analysis of Freud, Starobinski views the organizational structure of psychiatric diagnosis as a function of the way in which the distinction between action and reaction is invoked. In Louis Lambert he finds a textbook case of the phenomenon of reactive nostalgia as discussed by Jaspers. At the behest of Madame de Staël, Lambert is uprooted from his ecclesiastical uncle (with whom Lambert already lives as a consequence of a first, primitive uprooting from his father and mother) to "benefit" from an education at the Collège de Vendôme, Balzac's own school. There, the "'uprooted' flower" is subjected to "the miasma of communal life and continual punishments," to which he *reacts* by developing a pronounced melancholy, cultivating a retreat into interiority in which "he turns as white as the angels he contemplates" (AR, 238). The stoppage of will which ensues threatens to produce a violent explosion: at the theater, "Louis is overwhelmed to the point of paroxysm by the beauty of a woman he notices in the box next to his speaking affectionately with her lover. Lambert barely resists the 'almost overpowering desire' to kill this man" (AR, 239). Lambert is able to "overcome" this murderous desire only to the extent that it will ultimately result in suicide rather than murder.

Lambert's downfall, according to Starobinski, is due to "the disproportion between his spiritual capacity for motion and the material resistance he is incapable of overcoming" (AR, 240); here the model of "slackening" has been transferred to the social realm. The story culminates in an image of radical passivity which "represents both a triumph of the 'inner life' and the worst defeat of the Being of Reaction" (AR, 242). Louis fails to recognize the presence of the narrator, once his closest friend: "His face was perfectly white. He constantly rubbed one leg against the other, with a mechanical action that nothing could have checked, and the incessant friction of the bones made a doleful sound …" Louis is reduced to the state of a "child in arms. Suddenly Louis ceased rubbing his legs together, and said slowly—'*The angels are white*.'" (cited, AR, 242-43). Louis is "both an androgyne and a *puer senex*," and Starobinski asks whether we should read Lambert's degeneracy as embodying in its fusion of opposites nonetheless a grasp of "the law governing the world as a whole" (AR, 244). Literarily speaking, it is a short step from Lambert's *Treatise on the Will* to the cosmological speculation of Poe's *Eureka*, to which Starobinski proceeds. Do we see here, then, the initiation of a cultural ascendency of the couple of action and reaction comparable to the ascent from the first living point to "the spectacle of Saturn, the universe, and millions of centuries" which Diderot describes in *D'Alembert's Dream*?

Yet the organicism which supports Poe's speculative cosmology and drives the romantic movement at large is equally responsible, as already recognized by Benjamin Constant, for the "reactionary" desire to return to a previous political order. Here, in the context of the Enlightenment ideology of progress, a return to an earlier political state can only signify regression or "retrogression" (AR, 330). Constant's explanation for this desire is psychological and on analogy with the explanation of homesickness. "Here one finds, if not an excuse for those who foment political reactions, at least an honorable motive that credits the political adversary with an excess of sensitivity but that also attributes a weakness to him, assigning him a pathology" (AR, 331). The condition of Louis Lambert has been transported into the political sphere, where it poses a challenge for the triumph of reason over an excess of sensibility. The proleptic guard against such a potential retrogression is the anticipation of a further dose of rationality. As that same Madame de Staël, who in her fictional incarnation was responsible for packing Balzac's hero and self-representative off to the prison-house of college education, writes:

> Political science might one day acquire geometric proofs … . The organization of a constitution is always based on a fixed set of givens, since every kind of large number leads to ever similar and ever predictable results… . This revolution must end in reasoning. (cited, AR, 334)

In another work, de Staël compares the project of founding the state in a science of politics to Descartes' algebraic geometry: "The calculations of men are as subject to calculation as is friction in machines; in a certain number of cases, the return of the same events is certain" (cited, AR, 334). Here there is contrast as well as comparability, however, for we move from an exact calculus of equations to a calculus of probable actions and reactions. From the eternal recurrences of Poe's and Nietzsche's cosmologies, we return, at this earlier date, to the establishment of statistical recurrence theorems in the social domain. As Starobinski points out, such a project is not in the service of blocking the passions, but must in fact take liberation into account, so that "the politician becomes an ingenious mechanic, superior to the crowd" (AR, 335). A distinction is drawn between two types of reaction: that which "adjusts itself to motion" (cited, AR, 335), which can only be based on superstition and is hence properly "reactionary," and that which masters reaction through a knowledge of its laws. This latter type of reaction is one which insists that the science of politics be guided and applied to moral ends, again by way of appealing to the statistical law of large numbers: "Morality should direct our calculations, and our calculations should direct politics… . The moral sciences are susceptible only to the calculation of probabilities, and this calculation can only be based on a large number of facts, from which one can draw an approximate result" (cited, AR, 338). Probability has replaced Laplacean determinism (as already occurred in Laplace's own work), and from the psychological phenomenon of homesickness we have arrived at a statistical mechanics of the state, "reconciling" a hypertrophied freedom with a massive statistical determinism.

Conceptually speaking, it is but a short step to the twentieth century social sciences of demographics and polling, "doing the numbers." Set against these regularities, the historian faces a new problem of reaction which dramatizes an instability in de Staël's mandate that the science of politics should be morally driven: how are we to respond to the corrosive sense of statistical determinism which besets our confrontation with the past? In particular, if we are to see the development of history as a sequence of reactions, what room is left for the moral evaluation of this development? In *The Passing of an Illusion: The Idea of Communism in the Twentieth Century*, François Furet confronts this problem in the context of responding to the explanatory perspective offered by Ernst Nolte, who views fascism and, later, Nazism as resulting from a "chain reaction" in response to the victory of Bolshevism in Russia. Furet is troubled by the capacity for such explanatory forms to become the source of at least partial exoneration for these political developments, as exemplified by recent debates among German historians; and, as Starobinski remarks, "[w]hat Furet presents as a possibility seems to me to be a fact" (AR, 363).

The problem here is at least in part a function of the banalization of the vocabulary of reaction which Starobinski traces back to the context supplied by Marx's *Communist Manifesto*. In the historical transition from the period of the French Revolution, in which 'reaction' retained a neutral sense that was not immediately identified with a political ideology, to the post-revolutionary period, governed by antinomian terminology on both the left and right ends of the political spectrum, the term 'reaction' is rendered banal by virtue of its immediate tie to ideologies driven by postrevolutionary conditions. Reaction came to designate "the *aggressive* face of that which has no future" (AR, 346), and infighting among revolutionary groups came to be dominated by mutual accusations of reaction (AR, 351). The term 'reactionary', coined, as Starobinski points out, on the model of 'revolutionary', "is a partisan word used only polemically or disparagingly," and "[i]ts use is widespread, to say the least." But in addition to its use by enemies of reaction, it is appropriated by historians as well, "who, when they judge conflicting forces after the fact, effortlessly assess their respective merits." This effortlessness is a function of the historian's retrospective stance, and "a temptation arises to qualify as reactionary what did not succeed, what was defeated, and thus to confuse change with progress, triumphant necessity with real 'advance'" (AR, 347).

Uneasily faced with the options of accusatory and exonerative discourse exemplified by the situation of the historian, a third type of discourse of 'reaction' emerges, which Starobinski characterizes in terms of "the call to action" (AR, 363). Furet identifies a duty for reaction posed by "the historian's *attitude* and decision" (AR, 364). In exchange for renouncing the desire to govern history in the manner proposed by de Staël, Furet identifies a capacity to *react* against the illusive inertia of historical development:

> History appears all the more sovereign as we lost the illusion of governing it. But as always, the historian *must react* against what seems inevitable

at the time he writes; he knows too well that these kinds of collective givens are ephemeral. The forces at work toward the universalization of the world are so powerful that they trigger sequences of events and situations incompatible with the idea of the laws of history, *a fortiori* of possible prediction. Understanding and explaining the past is already difficult enough. (cited, AR, 364)

In a quietistic renunciation of the prediction and government of history, Furet locates the dignity of the historian in a *reactive* capacity to form future history that begs for comparison with the Calvinist doctrine of double predestination. Starobinski's diagnosis of this situation is delivered by focusing on "the play of words" through which "a circularity takes shape between the reacting subject and the intelligible side of the objective world, where causality will take on all the forms of action and reaction" (AR, 365). He locates, in particular, an indeterminateness in Furet's injunction which results from a blindness to the function of specific vocabulary, comparable to that found in existential analyses of feelings by such figures as Kierkegaard, Heidegger, Binswanger, Kolnai, Sartre and Lévinas:

> To be sure, such studies examined human experience in a way that sought to be concrete and grounded in lived experience. What has nonetheless remained imprecise is the role played, from the beginning, by the preexisting names and meanings given to the phenomena under observation. Nuances and variations of the experience in question were often interrogated only because they had an assigned place in the word's semantic field and because it was necessary to account for related words, for synonyms or antonyms, based on a "central" meaning assumed to be stable and in principle universalizable. (AR, 365)

By analogy, the suggestion is that what Furet has located as "forces at work toward the universalization of the world" should be investigated instead in terms of the specific function of semantic fields in the historical project. In both Furet's biographical recourse and in the existential analyses of feelings, Starobinski would counsel an attention to the way morals are drawn as a function of the specific language at issue. And so Starobinski will declare that

> what I have developed in this work belongs to an expanded semantic history, not phenomenology. Without losing sight of the phenomena preceding the theoretical attention that captures them, I have directed my gaze to the language in which these phenomena were described. (AR, 366)

Words are intellectual tools for use, and Starobinski has given us, in one particular instance, a history of their working: "'Action and 'reaction' (once the collateral meanings of 'action' are subtracted) are word tools, abstract entities that are easily manipulated" (AR, 367). They served as a substitute in popular science for calculation, and the success of these terms in a scientific context drove their integration into the vocabulary of lived experience. But the Romantic attempt to "re-enchant the world" through an organic use of the terms should be viewed as a reaction (!) to the world's disenchantment, and Starobinski, along with Paul Valéry, identifies any proposed "depths" of this vocabulary as an illusion: "There is nothing to seek in the 'depths' of the word 'reaction'.... . 'Action and reaction' belong to the intellectual lexicon, to the thought that objectifies emotion, not to emotion itself, however derivative it may be" (AR, 367). Such an identification of 'action' and 'reaction' as tools in an intellectual lexicon requires the renunciation of any desire to return to the depths of a home, whether it be the personal, biographical home of the historian, the phenomenological home of existential lived experience, or the illusory metaphysical home which momentarily seized Valéry:

> I caught myself in the act—in the process of *asking* myself the deep ... meaning of action and reaction, this principle drawn by Newton from experience! As if this relation between q[uantities] of motion was already closer to I know not what *secrets* than any experience from which one can deduce it. (cited, AR, 367)

TATTERED DREAMS

As we chart the trajectory from Balzac's *Louis Lambert* via Poe's *Eureka* to Valéry's *Monsieur Teste* and the *Cahiers*, we find a series of works which not only develop the vocabulary of action and reaction but also serve as closer and closer approximations to the attitude which Starobinski himself evinces. In each of the three above-mentioned cases we find either a portrait or a report of a treatise on action and reaction, yet in each of these three cases it is the form of presentation that Starobinski ultimately finds most revealing. In the case of Lambert's *Treatise on the Will*, itself a reflection of Balzac's own quasi-philosophical reflections, we are given, not the treatise itself, but rather "the 'intellectual history' composed much later by a witness who is not sure he has understood his brilliant friend or is able to communicate the full scope of his thought" (AR, 244). Are we being invited to compare the narrator's portrait of Lambert with Starobinski's own intellectual history of our linguistic couple, of which the "depth" is only an illusion? Balzac himself, not content simply with "borrowing from the scholars' lexicon," dreams "of teaching them a thing or two and even of surpassing them, promoting his own philosophical-scientific views on the soul, the body, the physical world, and the destinies of men," an ambition which Starobinski characterizes as "[i]mmodest and arrogant" (AR, 230). In this portrait of Balzac we find the antithesis of what Starobinski would himself counsel, and so it is no surprise that Starobinski would underline the fragmented character of this pretension as it enters into the literary works themselves. The doctrine of Action and Reaction which the narrator relates from memory in the course of the story is "far from clear" and "angelic in nature": "[i]t has in particular, the privilege of moving around in a region that lies beyond the obstacles and resistances of the external world" (AR, 235). Such is the reflection of indeterminateness that one finds in the literary representation of the philosophical treatise, and Lambert's final words about the whiteness of angels reflect the ambivalence associated to an identification with the indefinite.

And so it is in terms of just this indefinite register that Balzac is able to channel his "excesses of enthusiasm" into all the "telepathies and transmigrations that Balzac ... believed possible." This is the Being of Action, which "sees," "remains motionless," and may "travel in pure thought" (AR, 235). The Being of Reaction, on the other hand, is the being which lives and intervenes in the world, and so the being of practical effectiveness. Balzac thus divides the unity of action and reaction into a dualism of active and reactive beings, so that in his *Human Comedy* "[t]he tragedy of division supplants a monism of principle" (AR, 236). Louis Lambert internalizes this tragic division in his unsuccessful attempt to bring action to bear on the reactive medium of the resisting world, and yet "Balzac cannot articulate his defeat without mirroring it in a secret victory. In this way, Louis Lambert proves to have a mind powerful enough to conceive of a great system of human powers that could explain and predict the very adversity to which he succumbs." This is the absent *Treatise on the Will* which the story frames and which is consequently "a broken book, composed, or de-composed, in fragments, a book filled with lacunae, made up of remainders, in which Lambert's ideas appear only in tatters ..." (AR, 244). According to Starobinski, it is the case both that Lambert's fate itself is incomplete and that "those who speak of him profess themselves incapable of fully understanding him" (AR, 245). As such, Starobinski's description of the figure of Lambert could serve as an allegorical representation of the fate of the semantic figure he himself investigates. In contrast to Furet's vision of the task of the historian, Starobinski does not profess, indeed does not even seek, either the completeness or the full understanding of the intellectual history he provides.

Edgar Allen Poe's *Eureka* subjects the vocabulary of action and reaction to the organic imagery of the beating heart, and Starobinski points to the common features of Poe's work and Schelling's philosophical system, both of which find roots in "a common attraction to ancient cyclic cosmologies and a common penchant for 'speculative physics,' based on the cosmogonic theory of Kant and Laplace" (AR, 275). Schelling reformulated the theory of central mass found there and in the work of Maclaurin in the speculative metaphysical language of "a Totality of systems formed around a pulsating point" (cited, AR, 264). Valéry, as well, will view "the perpetual formation of the universe" as a process of "centrifugation, analogous to the gigantic centrifugation of the Kant-Laplace nebula" (cited, AR, 294) and refers in a letter to Gide to the "group Poe-Balzac" as "like the group Laplace-Ampère-Poisson, etc." (cited, AR, 431). Like Schelling as well, Poe's transformation of science into speculative, "poetic" language serves the end of reconciling "the poetic imagination and the rigors of calculating thought" (AR, 277), and this organic unity of language finds itself reflected, as well, in the systolic-diastolic coupling of action and reaction. Poe makes recourse to God's will to account for an explosion of matter out of a state of concentrated unity. This action, which Starobinski nominates "the big bang before it was called that" (AR, 277), produces time and space and initiates the cosmic cycle. But this dispersion has as part of its "condition" a tendency to return to unity, and so the expansion of matter cannot continue indefinitely. Poe attributes to matter a desire to return, and this desire is precisely the Newtonian force of gravitational attraction. Yet so that this centripetal tendency not immediately lead to matter returning to a state of concentration, God interposes a second force of a repulsive nature, which is what Poe takes to be observed in electrical phenomena. Nonetheless the concentration of matter leads to consolidations of enormous density, effecting "a series of catastrophes in which Poe's imagination takes great delight" (AR, 278). The ultimate "cosmic suicide" which eventually results indicates, nevertheless, a "rebirth" (AR, 279), and the cyclical cosmological movement repeats itself once again:

> Are we not, indeed, more than justified in entertaining a belief ... that the processes we have here ventured to contemplate will be renewed forever, and forever, and forever; a novel Universe swelling into existence, and then subsiding into Nothingness, at every throb of the Divine Heart?
>
> And now—this Heart Divine—what is it? It is our own. (cited, AR, 279)

Starobinski asks, however, whether the eternal repetition Poe describes is indeed life, or whether instead it is indicative of a Sisyphean inability to die. He then goes on to equate this possibility with the level of Freud's thought where the death drive is inscribed as a "tendency toward stability" (cited, AR, 280). Poe's cosmology revolves around "one far-distant center which is the Godhead" (cited, AR, 279), who according to Starobinski is "constrained by a double limit, for he knows neither the infinity of rest nor the infinity of expansion" (AR, 280). He compares this to the motif of the beating heart in Poe's "The Tell-Tale Heart," where this beating becomes "the unbearable hallucination following the dismemberment of a derisory Osiris." Thus,

> "Consistency," far from being the accord between Truth and Beauty, establishes a symmetrical relationship between the madness of a guilty man and the fable of the victim's survival. The guilty heart is ultimately the single heart that beats in the dismembered victim and in the murderer's conscience. (AR, 281)

As has the narrator of "The Tell-Tale Heart," Poe, it seems, has fallen victim in *Eureka* to the explicit presentation of his cosmological fantasy, and in this respect the tattered presentations of Balzac's Lambert and Valéry's Monsieur Teste seem more evenly tempered. The fate of Poe's narrator in "The Tell-Tale Heart" belies, in particular, the identification of the heart of the universe as "our own" in Poe's *Eureka*.

Valéry was himself an avid reader of Poe's *Eureka* in his youth, and wrote what Starobinski takes to be one of his finest essays about it. Valéry views Poe's cosmology as an anticipation of the theory of general relativity and traces its formation back to "a plan the profound symmetry of which is present, to some degree, in the inner structure of our minds" (cited, AR, 287). Valéry, however, in turn, proceeds phenomenologically to inquire into the mental genesis of this idea, which he takes to be grounded in the act of looking and in "motor consciousness" (cited, AR, 287). Thus the question of the world is made a function of the constitution of the ego. It is in thought, and indeed in all thought, that action and reaction are to be located, as Valéry boldly declares in a passage from the *Cahiers* in which the former is made a function of the latter: "The notions of thought, knowledge, and so on should be—rejected. That of act and reaction and so on should replace them" (cited, AR, 290). In "Manuscript Found in a Brain," which transfers Poe's "MS. Found in a Bottle" to the interior realm, Valéry describes a mental cycle on analogy with the cosmological cycle of Poe's *Eureka*. Thinking involves one's own self-exclusion, and Valéry's Monsieur Teste will declare that "I am a reaction to what I am.... 'What I am' is what appears to that which will be 'what I am'" (cited, AR, 291). In contrast to the vastness of cosmological expansion, Valéry writes: "I made myself a *Principle of the Finite* ... which consisted of a reaction of my mind against all expression or impression that came from itself or from *elsewhere* and that introduced things or values that were *inseparable from insoluble terms*" (cited, AR, 290). This is the heroism of Valéry's Monsieur Teste, the "witness," exemplifying "[t]hat in us which causes *everything* and therefore nothing—reaction itself, pure recoil" (cited, AR, 290)

As Starobinski recognizes, "'Reflex,' 'reaction,' 'response' are *explanatory* words for Valéry" by which we may "purify our ideas, too long attached to troublesome and illusory philosophical words" (AR, 293). In terms of reflex, Valéry is able to unify the domains of physiology and psychology, offering an inverse image of Poe's unification of imagination and thought. The ego is now understood as a quasi-algebraic "invariant" existing among a field of "impersonal, molecular reflexes;" as such, it is an "All" which is close to a nothingness (AR, 295). Yet beneath his "neoclassical rhetoric," Starobinski is still able to discern the presence in Valéry's poetry, in particular, of "the beating hearts of a whole era of Romanticism" (AR, 297). Valéry, the devoted reader of Poe, has ultimately only relocated the universal pulsation, assigned to God by Poe, in the multiplicity of individual human hearts. In so doing, however, the romantic dream of a Unity of Being is shred into those tatters which Valéry attempts to counter in the heroic solipsism of Monsieur Teste.

STAROBINSKI MY NEIGHBOR

Where in this history is Starobinski to be found? Taking his analysis of Valéry as a point of departure, Starobinski has this to tell us at the end of his book:

> I have called attention to Valéry's words at the end of his life: "I am a reaction to what I am." This is much more than a neutral statement; an obstinate desire commands this *activation* of the word "reaction." In the face of death, the thought that had consented to be merely an effect affirms that it is also a cause. As long as thought keeps vigil, the "I am" that reacts detaches itself from the "I am" that is no longer, and in declaring its difference, it traces out a mark that will survive. Within the confines of what happens, a decision, always and never the last, takes over from a state of facts. (AR, 371)

Applying this model to Starobinski's own work in *Action and Reaction*, we may characterize it as belonging to the history of semantic intellectual tools, terms like 'action' and 'reaction'. The tracing of this history is itself a decisionistic *activation* of these terms' historical trajectories, which itself ultimately demands to be understood on its own dynamic terms. This activation is the process by which linguistic facts, the historical uses of terms, are turned (by the intellectual historian at issue) into decisions, in this case the decision, in particular, to write a history of the use of these terms! As Starobinski writes in the preface to his book,

> At a moment when we are obliged to reflect on questions of necessity and nature, on the means and consequences of our reactions, I do not think it a useless luxury to give an account of the semantic history of a word we use so often. Everything that constitutes civilization may have, at one time or another, been considered a useless luxury. (AR, 11)

Starobinski registers a defensiveness in the face of the luxurious nature (which he confirms) of the history he traces, and he attempts to defend this luxury in terms of its value for civilization. This investment is reflected directly in Starobinski's hermeneutic credo, which appears a page earlier when he declares: "I believe that the semantic history of familiar terms—especially those that belong among our intellectual tools—helps us to understand better who we are" (AR, 10).

A more specific account of the impetus behind Starobinski's project may lie, however, in the way it allows him to respond to Furet's call for the historian's "reaction." As Starobinski points out, Furet's demand that the historian react is indeterminate, since it does not "indicate how to manifest this opposition or how to overcome the enormous adversity of the unjust and the inexplicable" (AR, 364). Starobinski transfers this demand for reaction to the level of investigating the language in which the history to which Furet demands response has been fashioned, and in doing so he endows the demand for reaction with a determinacy lacking in Furet's call. This program is, arguably, an extension of the one grounded in the tradition of the history of ideas to which Starobinski was exposed during his tenure at Johns Hopkins.

Yet in the course of the twentieth century, the tradition of history of ideas has confronted, repeatedly, in the work of such figures as Ernst Cassirer, the members of the Warburg School, Otto Pöggeler, Hans Jauss, Wolfgang Iser, Hans-Georg Gadamer, Paul Ricouer and, most significantly, Hans Blumenberg, a need to grapple with the indeterminate nature of appeals to the phenomenology of experience, figured in the absolute metaphor of the "lifeworld." In Furet's case this manifests itself in his appeal to the biographical dimension of the historian. Like many of the predominantly German contemporaries mentioned above, Starobinski reacts against this inevitable phenomenological indeterminacy by making recourse to the empirically particular status of the linguistic artifacts in which such appeals to phenomenological experience are couched. Such recourse may be identified, as well, in Pöggeler's appropriation of Heidegger's notion of "topology" to similar ends, to the focus of Jauss and Iser on reception, to Blumenberg's development of "metaphorology" and a "theory of nonconceptuality," and, in general, to a focus on the way in which language serves as a vehicle for understanding. All of these gambits derive inspiration, to a greater or lesser extent, from the notion of "topos-research" (*Toposforschung*) central to the tradition of the history of ideas, and exemplified by the work, in particular, of E. R. Curtius.

Where does Starobinski's initiative fit into this intellectual geography? Contrasting Starobinski with his fellow historian of the French revolution, Furet, we have seen that the determinacy Starobinski demands is taken to be a function of the recourse to concrete semantic tools. But behind this issue of determinacy, there lies an even more fundamental appeal to a "decisionism" on the basis of which such determinacy may be supplied. This is the model of "activation" (!) which Starobinski promotes in the penultimate paragraph of his book when he remarks that a decision must take over from the state of facts. In the final paragraph we are given an account of this process in which we may see the sort of history which Starobinski provides as a model of the freeing of our typical experiential path by way of its being rendered determinate and writ large, "civilized" as it were, to the highest degree. Here we have Starobinski's functional analogue of the man → Man transition. The significance of Starobinski's reinvisioning of this maneuver warrants extensive quotation:

> This tentative freedom discovers that it was itself—through its interpretation of the world—that set out to discover its origins, to the point of hoping to see itself being born. At the end of the causal chain we try to reconstruct—that is where our existence must lie. We hope to find the causes that made us live, and then made us emerge from animality and

respond to the challenges of the external world through calculation and reason. But it is first of all we ourselves who have set out in search of our origins. We are the origin of our search for the origin. The circle closes, and another action begins. (AR, 371)

Here we are left, simultaneously, with nothing less than a cultural explanation for, and yet also a renewed version of, the traditional metaphysical problem of free will and determination, written, no less, in terms of the vocabulary of the cultural tradition in which the problem must be both framed and explained. Given the embeddedness of this stance within the cultural tradition which Starobinski takes as his focus of concern, it is no surprise that the history of decisionism has a long and distinguished pedigree. At the inception of the modern age it is associated with the radical nominalism of those philosophers such as Occam who would insist on the absolute freedom of God and his lack of constraint by any antecedent laws of logic or reason. It is just this radical insistence, according to Hans Blumenberg, which serves as a point of psychological initiation for modernity: given the psychological untenability of living in the face of a God who transcends connection to any identifiable rational order, the modern project reconsolidates culture in an appeal to a minimal self-sufficiency of human reason grounded in the capacity for self-assertion. Yet it was this psychological untenability that modernity overcame in the positing of a minimal "emergency consolidation" in terms of the notion of human self-assertion.

The question of action in a modern context, then, is one in which we must ask after the connections between decision and the rational grounds for decision, and it is here that Starobinski leaves the reader with a host of unanswered questions. How is the determinacy which results from an appeal to the tools of the intellectual tradition to be understood? Why, that is, should we adopt Starobinski's faith in the hermeneutic efficacy of a history of semantic terms? If, indeed, as Valéry already asserts, the vocabulary of thinking should be *replaced* by the vocabulary of action and reaction, how, in the absence of an appeal to the "laws of thought," are we to justify the legitimacy of this new vocabulary? Failing answers to these questions, the guarantee of determinacy associated with a bare, volitional theory of decision can only look like a return to the psychologically untenable theory of the late medieval nominalists. And the successors of this theory within a modern context can be identified as progressively more *reactionary* as the modern age progresses, ultimately including among their ranks such figures as De Maistre and Carl Schmitt. In the context of such decisionism, as Hans Blumenberg has remarked,

> ... the choice of linguistic means is not determined by the system of what is available for borrowing but rather by the requirements of the situation in which the choice is being made. When Carl Schmitt characterizes De Maistre's political philosophy as the "reduction of the state to

the element of decision, and consequently to a pure non-reasoning and non-discussing, non-self-justifying absolute decision, that is, a decision created from nothing," then this is not the secularization of the *creatio ex nihilo*; rather it is a metaphorical interpretation of the situation after the revolutionary zero point.[149]

Once we recognize the metaphorical status of this maneuver in a context where it is not just the *history* of terms but their legitimacy and ownership which is at issue, the methodology of decisionism becomes much less credible. What it practices at the methodological level is an uncritical metaphorization of what it executes critically at the level of historical analysis. This recognition leads to various sorts of "deconstructive" critiques, yet the engine which drives them is not the "history of metaphysics" or the "history of terms" per se, but rather the lack of a fundamental confrontation with antecedent issues of methodological legitimation. Whether these issues *can* be sufficiently addressed is, of course, doubtful, but I maintain that Blumenberg has made a more serious effort in this direction than any of his (or our) contemporaries.

Starobinski's response to such decisionism must be that the understanding provided by the sort of intellectual history he supplies is, indeed, a function in part of the way in which the choice of linguistic means *is* determined by the system of what is available. But the fundamental metaphysical problem remains unaddressed, since it is still the case that to the extent that these "determinations" are "spontaneous" or "free" we may not understand them as a function of such systemic determination. Starobinski remains committed, then, to what we may refer to as a limited, "culturally contextual" version of decisionism, and it is the paradoxical character of such a "limited decisionism" which is reflected in the final image of his book: "The circle closes, and another action begins." We are left with another version of the myth of eternal recurrence, but with a difference: for while the circle itself repeats, we have no reason to assume that the actions do. Nonetheless, it is by a slender and unprotected thread that Starobinski's position differs from an overtly quietist form of historicism. The *activation* of which Starobinski speaks at the end of his book is a function of the hermeneutic faith he affirms at its beginning, but closes no circle, and therefore warrants no action. This, however, is not merely a dilemma for Starobinski, but one faced by the contemporary intellectual at large, and so we may thank Jean Starobinski for the rigor with which his work lays this problem bare.

---

149. Blumenberg, LMA, 93.

5

Daily Rhythms

> Today scholars may believe they have explained everything. But our explanations and glosses, even in paperback, are thick, stiff, and heavy; they do not bend. (NTAP, 135)

EISENSTEIN, AGAIN

In this chapter, we move up the scale of pacing from motion and action to rhythm, which involves not just the dynamics of motion and impact but the *relation* of motive "strands" into a complex pattern of phases. To find a home for this second chapter on Angus Fletcher's recent work within the overall project of this book, I would like to begin obliquely by extending the discussion of Eisenstein as a "precursor" of Fletcher which I began earlier. Like Fletcher, and also like Harold Bloom, Eisenstein is particularly exercised by Shakespeare and by Whitman. In one passage he provides a telling point of comparison for their respective "montage techniques":

> With Shakespeare, everything is so harmoniously integrated on a human scale—as opposed to a superhuman scale, as is the case, for instance, with Walt Whitman, where it is precisely this which enables the structural ligatures of his technique to be laid bare. (SW II, 188)

For Eisenstein, Whitman is "Shakespeare writ large"—though this is only the beginning, hardly the end, of Eisenstein's story. Yet the insight still helps us to track the differences between Shakespeare and Whitman along the lines of the man → Man transition, where issues of scale, metaphorization and legitimation intersect. Whereas Shakespeare (in this regard like Pushkin in Eisenstein's estimation) can create the dramatic sense of a scene through the combination of a small number of well-chosen details, Whitman's more Rabelaisian penchant for unending lists assumes more gigantic proportions.[150] Eisenstein devotes attention particularly to Whitman's "Song of the Broad-Axe" and shows how Whitman's poem engages an ax → Ax transition. In a passage of immense straightforwardness and worth, Eisenstein lays this transition out in its multidimensionality:

> Whitman wants to sing a paean to America, the America of the pioneers. He wishes to hymn his country through the emblem of the pioneers' first working tool, the axe. He does so in his 'Song of the Broad-Ax' [sic]. But an axe is an axe. An emblematic axe is an emblematic axe. He needs to make an Axe with a capital A, an emblematic Axe, out of an axe with a small a, out of a real axe. How does Whitman set about it? Like a true montage artist. Taking as his 'long shot' the *real, physical axe*, he splits it up into a multitude of 'montage fragments' of *what an axe can do*, what can be done with an axe, giving rise to endless enumeration of a cunningly juxtaposed succession of items which brings to life a whole sea of association. They are strung out along the powerful rhythm of the embodiment of an idea. In the perception of the reader this endless series is reassembled into a unity; but what emerges is not the axe-as-object, a merely pictorial rendering, but a new quality of axe, the Axe-as-emblem, the Axe-as-image, encompassing in its generalising sweep the image of the young American democracy, whose thousands of axes created the state by laying a path for its power through the dense, impenetrable forests of North America (SW II, 146-147).

What Eisenstein said before of Shakespeare applies equally to Whitman as well: the montage is directed not merely to the juxtaposition of images but to the creation of an ultimate phasal rhythm. In the case of a poem like "Song of the Broad-Axe," the sweep of this rhythm is relatively crude and easy to hear, "writ large," but in the major masterpieces of Whitman's poetry this rhythm is intricate and evasive in its effects. It is the central, but far from the only, merit of Fletcher's recent book to provide more articulation of these rhythmic effects than has heretofore even been conceivable. In taking Whitman as central American bard and looking toward the future of American poetry, Fletcher charts a future path for poetry of tensile strength, whose reading will require the sorts of virtues he strives to cultivate.

---

150. Tellingly, Harold Bloom is overtly displeased with Whitman's lists: "No reader is happy with Walt in his dreariest cataloguings, his Songs of the Answerer, Joys, the Broad-Axe, the Exposition, the Redwood-Tree, Occupations, Rolling Earth—on and on and on." *The Anatomy of Influence: Literature as a Way of Life* (New Haven: Yale, 2011), 298. I return to this aesthetic dispute below.

THE FUTURE OF AMERICAN POETRY

Angus Fletcher's *A New Theory for American Poetry: Democracy, the Environment and the Future of the Imagination*[151] is both a blueprint for the poetry of the American future and a manual for the reading of such future poetry, anchored in extended, historical appreciations of the poetry of John Clare, Walt Whitman and John Ashbery. Along this historical route Fletcher discerns an alternative to the aftermath of that High Romantic trajectory which he sees as now in its endgame. At the close of his volume he declares, "We live at the end of the long twilight of Romanticism, and this book has presented a theory of the poetry to come" (NTAP, 225). According to Fletcher, this alternative poetry, and the theory he charts to meet it, are diurnal in their rhythms, reflecting the fundamental conditions of our natural environment, and they chart a development in the power of linguistic description which stands in a special relation to explosive early modern developments in the mimetic and dramatic. But while Fletcher's emphasis on description is wholly salutary, it is but a first step toward the need for a theory of the pacing of modern literature, for the rhythms of the most advanced modern language are fixed not only by our environment, even in its most sophisticated sense, but by our epochal condition: those rhythmic figurations which exemplify our advancing modernity.

Fletcher's *New Theory* is divided into fourteen chapters, which he hopes compare to the condition of William James' house as described by his sister, Alice: "It's the most delightful house you ever saw; it has fourteen doors, all opening outwards" (cited, NTAP, 6). But perhaps even more important is the rough division of the work into six parts which Fletcher describes in the Introduction, and which I will use to sector this chapter as well:

> We begin with the *concept of horizon*, which implies the immediate boundary to any environment. Next, the argument turns to the broad question of *the poet's way of being in the world*, when this world is defined as an ecological surrounding. Then, concentrating on Whitman, my central chapters develop a dynamic theory of *poetry as environmental form*. A fourth main division of the theory shows *the power of underlying rhythms* in this unique poetry. A fifth section of the whole account is devoted to the exemplary work of John Ashbery, treating him as a philosopher of *the poetry of becoming*. Finally, in sixth place I show how a *theory of coherence* yields the value-system of the bonding of literature and the environment. (NTAP, 5-6)

Two parts each follow under the stars of Clare, Whitman and Ashbery, respectively. With this schematization Fletcher's book itself already begins to

---

151. Angus Fletcher, *A New Theory For American Poetry: Democracy, the Environment, and the Future of the Imagination* (Cambridge: Harvard, 2004).

take on the shape of the sort of "fluid diagram" which he discerns as the formal scaffolding which must underpin his central poetic object, the "environment-poem." Ultimately the scaffolding and the poem itself merge into one: the "grand or merely pragmatic plan ... turns out to be the poem itself" (NTAP, 210), the words of which are, following Empson, the "bones of the situation" (NTAP, 223). The balanced power of the environment-poem which Fletcher praises is a flexible power to which the reading of the environment-poem must also aspire. That the world of the poem meets the world of the reader is at once a defining feature of the environment-poem and its deepest challenge, both to the reader and to the nature of poetry. It is this challenge which Fletcher's "new theory" articulates.

HORIZON

"One day, when he was a small boy, John Clare went looking for the horizon" (NTAP, 17). So begins the body of Fletcher's book. This horizon is something we must understand both as grounded in the land we inhabit and in terms of the perceptual condition of this inhabitation. It is part of the nature of a horizon that it recedes as we approach it. So Clare ventured out into the woods and the heath beyond: "I had imagin'd that the worlds end was at the edge of the orison and that a days journey was able to find it" (no end punctuation, cited, NTAP, 18). For Fletcher, Clare's poems are *paradigmatically* the description of this experience. But as is the case with the American landscape (captured, in this regard, by John Rogers Cox's *Grey and Gold*), the terrain which Clare traverses is, paradoxically, nondescript: "In Clare's fenland and across America place is the space of the nondescript, whose paradoxical mode of description can only emerge when the poet "observes" the uncanny" (NTAP, 56). So the description of the vanishing horizon must go by way of careful attention to the details encountered along the pursuit of its path, and in the paradoxical observation of these insignificant, yet thereby significant, details, the poet uncannily yokes together the "mixing of outward and inward apprehension" which characterizes our horizonal condition. Fletcher recalls Husserl's phenomenological characterization of this condition in terms of the quest for "immanent transcendence" (cited, NTAP, 17). Yet Husserl's understanding of this orientation in terms of the horizon marking "the idea of end as purpose" (NTAP, 17) is perhaps less appropriate to the new ontological status of the environment-poem than to the poetry of consciousness which it historically displaces, at least on Fletcher's reading, and several pages later Fletcher instead sets Clare's "ontological experiment" next to Tolstoy's (NTAP, 19). Clare's own, unique version of such ontological experimentation, however, would not take the route of Tolstoy's "mastery of strategy and large-scale forces" (D.M. Thomas, cited, NTAP, 19), but would instead collapse a lifespan into a "*single* moment of immanent transcendence; he was always walking toward the horizon, which maybe he learned to do early, from his flat fenland home" (NTAP, 19). Here, instead of the battlefield of world-historical forces, we have a broad landscape intimated by selection of minute detail.

Yet in Clare's case, as well as Tolstoy's, the "ontological experimentation" at issue intrinsically involves issues of *scale*, and in Clare's case in particular a mad rush "toward the unbounded":

—On roars the flood—all restless to be free

Like trouble wandering to eternity (cited, NTAP, 18)

which Fletcher also characterizes as a "chase after 'astonishment'" (NTAP, 18). Rather than the large scale of dramatic event, Clare (in this respect like Dickinson) focuses on the seemingly inconsequential details of apparently random encounters. This paradoxical description of the nondescript unleashes the power of the uncanny precisely by way of the portrait of the empirically delimited (NTAP, 21), and it is the mystery of the factually contingent which is sharpened: "'I never unriddled the mystery,' he once reminisced about another search for the fact" (NTAP, 21-22). However, in the face of this most ordinary, and yet therefore most impinging, of mysteries, the attentive appeal to delimiting fact not only elicits the mystery of the "uncanniness of the ordinary," but also sets our feet firmly on the ground, since the requisite attention embodies not just our standing over against a horizon but also the perceptual focus which is required for environmental orientation. "[H]orizon carries us outside of ourselves, yet keeps our feet on the ground" (NTAP, 22), and the environment-poem must do no less. The environment-poem, grounded in the poetry of Clare, accomplishes this through what Fletcher calls "description," but which we must always understand to include the description of the seemingly nondescript. In this sense, "description" is what binds the environment-poem to our factual, horizontal condition. "When I speak in later pages of description, I am speaking about this almost genetic connection between poetry and natural fact" (NTAP, 22).

SURROUND

Understanding the genetic connection between poetry and natural fact requires a focus on the common details to which Clare points us, and "[u]nderstanding *the common* as a function of poetic form and language—the subject of Wordsworth's Preface to the *Lyrical Ballads*—requires an ecologically detailed accounting for its expression ..." (NTAP, 25). But Fletcher finds such an accounting largely lacking in Wordsworth and the High Romantic tradition to which he belongs. In contrast to Clare, who "was precisely unlike a tourist, the paying traveler one suspects of not much liking his own home" (NTAP, 22), Fletcher sees Wordsworth as "virtually an eco-tourist, prospecting for higher laws" (NTAP, 69). Just as the value of description must ultimately be sought in the nondescript, so the value of environment is to be found at home—as in A. R. Ammons' back yard—, not in traveling to seek out exceptional vistas. The environment is "what is *around*," "what is *surrounding* the poet's seeing eye" (NTAP, 25), the nondescript subject to description. And just as we must distinguish between (low) nature and (High) Nature, so we must distinguish between various uses to which description may (or more significantly, may not) be put. Fletcher charts a course, through Clare but stretching back into the eighteenth century, for a Low Romantic attentiveness, and the heart of his polemic against the High Romantic tradition is embodied in the failure he finds there to *describe nature*. Wordsworth and his friend Jones covered 2000 miles on foot during their summer hike through France and Switzerland; as Fletcher remarks, "[t]his was not walking: it was running" (NTAP, 66-67). Wordsworth's effort lies in a *displacement* of the environment which he nonetheless poetically extols in search of his mastery of it, and the disjunction of these two moments is exemplified by the fact that "Wordsworth depended upon his sister Dorothy to learn how to observe, though not to formulate his grand ideas …" (NTAP, 62)

The Low Romantic path, by way of contrast, extends the eighteenth century preoccupation with description. In his treatment of antecedents, Fletcher focuses on the traditions of topographical poetry, on the one hand, and the condensed descriptive capacity of the couplet, on the other. In the first regard he mentions Sidney's *To Penhurst*, Denham's *Cooper's Hill* (NTAP, 32) and Drayton's *Poly-Olbion* (NTAP, 23)[152] but discusses more extensively the eighteenth century precedent provided by James Thomson's *The Seasons*. In revising his own work Thomson's interest in meteorology and "Newtonian notions of the optics of light" is progressively displaced by the need to "suggest emotional or moral atmospheres rather than the cultural atmosphere of scientific observation" (NTAP, 33). Yet, like the stylistic example canonically provided by Bishop Thomas Sprat's *History of the Royal Society*, Thomson's emphasis on description grappled with an economy of number in the descriptive realm that would favor equation over metaphor, emphasizing a "precision that was to reach its acme in Cowper, Crabbe, and Clare" (NTAP, 84). Just as is the case for Empson,[153] here metaphor, "the cardinal inward burning source of poetry, is a kind of bad equation, an equation without numbers" (NTAP, 84). With Thomson "description creates a discursive paradox of vision and fact *inmixing* with each other" (NTAP, 84), yet it is still "the light-centered universe of Newton's theory of gravity" which "holds all together for Thomson" (NTAP, 83). Poetic coherence, while overstepping the bounds of mere natural description, is nonetheless grounded in

---

152. See also Fletcher, *Allegory*, esp. 235, 358.

153. See William Empson, *The Structure of Complex Words* (Cambridge: Harvard University, 1989), 331-49.

the coherence of natural law. Thus poetry is ineliminably rooted in the description of nature.

A different, but related, tradition of description is to be found in the development of the eighteenth century cultivation of the poetic couplet. Already "with Drayton and Daniel and other late Elizabethans, the description of nature falls comfortably into heroic couplets," beneath whose "bipolar structure ... there always lurks a desire to define, to enclose, to delimit" (NTAP, 35). The couplet points in the direction of a symmetric balance whose "tension permits a power of defining both edge and volume" (NTAP, 35). Fletcher characterizes "the dance of the couplet" in the masterful hands of Alexander Pope as depending upon "the pirouette, as if in its poetic form the couplet were describing a circle" (NTAP, 35), and continues:

> It is tempting to speculate that the heroic couplet contracts discourse to its ultimate hermeneutic circle, to our understanding that when Alexander Pope plays often on the theme of the part and the particle, he is poetically projecting Schleiermacher's vision of interpreting texts, namely, that within the hermeneutic circle we must understand the whole to understand the parts, and we must understand the parts to understand the whole. (NTAP, 35-36)

Fletcher's ultimate suggestion is that "the encircling horizon of nature parallels the circle of hermeneutic enclosure, suggesting that the latter derives from the former" (NTAP, 36). And so, in a sense, the heroic couplet becomes the most controlled poetic laboratory for a description which would give our experimental relation to nature its due. Hermeneutics would inherit its horizonal structure, as would Husserl's phenomenology, from the embedded nature of our experience, so that "the descriptive poets and authors of the past were directly or indirectly writing about nature, which they perceived as whatever surrounds us" (NTAP, 36). Ontological experimentation precedes phenomenological hermeneutics.

Yet, just as Thomson's topographical poetry would move dynamically from description to vision, seeking "enlargement of scope" in a recourse to large, musical forms (NTAP, 34), so the tradition of descriptive couplets "could not generate adequate energy unless daimons or personifications were introduced" (NTAP, 37). In both cases the drive is toward an enlargement of scale, whether it be in the recourse to large-scale forms or to personifications which "speak for a horizon beyond the scene described and the passage describing."[154] This suggests that it is not so much a traditional problem of the part and the whole we face as it is a problem of the relentless displacement of any unit in favor of a larger unit, itself incomplete in turn, only indicating the further shift in the scale of the implied horizon. Ultimately

---

154. See also William Empson, *Seven Types of Ambiguity: A Study of its Effects in English Verse*, revised edition (New York: New Directions, 1947), on Pope, 128.

this dizzying horizonal instability is most powerfully achieved by the immersion of the observer into the descriptive surround. Fletcher draws on the example of the "later landscapes of Constable, Turner, and other masters of what Turner called 'indistinctness',"which "place observation in the midst of its surround, so that the artist in a new way appears to be part of what he is observing and depicting" (NTAP, 62).

In this way the description of the nondescript reaches a higher level, for the description at issue is not just of the nature of the nondescript but even of the *in*descript. The paradigm for such "indescription" will be the wave (in French *la vague*, from Latin *vagus*, wandering, vague), which absorbs the particulate into its multiform undulation. Beyond a rooting of the hermeneutic circle, we achieve here a construction of the temporal continuum. Instead of the "single moment of immanent transcendence," "[t]he radical repetition of one moment in the next is the source of our life in nature, but we thereby are born to accept an indistinct, imprecise, wavy existence" (NTAP, 78). "There is no grand perspectival Claudian withdrawal to a high point of survey; there is thus no 'general view of a situation in its entirety'" (NTAP, 87).

Beyond the topographic poem, we shift to the poem itself as environment, and beyond the personification of nature we move in the direction of a poetic analogue of multiple personality disorder. The difficulties of adequate description are reflected in Ashbery's poem, "For John Clare," which tells us "how it is almost impossible to hold in our mind's eye the multiple pictorial truth of all we so readily perceive, so quickly does our perception resolve into an excess of detail" (NTAP, 63). The need to handle a proliferation which threatens us with dizziness can only be managed by recognizing that "[w]e are of many minds, an odder situation than one might think, since it would follow, at least from the Parmenidean principle that "thinking and being are one," that our many minds imply many worlds all at once existing everywhere" (NTAP, 63-64). So we move toward the paradoxical structure of the environment-poem, which, too, is "[s]tranger than one might at first imagine" (NTAP, 103).

ENVIRONMENT-POEM

As Fletcher tells us at the beginning of the book, *A New Theory For American Poetry* grew out of work on Whitman, work which is most focally represented in a chapter on "The Whitman Phrase" (NTAP, vii). Fletcher identifies the phrase as the constituent unit of Whitman's poetry, which billows out in a largely paratactic proliferation of these units. In so doing, Whitman's poem avoids the hierarchical structure typified by the grammar of superordinate and subordinate clauses, reflecting instead the more democratic organization of the new Jacksonian democracy which the poem inhabits. But it would be misleading to take the poem simply to be a reflection of this reality, only a mirror image of the Jacksonian environ, for in its outward drive toward the linguistic frontier of the paratactic, the poem *itself* becomes an environment: no longer merely representative of reality, but directly participant in its own reality on the terms which the poem sets for itself. In so doing the poem approaches the linguistic frontier as well, and Whitman becomes "master 'of a larger, more intuitive linguistic medium than any particular language'" (NTAP, 110, citing Fletcher's *Colors of Mind*, on Sapir on Whitman). Fletcher points out also that Randall Jarrell called Whitman "the poet of parallel present participles" (cited, NTAP, 158), and compares the intensification which such linguistic stress generates to the capacities of Hopi grammar as studied in the work of Benjamin Lee Whorf:

> The Hopi were able through their grammar to express a universe full of vibrations ("vibratile phenomena") which were becoming the primary concern of modern physics. But the grammar allowed primitive intuitions to go beyond any language possessed by "normal standard English." Whitman is a born Hopi. (160)

The form of the environment-poem which Whitman fashions becomes the privileged carrier of a language adequate to the new condition of Jacksonian democracy, and as such the chief linguistic innovation for inhabiting this new reality.

In a world in the process of losing its traditional, hierarchical social structure, social cohesion becomes a pressing concern, and this concern is consequently exemplified in the environment-poem. Early on Fletcher points out that "'cohere' was one of Whitman's favorite terms for what he was attempting" (NTAP, 11) and so Fletcher's chief task in articulating the "Whitman grammar" lies in characterizing the manner in which Whitman navigates the horizontal grouping of phrases in order to generate a cohesive environment. A model lies to hand in Whitman's notion that "these United States are the greatest poem" (cited, NTAP, 97), and in particular in the "special pressure upon the Union of free and slave-holding states" (NTAP, 97) which Whitman's poetry also seeks to achieve. Whitman's poetry becomes the chief exemplification of his vision of American democracy as "life's gymnasium" (cited, NTAP, 99), in which he seeks to counterbalance the depersonalizing forces of monetary acquisition by a vitalization of "man's free play of special personalism" in the service of "preserving cohesion, ensemble of Individuality" (cited, NTAP, 99). The environment-poem which Whitman promotes is not, however a "literal fact," but rather "as any good poet would know, an imaginative discovery and an imaginative product" (NTAP, 116). The cohesion which it embodies is not meant, then, as a political panacea, but rather as a vision of a democratic order against which political reality may measure itself. As figured in the poem, the world and, in particular, the body become loci for presenting a picture of the "self-reflexive awareness" (NTAP, 132) that derives from the self's being surrounded by a world. In this figuration the "environmental array" may be "humanized" in a way reminiscent in some regards of the sort of personification Fletcher has described previously in an eighteenth century context, and this humanization allows the environment to engender "reveries of a coherent society" (NTAP, 132). Here, as well, we find the personification of the environment associated with dramatic shifts in scale, and it is this scale-shifting which leads to the heart of the environmental attitude, for "in environmental studies *scale* is everything" (NTAP, 137). In the environment-poem we find shifting scales in an age of democratic transition. Fletcher continues by asserting that, "[t]hough it may not be fashionable to speak in such words, I would say that this scale-shifting has a spiritual aspect, which in our poetry is signaled by the descriptive use of personification, along with other signs of animation in the scene" (NTAP, 138). This depicts a crux which is equally to be identified in terms of a central technical dilemma of poetic description, for "[s]omething has to shift us beyond the materiality of observed fact, and yet hold its specificity in a representation of the passing of real time" (NTAP, 138).

The solution which Fletcher identifies lies in the descriptive capture of impressions, seized in a moment which nonetheless conveys dynamic, hence specifically temporal, effect. Most dramatically, Fletcher describes this process as seeing "the Zenonian trajectory," reminiscent of Eisenstein's "image of movement": "Whitman's hammer never hits the nail. Instead, he catches, as in a snapshot, the hand holding the hammer in midair in all its intrinsic hammerness" (NTAP, 108).[155] This "snapshot" effect is captured in particular by Whitman's insistence on participial constructions and, more generally, by what Fletcher calls the poetry's "lack of transitivity," which is "staggering in its consistency" (NTAP, 108). Instead of thinking of seeing as an act in which a perceiver perceives a perceived, we must reconfigure our notion of vision into something which is carried along by the environment, so that Whitman may ultimately remark that "the sea whispered me" (NTAP, 130). Seeing, which as for Donne is meant here to signify "*All* the senses" (cited, NTAP, 95), is seeing in its prophetic sense (NTAP, 108), and Fletcher will go on to identify the Whitmanian vista with "confluent seeing, such that inhabitants dwell where paths and rivers meet, as they do in New York City" (NTAP, 121).[156]

"Thinking in vistas is a general sight" (NTAP, 95), and Fletcher's linking of sight and thought points to the original sense of theory, which he

---

155. Here we see a first intimation of space as a "modality of time" (NTAP, 18), a preoccupation of Fletcher's to which I return below.

156. That Fletcher's recourse to Donne on sight as omnisensational is not entirely coincidental is suggested by the fact that in his *Symphonia: Sum Fluxae Pretium Spei* Elliott Carter equally draws on the work of the seventeenth century poet Crashaw as a source for the notion of an environmentally carried locative presence, in Carter's case bubbles.

stresses in his reading of Whitman but which ultimately extends to the sense of theory involved in Fletcher's own "new theory for American poetry." This is not "what scholars have been calling 'theory' ever since about 1965 or so," but rather "the theory of the making of poems, which are *made* symbolic objects, *poemata*" (NTAP, 97). Whitman invokes theory in the context of his hopes for poetry as a countermeasure set against the "seething currents, cross and undercurrents, vortices" of demagoguery and greed, the "blind fury of the parties," the "scrofulous wealth, the surfeit of prosperity, the demonism of greed" (cited, NTAP, 99) registered in American society as he finds it. Against this Whitman proposes that "a new theory of literary composition for imaginative works of the very first class, and especially for highest poems, is the sole course open to these States" (cited, NTAP, 100), and we should no doubt take Fletcher to be following Whitman's recommendation, albeit perhaps in a more modest way. In any case, what is most important to stress is that the theories which Whitman and Fletcher, respectively, propose are themselves integral elements of both the historical and poetic condition as they find it. And, as I will argue below, Fletcher may be taken in particular as attempting to supply the vistas for Ashbery's poetry and its future which Whitman hoped to supply for himself in his own *Democratic Vistas*.

WAVES

The language of phrases is the language of units, and of the aggregations of these units. Viewed in terms of such aggregation, this, we might say, is a static language. But in fact, a key source for Fletcher's notion of aggregation is the way in which this term is used to describe the concluding phase of an initiation ritual, in which the initiate comes to take his (or her) place in the larger community as a full-standing member. Aggregation, then, is the final phase of the three step procedure of "separation, liminal passage, and aggregation" (NTAP, 112). By analogy, "the poem following this plan would reach closure and climax when the protagonist reaches a higher level of insight, status, or home and belonging" (NTAP, 112). In the environment-poem there is a general displacement of the function of the hero onto the function of the reader, and so the insight at issue is whatever might come over the reader in her (or his) reading of the poem. This model of aggregation is directly tied to the "spiritual aspect" of scale-shifting mentioned above, and in both social and poetic context we might describe the limiting case of such integration as an experience of the oceanic, of waves.

It should come as no surprise, then, that Fletcher describes the formal composition of the environment-poem out of units in just such terms:

> Aggregation and the forming of the ensemble allow the phrase to become the centrally natural linguistic expression of democracy, for good or ill. The phrase bespeaks thought in its most immediate, unreticulated,

even fragmentary form, which in a later chapter I will identify with Whitman's use of waves deriving from particles. (NTAP, 112)

In a discussion of wave-particle duality in physics, Fletcher concludes that "there is no doubt that the Whitman phrase is a kind of linguistic particle, while his main larger effect is to create waves of expression and meaning" (NTAP, 144). The task, then, is to understand this "transition" from particle to wave; what we have seen above indicates that this is to be understood in terms of a shift in scale.

In this light, it is all the more interesting that Fletcher's chapter on these issues should carry the title "Waves and the Troping of Poetic Form," for these two central concerns are both related to a shift in level: in scale, in the first instance, as we have already seen, and in the second instance in a shift from poetic content to poetic form. Understanding the cooperation of these two shifts will help us to understand that Whitman and company "write less *about* waves than they actually write *in waves*" (NTAP, 154). Given that the emphasis in the environment-poem is on process as against substance, the waves in which the environment-poem is written are the carriers of process (NTAP, 171) as opposed to the ontological establishment of the poem: which is to say, they are ontologically experimental in the above sense.

The wave is oceanic, too, in its creation of a sense of "the surround." Focusing again on Whitman's use of the present participle, Fletcher remarks that "[t]he intensifying present participle makes the *sight* of process *resound* in our ears, with a sense that something is ongoing, continuing, flowing, moving through a moment that knows no start or finish" (NTAP, 174). Here, sound registers a temporal "activation" of the "Zenonian trajectory," and "the reader should remember that only under special circumstances does sight envelop the viewer, whereas sound always surrounds us, as it resonates" (NTAP, 173). The frozen intransitivity of the raised hammer is thawed into a sense of passage, establishing what, from a grammatical perspective, Fletcher will refer to as "the middle voice." This passage from the "omnisensational" impression to the surround of sound marks the aggregative closure of poetic effect, as the particular phrases of the environment-poem wash over us in waves, and with such closure the environment-poem is, paradoxically, brought into being. The environment-poem is a symphonic conversation of particulate phrases carrying its reader along, like a bubble in air. But this closure into birth is in no traditional sense an ending, for as Fletcher insists, "the environment-poem always drifts off toward the horizon, which in turn leads to another more distant horizon" (NTAP, 120). Indeed, even this movement is already embedded in Clare's anticipation of the environment-poem in three of his sonnets. As Fletcher remarks,

> [t]here is perhaps no final horizon of our ideas, although within the sphere of our senses there is that narrower perceptual horizon toward

which our senses carry our thoughts like an invisible cargo of selfhood. If finally this ineffable cargo never reaches port, it fails because space at last becomes a modality of time, as Clare's three great sonnets on a winter flood once showed in one wild scene" (NTAP, 18).

In fact, Fletcher explicitly addresses the apparently contradictory nature of the poetic conception implied by the environment-poem:

> There appears something impossible about this descriptive notion of a shared conversational poem that simply *is* an environment. For the claim to be literally true, the reader would have to be actually living inside a verbal construct. That can happen in science fiction, but can *such living* occur in ordinary life? The answer would be yes, if the imagined union of the poetic form and the reader's experience is in fact the most imposing aspect or part of that experience. (NTAP, 172)

Here, we encounter dramatically the second shift of level registered by the environment-poem: no longer *the description* of an imaginary world into which the reader may retreat, the environment-poem *as form* comes out to greet the reality of the reader. And it is for this reason that it is important for Fletcher to stress, enlisting John Hollander, that "poets do not so much imitate the world, as *they trope poetic forms*" (NTAP, 148).[157] Along these lines, what happens in the environment-poem is that what has always been the implicit source of activity in poems (the way in which they trope previous poetic forms) is now made the overt principle of their poetic construction. This generates what is arguably one of the most interesting criticisms of Harold Bloom's poetic tropology, for Fletcher acknowledges the focal role of troping in the theory of poetry, but sees it aligned with the capacity for poetic description rather than with the stance of one poet relative to another precursor poet. What is at issue, then, is not poetic belatedness, but rather poetic descriptiveness. With an obvious if tacit swipe at Bloom, Fletcher puts it this way:

> In my enlarged sense of *descriptive poetry*, tropes are also no longer local decorations or particular swerves of particular meanings; tropes go beyond any turbulence in the text. Whitman and Ashbery, who is so like him, take the object of description and turn it into an *objectified form of the object of description*. They get the object to speak. (NTAP, 151)

In this way, we can understand that in the most nearly literal sense possible, the environment-poem establishes a conversation between poem and reader; in reading, environment-poems become *our* environments, the "poems of our climate." In an inversion of Platonism where impressions are substituted for ideas, the environment-poem is where we live when we are most real.

---

157. Harold Bloom also speaks of Whitman's "titanic innovations in what John Hollander teaches me to call 'the trope of form'," AILWL, 236.

POETRY OF BECOMING

Environmental poetry, in Fletcher's sense, is a poetry of emerging relations: rather than being about things, it is about what happens when things encounter each other. This means that the construction of the environmental poem is governed by metonymy, and in John Ashbery, Fletcher finds an exemplary poet of what might be called "metonymic drift." Drawing on an early article by Jakobson on Pasternak, and pointing out that Ashbery chose an epigraph from Pasternak in his early volume, *Some Trees*,[158] Fletcher shows how metonymy promotes a poetry of becoming. Appealing to the notion of *Stimmung* (tone or mood, also a keyword in the philosophy of Heidegger), "whose theory is a semantic version of ecology," Jakobson "wanted to show how poems actually shape the *Stimmung* effect" (NTAP, 185).[159] In Pasternak's case, Jakobson "identified personal character with the environment surrounding the person, and hence he thought that action could be replaced by topography, and figuratively in realistic literature by metonymy" (NTAP, 186). Jakobson identifies a technique here which is fundamental to the "*Stimmung* effect" of the environment-poem: the displacement of the persona of the poet by that of his environment, and the presentation of this latter through a process of descriptive juxtaposition.

In a passage made all the more interesting by comparison with his early work on allegory, Fletcher remarks that the "predominance of this figure of adjacency leads to a new and original kind of allegorical writing, an instance of what we might call postmodern allegory" (NTAP, 188), but which might with equal justification be called reverse allegory. For whereas traditional allegory "projects the *received ideas* of a culture, and when inspired, brings to these orthodox ideas a new and pleasing analysis" (NTAP, 188) whose aim is "to provide a fiction of ideas in action" (NTAP, 189), conversely, Ashbery in particular "plays a parodic game with the stereotyped tokens of what 'most people think'," with the consequence that "he invents what one might call *allegory without ideas*" (NTAP, 189). Although Fletcher does not point it out explicitly, we might see this as the formal consequence of the development of poetic description to that point where its inevitable "reverse Platonism" is necessarily driven out into the open: unable to hide any longer behind the sheltering storm of ideas, the poem emerges into its own climate. The persona of the poet is distributed across this weather system: as Fletcher notes, Ashbery has "on many occasions spoken of his fluidity, even loss of personal identity, as a clear and strong ego" (NTAP, 185).

---

158. For the poem, "The Picture of Little J. A. in a Prospect of Flowers," *Some Trees* (New York: Corinth Books, 1970), 27-29.

159. See also Leo Spitzer, *Classical and Christian Ideas of World Harmony: Prolegomena to an Interpretation of the Word "Stimmung"*, ed. Anna Granville Hatcher (Baltimore: Johns Hopkins, 1963), reprinted from *Traditio* **2** (1944): 409-64 and **3** (1945): 307-64.

Kenneth Burke indicated, if I recall correctly, that he wished to entitle the third volume of his literary summa, the poetics to follow *A Grammar of Symbolic Form* and *A Rhetoric of Symbolic Form*, not *A Poetics of Symbolic Form* but rather *While Everything Flows*. It is perhaps testimony to the difficulty of describing such fluidity that Burke was not able to finish such a volume, at least as such.[160] Ashbery and Fletcher both take up the gauntlet: Ashbery most obviously in the book-length *Flow Chart*, and Fletcher in his attempt to develop a theory of poetry adequate to it and the future to which it points. Not surprisingly, the formal predicaments associated with shaping the environment-poem, and particularly in arresting its fluid development, are major concerns in Fletcher's new theory. Given the nature of the environment-poem, we should not expect a definite theory of "poetic closure" here, but Fletcher does have much to tell us about the development of such a poem. Already in the discussion of the Whitman phrase he admonishes the reader to keep in mind that "Whitman writes poems which seem unbounded, but are in fact enclosures" (NTAP, 104). As mentioned previously, we must not mistake the environment-poem for a literal fact, always bearing in mind rather its status as imaginative artifact. Hence, in the most basic and literal sense, the poem by Whitman or Ashbery does end, even if Walt or John is waiting for us somewhere on the road up ahead. Fletcher is inclined to see the basic structure of the environment-poem in terms of an expansion of the middle (NTAP, 253), and Ashbery consciously begins *Flow Chart in medias res* ("Still in the published city but not yet / overtaken by a new form of despair ..." (cited, NTAP, 196)). But before attempting to understand, as Fletcher puts it, how Ashbery was "to control the poem's meander" (NTAP, 219), we must return to an earlier stage, and look at the dynamics of the environment-poem as they are already manifest in Whitman's case.

"The trick for Whitman, and those like him, is to express enormous force driving toward a conclusion, but then to allow this force to dissipate as the poem reaches its ending" (NTAP, 120). Given Whitman's intensification of the phrasal unit by leaning heavily on the present participle, "the sense of tidal outflow increases subtly" (NTAP, 120), and the poem drifts out to sea. In a poem like "Song of Myself," this outrush leads the poem back to the point where it first began, and the cyclical structure establishes "an environment perfectly balanced between inner and outer" for "the outer world in its letter gives the coordinates of the inner world, with its thoughts" (NTAP, 120).[161] This is a sense of conclusion, or rather ending, which is established by

---

160. See, however, Kenneth Burke, *Language as Symbolic Action: Essays on Life, Literature, and Method* (Berkeley: California, 1966). Much of this volume, along with the earlier essays collected in *Philosophy of Literary Form*, could be taken as preliminary contributions to such a project.

161. Fletcher's book, too, possesses such a cyclical structure, returning in its last section "to our point of departure, the horizon" (254).

way of a balance rather than through any narrative or topographic resolution: just as the tide washes out, "[a]pproximating conclusions only, the environment-poem always drifts off toward the horizon, which in turn leads to another more distant horizon" (NTAP, 120). In "Song of Myself" the figure of the poet itself registers a metonymic displacement of the poem's horizon, on the other side of which Walt stands, looking back for us or up farther still.

But the tendency of the environment-poem to "drift" is a constant concern, for how is diversion itself to be diverted? Many traditional poetic methods of control, which would reduce such topographical wandering to the allegorical presentation of a conceptual scheme, are incompatible with the productive strategy of such poetic drift, which seeks to avoid external control so that its self-confident meandering may generate emergent order on its own terms. Before addressing the "diversion of diversion," Fletcher must provide an account of the (potentially) productive capacity of drift, and here he faces a problem common to many areas associated with the study of complex adaptive systems. He therefore enlists the burgeoning science of complexity to supply a vocabulary for describing such emergent order and the productiveness of relations established "on their own terms." Following the heuristic characterization of John Holland, Fletcher distinguishes seven requisites for a complex adaptive system: *aggregation*, *tagging* of the most valuable components, *nonlinearity* as a productive form of interaction among components, *flow* as a pattern of changing adaptations, *internal diversity* as promising a diversity of interacting agents in the system, *an internal model* which provides a representation of the system within the system itself, and *building blocks*, the fundamental units out of which the system is composed. Many of these features are already familiar from Fletcher's analysis of the environment-poem, but with these terms we may begin to describe the "drift" of a complex system in terms of the capacity for the system "to develop its own ensemble character, much in the manner of small chamber groups of musicians who play without a conductor, as in the eighteenth century" (NTAP, 206). To extend the analogy, we might even say that the listener comes to occupy the position vacated by the "conductor," establishing an intimate connection with the ensemble unmediated by any interpretative imposition. We might say further that our responses meet the horizon of the ensemble, pushing the observer "inside the system," or perhaps even better, bringing the observer up to its edge, to seek "what Donne called emergent occasions" (NTAP, 207).

Again, however, we must recall that the environment-poem is not a "literal fact" but an "imaginative product," and Fletcher proposes that, at least in the particular case of Ashbery's *Flow Chart*, it "risks one aesthetic disadvantage—the days resemble each other too closely" (NTAP, 207). Eisenstein noted that in Whitman's poetry (as also in Zola's novels), there is a risk of "numbing the mind" and also of generating a comic impression, brought on by the element of repetition (in both these regards, one thinks of Gertrude Stein's work as well).[162] These threats face montage generally, which may lead not only to "self-enclosure" and a certain "drowsiness," but more generally to what Eisenstein calls *"the solipsism of audiovisual drama."*[163] In order to avoid the risk of tedium associated with diffuse sameness,

> "[t]he poem needs what in music would be called a *stretto*, a concentration of themes in one massively converging contrapuntal treatment. This amounts to placing a monument in the scene, to interrupt the flow of reverie, so that in itself the flow will be sensed as the idea of the poem, by virtue of the aesthetic contrast. (NTAP, 208)

The monument establishes a scalar constant which dominates the environment it graces and hence serves as a point of focus around which the inspection of the environment may be organized. In the case of Ashbery's *Flow Chart*, this monumental "diversion of diversion" comes in the form of a technical tour-de-force, a double sestina composed on a set of end words which Ashbery inherits from Swinburne's "Complaint of Lisa," which in turn derives from an episode in Boccaccio's *Decameron*. In fractal fashion, the six-part structure of *Flow Chart* is reinscribed in the six-fold character of the double sestina (as it is, as well, in the six sections of Fletcher's book), establishing a reverse sense of scaling: the monumental sestina is itself a miniature "version" of the environment-poem at large, so that "the whole six-part meditation of *Flow Chart* is, in fact, one immense sestina" (NTAP, 223). The "late placement" of the double sestina controls "the larger flow by looking back over a broad stream of pages preceding it. Yet it must be followed by a final denouement …" (NTAP, 208). In this way Ashbery resolves the problem of the ebbing of the environment-poem differently from Whitman, but no less successfully.

COHERENCE THEORY

Philosophers often debate the relative merits of a correspondence theory of truth—one in which a statement is taken to be true if it corresponds to a state of affairs obtaining in the world—, versus a coherence theory of truth—one in which a statement is taken to be true if taking it to be true meshes with the truth values we assign to other statements in the language. But, at least from the perspective of the fashioning of poems, the distinction between

---

162. Sergei Eisenstein, *Nonindifferent Nature*, trans. Herbert Marshall (Cambridge: Cambridge, 1987), 83, 85. Eisenstein draws the charge against Zola of "numbing" from B. Reizov, "The Utopian Novels of Zola," *Literaturnaya Ucheba* [*Literary Studies*], Moscow, 1934.

163. idem, 387, 386. Eisenstein's term 'audiovisual drama' need not be limited to film or even the literally dramatic, but should be taken to include more broadly dramatic audiovisual effects in all art. In Eisenstein, the status of the problem of "montage solipsism" is complicated by political requirements that he disavow his more extreme experiments in montage, as in the 1927 film *October*.

correspondence and coherence theories of truth is best seen as one which distinguishes between easily containable, "model," linguistic situations and less easily containable situations of language "in the rough." To the extent that the environment-poem is grounded in description of the world narrowly conceived, it will need to correspond to the object of its description. Yet, as Fletcher points out, when pressed far enough the poetic representation of environments leads to the poem itself actually *becoming* an environment (NTAP, 227), so that the environment-poem is ultimately not so much a poem about the world as environment as it is itself its own environment. And in the case of an environment fashioned out of words, the practical condition of their interaction will be one of coherence, not correspondence. The last section of Fletcher's book is devoted to the description of these coherence conditions in the world of the environment-poem.

There is, as well, an extra-poetic ground for the dominating concern with coherence which Fletcher identifies in the environment-poem. Coming, as it does, in the "long twilight of Romanticism" (NTAP, 225) which we now inhabit, the environment-poem is both a privileged articulation of and response to a world in which the complexity of our social and environmental condition has reached staggering proportions. In all dimensions, this complexity is reflected in numerical largesse: of populations, of monetary resources, of information, of demand on environmental resources. As Fletcher puts it dramatically, "[t]o an extreme degree the numbers themselves are the essence of the coming environmental reality" (NTAP, 238). The numbers themselves "become the new main issue, as any economist will tell us," (NTAP, 238), and so "[a] poetry written within the new environment of human propagation had to discover new integers" (NTAP, 239). Fletcher identifies this as "exactly the Whitman quest" (NTAP, 239): it is a problem which finds its quintessential political representation in American democracy and, in particular, the need to distinguish the individual and the idiosyncratic from the undifferentiated mass. Fletcher reiterates that the Whitman phrase lies at the grammatical heart of this project, which would seek to carve out individuals from the stock of language, when he asserts that "[a] *phrasing* of our democratic existence seeks to preserve such idiosyncrasy, as if in response to Tocqueville's worry that Americans tended paradoxically to conform" (NTAP, 246). Like the days themselves, Americans may come too closely to resemble one another.

There is both an irony and a danger here: in order to do justice to the role of the individual in the democratic state or, analogously, the phrase in a Whitman poem, we must read "environmentally," which is to say, by invoking either a political or poetic equivalent, respectively, of the law of large numbers. We have seen how Fletcher's approach to the environment-poem as complex adaptive organism seeks to do just this. But in such a procedure there is an inevitable tendency to abstract from the individual unit, to consider the relations among units rather than the merit of the individual units themselves. By the time we reach the poetry of Ashbery, this tendency has become something of a necessity: although Fletcher insists that "[m]ost of the poetry is perspicuous to a careful reading," such careful reading must be conducted in a context qualified by the recognition that "Ashbery plays subtle polyrhythmic games with sequential order" (NTAP, 141). And if the "relatedness is all," then this added condition is not an external rider, but the key fact about an Ashbery environment-poem. A new kind of reading is required: not one, of course, which is lax with respect to the duties and obligations of reading, but one which is vigilant in a new and improved way: "The environment-poem requires us, in both writing and reading, to practice a casual, unauthorized, but always intensely focused noticing" (NTAP, 238). This new reading must passionately attend to the multivoicings and subtle equivocities of a poetic language which reflects the complexities and shadings of our post-Romantic environment. As Fletcher puts it,

> Our own multifaceted thoughts surround us with dream-like perceptions. When our personhood splits several ways, we paradoxically are enabled to follow a new perseveration of Being, resulting from various voices all living together—at least, that seems to be the model. By saying to ourselves as readers, "Let's move in," we get to be where we need to be, where Being is tested in experience, as it always is for children. They, unlike the poor grownups, do not experience buyer's remorse. (NTAP, 142)

The flexibility of a child's environment, which the environment-poem resurrects as an homage to the complex shading of the larger, worldly environment it inhabits in turn, is bought at the price of a fluidity of reference—for as we all know (but are constantly in the process of forgetting), the lack of referential fixity is a hallmark of the world of the child. And in the world at large, the complex shading and referential fluidity of our post-Romantic environment is a function of the complicated and "polyphonic" way in which we, as humans, inhabit it. How much of this complexity can the environment-poem convey?

"Ecology," Fletcher tells us, "may appear to depersonalize social thought, but ecology is nevertheless the sadly correct concept for initiating adequate *global* analysis" (NTAP, 190). The turn away from Romanticism which Fletcher recommends is not one in which we avoid the human condition or escape our inevitably perspectival perception, but it is one in which we must refuse to *start* with the Romantic paradigm of subject-centered consciousness. In moving away from such a consciousness-centered perspective, we do inevitably depersonalize our orientation, but we do so in order to respect the complexity of sensation, information, interaction and surrounding within which any individual person is oriented. Here, too, in moving away from paradigmatic experiences of Romantic epiphany, we confront an experience of poetry "in the rough," and so one which partakes of the mixed blessing of all things not under rigorous control. In so doing, we move away from the Romantic picture of the poem as dream into a multiconscious state of intense, yet fractured, reality: "[i]t is as if the dream had become real" (NTAP, 227). We are no longer in a position to draw a clean distinction between idea and thing, and so in no position to follow out in any terms a correspondence account of the relation between poetic language and worldly referent. Yet the intensive preoccupation with coherence does not register a defeat of realism, but rather a commitment to a *hyperrealist* ambition. Fletcher sees in this a poetry which is appropriate to the scientific worldview, so that "the consequence of an interest in science will be a metaphysical blurring and uncanny fragmentation of the unexamined manifold of 'things we all know to be the case'" (NTAP, 227).

Concomitantly, in its hyperrealistic ambition, the demand of the environment-poem for coherence must also not be limited by the constraint of a narrowly rational consistency. Instead, the environment-poem will sacrifice such consistency for "a loose and notably inconsistent completeness" (NTAP, 227). The condition upon which the reader may be invited into the linguistic reality of the environment-poem is, we may say, that the flange over which the reader must step to enter the poem is marked by an overt contradiction, which allows the reader to breathe inside the poem only on pains of inconsistency. This inconsistency, which underwrites the amplitude of the poem as environment, must lead, ultimately, to the disintegration of the poem: the disaggregation of the units of the poem itself, and hence to the denouement of the poetic experience of the reader. As Wallace Stevens remarked in a passage cited by Fletcher, "It seems to me that Whitman is disintegrating as the world, of which he made himself a part, disintegrates. *Crossing Brooklyn Ferry* exhibits this disintegration" (cited, NTAP, 251). This is, however, the appropriate conclusion for an environment-poem, for "here, as if we were returning to Heraclitus for instruction, conclusion means not *finishing off* the parts" (NTAP, 253). The environment-poem leaves itself open to its own undoing, rather than engaging in the "mechanical consistency" of an "obsessive ritual of self-defense" (NTAP, 254). We, in turn, cannot expect to bring it under our control, possessing of it only "the layering it leaves, the minute encrustations of an allusive drift" (NTAP, 255). The complexity is conveyed by whatever we happen to find there: not guaranteed in advance, nor written into its own future, it is the reward of its own reality. In this, it is quite simply *of our world*.

DAILY RHYTHMS

When I first began contemplating this chapter, I thought of entitling it "Daily Themes," taking on the name of the Freshman Composition Course at Yale University. But rereading Fletcher's book, I learned that this was precisely *not* the right title, and in a way which proves instructive for the understanding of Fletcher's project. For a great benefit of the environment-poem, according to Fletcher, is that it "allows us to get beyond the vice of slavish thematics; it allows us positively to find patterns arising from the complex, seemingly undirected array of elements in the poem, as the poet found these when tracing her walk to the horizon" (NTAP, 237-38). Fletcher prefaces his presentation of this benefit by remarking that "this approach to poetry and literature in general is not any more abstract than is music," and so, by analogy, my new title suggests that we think of the patterns to which Fletcher refers as rhythms.

As environment, the unit of the environment-poem is the day, and Fletcher traces its legacy back to Hesiod's *Works and Days*, whose "virtually epic subject" is "how resources are to be allocated for human survival" (NTAP, 231). At the other end of the historical continuum, Ashbery's *Flow Chart* grew out of "an almost daily journal" leading from the day of his mother's death to the poet's birthday on July 28, 1988 (NTAP, 197). The diary, whether poetic or prosaic, is a privileged linguistic forum for the tabulation of the minute details of everyday life, and so a privileged linguistic space for the cultivation of description; how much of the environment-poem is rooted in the cultivation of the diary form is open to speculation, but the formal and functional correlations are clear.

As in the rhythm of seasons, the diurnal rhythm is a cyclical one, and so lies at the rhythmic root of the inward and outward drift of the environment-poem (and as the last word of Fletcher's book is 'drift', so its first two are 'One day'). Clare (as also Hölderlin[164]) is a poet of the rhythm of walking. In conversation, John Hollander once described to me the effect of a poem by Ashbery as analogous to taking a walk in a large city: the experience is in some sense continuous, but you turn a corner and move into a new scene, or walk along a series of blocks which shift from fancy to fallen and back again. And as Fletcher has identified the Whitman phrase as the grammatical motor of his poetry, so Hollander spoke of Ashbery's control over what, usually in the analysis of prose, are referred to as *periods*. In "Little Boy and Lost Shoe," Robert Penn Warren finely evokes the way in which walking is a daily rhythm in both the traversal of space and time:

> Under the sky he walked and the sky was big.
> Sunlight touched the goldenrod, and yellowed his hair,
> But the sun was low now, and oh, he should know
> He must hurry to find that shoe, or the sun will be down.[165]

---

164. Pierre Bertaux, *Hölderlin* (Frankfurt am Main: Suhrkamp, 1981), 284-87.
165. Robert Penn Warren, *The Collected Poems of Robert Penn Warren*, ed. John Burt, with a forward by Harold Bloom (Baton Rouge: LSU, 1998), 307.

As Fletcher recognizes, the greatest American walker is Thoreau (NTAP, 26), and he identifies Thoreau's "key to the method, for poetical purposes," in "the quiet or even the complete solitude of the walker. In this sense the walker, the rambler, the explorer, has a kind of love affair with perception itself" (NTAP, 27). One senses that, whether literally or otherwise, Fletcher is also such a walker, and that here we approach the personal core of his book.

Daily rhythms, then: no slavish and much dreaded undergraduate themes, but rather the opening and closing of fields. Such is our environment, American and poetic.

MONTAGE, COMPLEXITY, CONTRADICTION AND ARCHITECTURE

As I began this chapter, so I would like to end it with a "montage" of Eisenstein and Fletcher, also briefly invoking as a third element in this "audiovisual drama" the controversial architectural theory of Robert Venturi and associates, as presented in the volumes *Complexity and Contradiction in Architecture* and *Learning from Las Vegas*.[166] Venturi's work serves as a helpful point of comparison, in particular, for Fletcher's development of the notions of complexity and contradiction. Venturi recognizes, for example, that what he calls contradictory "both-and" structures can promote "rhythm and also complexity of scale in the giant order,"[167] and develops a notion of the contradictory "difficult whole"[168] which offers interesting points of comparison with Fletcher's coherence theory. The modern architectural "purism" against which Venturi reacts tended to eliminate "contradictory juxtapositions"[169] and "superadjacencies" in which "juxtaposed directions create rhythmic complexities and contradictions."[170] The resonances of juxtaposition with Eisenstein's montage are immediate, and both positions share Fletcher's emphasis on a richness of elements which may accommodate both continuity and discontinuity.[171]

A montage, especially of the sort which emphasizes the *Urphänomen* of movement, combines complexity—a manifold of "shots"—and contradiction—or juxtaposition—in an effort to create an intricacy of aesthetic rhythm otherwise unavailable. But like architectural theory, montage theory

---

166. Robert Venturi, *Complexity and Contradiction in Architecture*, 2nd ed., with an introduction by Vincent Scully (New York: The Museum of Modern Art, 1966, 1977). Venturi's later volume, with Denise Scott Brown and Steven Izenour, *Learning from Las Vegas*, revised edition (Cambridge: MIT, 1972, 1977), extremalizes many of the claims from the earlier volume, in many cases leading to a reductio ad absurdum.

167. Venturi, *Complexity and Contradiction in Architecture*, 35.

168. idem, 41.

169. idem, 66.

170. idem, 61.

171. idem, 98.

as Eisenstein develops it is "compositional" in orientation. In the most literal, and therefore most basic sense, neither buildings nor films "move." The holy grail of film is not movement itself but rather the *image* of movement, and we have seen Fletcher emphasize a similar point in his analysis of Whitman's presentation, not of movement itself, but of the "Zenonian trajectory." The problem with the Modern "articulated" architecture Venturi and company oppose is that it is "like a minuet in a discotheque" (LL, 139). Complexity and contradiction are not *desiderata* of this process, but rather necessary *tools*: the goal is the production of a contemporary aesthetic *rhythm*, and it is for this reason that Fletcher's book rightly returns in its last paragraph to his focus on the diurnal: "With disciplines of thought we hardly grasp, we would transfigure sleeping and waking, sitting still and walking around."[172]

Architecture and cinema are right in this diurnal context to serve as supporting pillars for an appreciation of modern poetry because, unlike modern poetry—at least for most of us—buildings and the movies are our daily habitation and recreation respectively. There is a massive and largely unacknowledged praxical contradiction in Fletcher's new theory for American poetry: at a time when it is called on to transcribe the complexity of our daily rhythms, the experience of poetry has itself *never* been so far from our diurnal condition.[173] In an era when ever more contemporary poetry is published and yet assumes an ever more peripheral cultural significance than ever before—with a sea of good but rarely excellent poetry drowning out the most serious attempts to create poetry of longstanding value—Fletcher's celebration of American poetry threatens to become a pipe dream only serving to assuage fears of the irrelevance of the traditional arts and the thorough displacement, in particular, of literature by the "movie." Octavio Paz surveyed the situation of poetry at the end of the twentieth century and came to the conclusion: "I am not worried about the health of poetry, but about its place in the society we live in."[174] Here again, the assumption is that the two issues, even if not independent, can nonetheless be considered distinctly. This assumption holds up to a point, but not one that would consider the overall dynamics of modernity's pace. Paz poetically, but ineffectually, laments, " ... our present is a weightless thing: it floats along, it does not rise, it moves but makes no headway... Our present is a time that has no

---

172. Fletcher, *New Theory*, 255.

173. A related concern faces Stanley Cavell's celebration of the "ordinary," yet Cavell, at least, recognizes the pre-eminence of cinema as a popular art form in our time, and in this regard his celebration of ordinariness is more consistent. Unlike Fletcher, Cavell is not engaged in promoting advanced contemporary poetry (though perhaps he should be).

174. Octavio Paz, *The Other Voice: Essays on Modern Poetry*, trans. Helen Lane (New York: Harcourt Brace Jovanovich, 1991), 120; see esp. "The Few and The Many," 77-98, and "Quantity and Quality," 99-118.

north to guide it."[175] Eerily, the passage echoes, but in another key, the "minute encrustations of an allusive drift" with which Fletcher ends his book.[176] Fletcher's analysis of poetic rhythm is more sophisticated than what we may extract from Eisenstein or Venturi, but film and architecture are (and typically in the lowest sense) our diurnal arts, not poetry.

So far from arguing for an abandonment of the high art of poetry, however, I am instead insisting that Fletcher has not faced the dilemma of democracy and poetry sufficiently squarely. The more overtly political dimensions of his volume celebrate Jacksonian democracy as *over and against* the legacy of the federalist tradition, with insufficient recognition of the balancing role these two traditions have played in American political history. What is the analogue in our tradition of poetry? This question is not on Fletcher's map, yet desperately deserves to be. In his celebration of Jacksonian democracy, Whitman was equally aware that the worst excesses of the Gilded Age were an integral part of this legacy, as is made clear in manifold passages from his *Democratic Vistas*. Fletcher, of course, is aware of this, too, but both Whitman and Fletcher have much less to *propose* about it. Historically between the two, Robert Penn Warren's *Democracy and Poetry* is better in this regard, because more realistically and concretely political.[177]

In a different, but related, sense of politics, both Eisenstein and Venturi struggle with these issues more overtly than Fletcher does. Eisenstein's battle with Stalin is much too complex to summarize here, but for current purposes it suffices to say that Eisenstein struggled (whether for better or worse) to maintain some simultaneous sense of cinema as both a popularly social and a high aesthetic force. Venturi's rejection of the most "utopian" (read: impractical) aspects of the International Style of architectural modernism led him in directions which some of his critics have characterized as "Nixonian."[178] In "the brutal automobile landscape of great distances and high speed, ... the subtleties of pure architectural space can no longer be savored" (LL, 119). The twinkling, labyrinthine darkness of the Las Vegas casino is emblematized in Rick's fictional-but-famous Café Americain, where architecture becomes a symbol of the pace of modernity. In the gambling den, "you are no longer in the bounded piazza but in the twinkling lights of the city at night" (LL, 50). (Rick's may be *set* in Morocco, but it undeniably *exists* only on a 40's Hollywood film *set*.) This is the architectural-cinematic

---

175. idem, 114.

176. Fletcher, *New Theory*, 255.

177. Robert Penn Warren, *Democracy and Poetry* (Cambridge: Harvard, 1975); the book originally derives from the 1974 Jefferson Lectures, and takes as its epigraph from St.-John Perse: "And it is enough for the poet / to be the guilty conscience of his time."

178. Venturi et al., *Learning from Las Vegas,* respond that " ... there is a fine line between liberalism and old-fashioned snobbery" (LL, 155).

space which is trying to *escape* from the subtle thoughts needed to control our daily rhythms in an age of domestic anxiety.

In an age of often brutalizing efficiency (especially of the economic and informational varieties), any rejection of the ideal of modern self-assertion threatens to become a form of pre-modern reaction, yet this reactive status in turn *enforces* the modern condition with unprecedented *efficiency*. To take a supremely dramatic example, Islamic and other "fundamentalist" terrorisms are reactive against modern ideals, but of historical necessity themselves also a quintessentially modern phenomenon, quickly absorbed into the modern dialectic of "freedom and terror." The "enemy," noble or ignoble, is not so much in opposition *to* as it is a contributing part *of* this modern dynamic. Ashbery's poetry, but not Whitman's, expresses this condition, yet Fletcher's treatment of Ashbery largely misses this set of issues—so much so, that one wonders why Fletcher didn't choose to consider instead the distinguished poetry of A. R. Ammons, who is a more obvious exemplar of the tradition Fletcher represents. Ultimately, Fletcher's book charts the rhythmic implications of Whitman's *legacy* with astonishing precision, but fails to deliver a full account of the *overall* rhythmic complexity of our contemporary condition.

Faced by such a barrage of rhythmic "angles," an accelerating need is also felt for a wisdom appropriate to this advanced modern age. In contravention of Blumenberg's legitimation of the modern age as a successful overcoming of Gnosticism, Harold Bloom proposes that it is precisely in Gnosticism that modern wisdom shall be found. My discussion above, both in the chapter on Blumenberg and at the end of this current chapter, already suggests that this is a predictable and integrable component of the overall pace of modernity. On the descending slope of this book's waking dream we must face the reactive force of modern wisdom, as exemplified in the work of Harold Bloom.

6

Divagation at the Crossroads: In Search of Modern Wisdom

In a volume written after a brush with death and the abandoning of prior draft material, Harold Bloom has taken up the tradition of wisdom literature in the West and outlined a highly personal canon to which he finds it most necessary to return: "*Where Shall Wisdom Be Found?* rises out of personal need, reflecting a quest for sagacity that might solace and clarify the traumas of aging, of recovery from grave illness, and of grief for the loss of beloved friends."[179] It is the work of an elder statesman of the literary tradition, reflecting a lifelong preoccupation with the standards of reading proper to the literary canon and, here, specifically, to the vein of wisdom literature found within it.

Bloom's volume serves as a genealogy of the Western canon in particular so far as the relation of religion and literature is concerned, and given Bloom's growing sense of himself as a religious as well as literary critic, it offers a fruitful point of departure for considering recent developments in Bloom's own canon. In the next chapter, I will return to Bloom's earlier tetralogy (*The Anxiety of Influence*, *A Map of Misreading*, *Kabbalah and Criticism*, and *Poetry and Repression*) in an attempt to map out an alternative to the religiously governed trajectory Bloom follows in the second half of his career. The alternative I propose moves from literary figuration into mathematical extensions of language, and so offers a "centrifugal" alternative to Bloom's increasingly "centripetal" perspective. Given my concurrence in Blumenberg's insistence on the lack of any religious appeal in the legitimation of the modern condition, such an alternative will be necessary for the reading of a modern literary pace, which I try out on a particularly advanced text, John Ashbery's *Three Poems*, in the final chapter of this volume.

---

179. Harold Bloom, *Where Shall Wisdom Be Found?* (New York: Riverhead, 2004), 1.

Bloom's choice of wisdom literature begins predictably enough with the Hebrew Bible—"(no Jew should call it the Old Testament)" (WW, 101)—focusing particularly on the Books of Job and Ecclesiastes. Yet as a bardolater of long-standing it should come as little surprise that Bloom identifies the Shakespearean corpus as the central body of Wisdom Literature in the Western tradition. Although, as he admits, he "cannot recall ever reading (or listening to) an account of Shakespeare's wisdom," nonetheless Bloom asserts that Shakespeare, this "most inventive of writers," is "also the supreme creator of wisdom literature" (WW, 103). A considerable part of the challenge facing the reader of Bloom's recent volume is to come to some understanding of just what is intended in this context by "wisdom literature." What becomes apparent in the course of the book is that Shakespeare's concomitant first rank as imaginative and wise is anything but a coincidence: Bloom's conception of wisdom literature is a romantic one in which wisdom is the fruit of imaginative labor. But there are various strains of romanticism, and Bloom's ultimately does more justice to the legacy of Emerson than to the Shakespearean one he professedly most admires.

The book is divided into three main parts. After a brief introduction, the first part, "The Power of Wisdom," itself divides into three sections. In the first section of the first part, Bloom provides the discussions of Job and Ecclesiastes mentioned previously, which are followed by a section on the ancient Greek tradition, focusing on Plato's quarrel with Homer. The third section of the first part, rounding out the "foundations" of wisdom literature in the West, is devoted to the twinned figures of Cervantes and Shakespeare. In the second part, "The Greatest Ideas Are The Greatest Events," Bloom again pairs off figures, this time into four sets: Montaigne and Francis Bacon, Samuel Johnson and Goethe, Emerson and Nietzsche, Freud and Proust. In the third part, Bloom returns from the modern to the earlier tradition of "Christian Wisdom," providing a reading of the gnostic Gospel of Thomas followed by a chapter on "Saint Augustine and Reading." The book is rounded out by a short coda, "Nemesis and Wisdom."

Across Bloom's volume there is a further division which pertains to the entire investigation: the distinction between a wisdom of the covenant and a wisdom which stands outside any such relation. In the introduction, Bloom cites a number of proverbs from the *Pirke Aboth*, the "Sayings (or Wisdom) of the Fathers," itself a late addition to the Mishnah or "Oral Torah" (WW, 4-5). As his favorite aphorism Bloom selects the admonition, "You are not required to complete the work, but neither are you free to desist from it," and recounts that, "however many classes had to be taught and however much writing had to be done, when I was ill, depressed, or weary, I rallied, with Tarphon's cognitive music in my inner ear" (WW, 6). Bloom closes with a passage from Rabbi Akiba, "the greatest figure among the founders of Judaism as we know it today" (WW, 6), remarking of it, "if wisdom is trust in the Covenant, then I cannot see how wisdom can go further" (WW, 7). That Bloom identifies Shakespeare as the greatest of wisdom writers indicates that wisdom does go further, but only at the expense of the breaking of the Covenant. As a work about wisdom, Bloom's book is itself a story of this breaking.

THE POWER OF WISDOM

Already in the *Book of Job*, that Covenant which "the Hebrews strove to trust in" (WW, 48) is severely questioned. Leviathan, which as depicted in *Job* dramatizes "the sanctified tyranny of nature over man" (WW, 15), "makes no covenant with anyone, and the Book of Job is skeptical as to whether its God is still interested in covenants" (WW, 18). Of the writer of this book, Bloom remarks, "whoever the poet was, he strikes me as no more pious than Herman Melville, who did not exactly trust in the Covenant, any more than Captain Ahab did" (WW, 15). Just as Melville called *Moby-Dick* "a wicked book," Bloom reads the wisdom of the *Book of Job* as "more wicked than not" (WW, 15). Wickedly, Yahweh taunts Job, asking him of Leviathan, "*Will he make a covenant with thee?*" (cited, WW, 15). Bloom reports: "Even as a child, I blinked at this divine sarcasm" (WW, 17). Pointedly, brutally, we are taught to acknowledge the natural limits of the human condition, and at the beginning of his book Bloom effectively defines the genre by remarking that "wisdom literature teaches us to accept natural limits" (WW, 4).

To further his reading of *Job*, Bloom enlists two pillars of the Protestant reception, John Calvin and Kierkegaard, whom together Bloom calls "the most powerful commentators on Job's book, for me" (WW, 13). Bloom reads Calvin as the lobbyist for "Job's Comforters," who "take joy in God's wisdom, but pragmatically ... are more satanic than the accuser" (WW, 18). Such extended satanism is the consequence of reveling in God's wisdom in "a poem where God knows only the wisdom of force," and Calvin serves as their apologist, "who strengthens their case with a kind of mad eloquence" (WW, 18). Kierkegaard, "subtler than Calvin," diagnoses this exacerbation, the sadomasochistic wish for an extension of force, as our *desire*. Rather than being overcome by Leviathan, for Kierkegaard it is the Creator who overcomes Job, and us. But Kierkegaard turns the internalization of that "fear of the Lord which is the beginning of Wisdom," and which begins as a covert desire for punishment and self-abasement, in the direction of the cultivation of sincerity: "So be sincere with yourself, fix your eyes upon Job; even though he terrifies you, it is not this he wishes, if you yourself do not wish it" (cited, WW, 19). The cultivation of such sincerity in the face of force opens onto a sublime experience of that which transcends our power: "Leviathan and Behemoth are *beyond* Job, even as the Creator is," and thus "the Book of Job offers wisdom, but it is not anything we can comprehend" (WW, 19).

Bloom's last citation from *Job* ends: "And unto man he said, Behold, the fear of the Lord, that is wisdom; and to depart from evil is understanding" (cited, WW, 20). As the experience of a sublime wisdom, the effect of *The Book of Job* as Bloom understands it is specifically literary. Commenting on works of Blake and Melville deriving from the tradition of *Job*, Bloom remarks: "Truly the beasts *are* the poem, and are the emblems of the incommensurateness of Yahweh's wisdom and humankind's" (WW, 21). Poetry is a power of contagion, by which, to borrow a line from Shakespeare which Bloom weakly misreads elsewhere, we are struck "more dead than a great reckoning in a little room."[180] Poetic wisdom is as much or more a power of death as a power of life.

Bloom's commentary on Koholeth's Ecclesiastes is even more personal, and takes as its pivot the Paterian recognition that "we have an interval, and then our place knows us no more" (cited, WW, 1). The repeated insistence upon this transience opens up depth upon depth, in famous passages Bloom cites at length. "If wisdom in Job costs too much for its confirmation, so in Koheleth all wisdom becomes personal, fragments of a confession" (WW, 28). In this personalism Bloom discerns one of the roots of Shakespeare, for the repeated revelations of depths beneath depths engenders an abysmal dizziness and finally a recognition that "this is the wisdom of annihilation, of Hamlet and Lear, and perhaps of Shakespeare himself" (WW, 30). It is ultimately to our own bounded existence that this wisdom refers, and "few can come into their seventies without a chill at these repetitive rhythms" (WW, 26). In the context of such wisdom, nihilism is incarnated most focally in the recognition of personal annihilation, as Hamlet and Lear evince most powerfully, extending the wisdom of Koholeth.

From the treatment of Job and Ecclesiastes, Bloom turns to a chapter on the Greeks, tracking "Plato's Contest with Homer." Here Bloom attempts to defend literature from philosophy and so rescue Homer from Plato. But this defense comes in the paired assertions that, on the one hand, Homer needs no defending, and, on the other, that we are all shaped by the literary (if not the philosophical) legacy of Plato. Bloom openly and unapologetically declares himself "*alogos*, averse to philosophy, since first I fell in love with the poetry of William Blake and Hart Crane" (WW, 36); as he reports elsewhere, the reading of Crane began in his tenth year, and a volume of Crane's poems, given to him by his sister on his twelfth birthday, was the first book he ever owned.[181] Just as Bloom identifies Plato as the fountainhead of the school of resentment, it is clear that he himself resents Plato,

---

180. The line is Touchstone's in *As You Like It*. Incomprehensibly, Bloom follows the weak interpretation of the line proposed by Charles Nicholl; see Harold Bloom, *The Anxiety of Influence: A Theory of Poetry*, 2nd ed., with a new preface (New York: Oxford, 1997), xlv.

181. Harold Bloom, *Agon: Towards a Theory of Revisionism* (New York: Oxford University, 1982), 252.

remarking that he regularly rereads *The Republic* "to receive a wisdom that chastens my fury against all ideology" (WW, 36).

Yet how is this all to work? The dilemma, as Bloom recognizes it, is clear: "wisdom and literature cannot be brought together either with or without Plato and his Socrates" (WW, 45). Wisdom and literature cannot be brought together *with* Plato because Plato himself promotes philosophy at the expense of the poets, and most specifically Homer. But the two also cannot be brought together *without* Plato, since "all of our still current Alexandrian culture—pagan, Jewish, Muslim, Christian—was and remains Platonist, and you cannot harvest Hellenism without incessantly reading Plato" (WW, 51). Bloom stops short of declaring that the Platonic legacy is a form of ideational contamination, but following Emerson he does suggest that Shakespeare's Hamlet descends directly from the Platonic quandary, and "Hamlet, like Plato, I regard as fascinating bad news" (WW, 51).

Invoking Pierre Hadot's recently translated work, *Philosophy as a Way of Life*,[182] Bloom sets the battle between poetry and philosophy yet another way: philosophy is best when it is practiced as a way of life, but the study of philosophy "is death;" in contrast, "I do not think that poetry offers a way of life (except for a handful like Shelley and Hart Crane)" (WW, 62), but the exoteric implication of Bloom's volume is that the study, the reading, of poetry is life-engendering. Here we have a curious reversal of the "esoteric" character of philosophy which excludes Bloom by his own self-avowal: "We cannot all become philosophers, but we can follow the poets in their ancient quarrel with philosophy." Poetry cannot offer a way of life because of its largesse: "it is too large, too Homeric, for that" (WW, 62). Despite Bloom's insistence that we "need not choose," the practical moral is that the esoteric lifestyle of philosophical pursuit is but the resentful projection of an unattainable Homeric greatness:

> Homer's is poetic argument, and not the mode of Plato's Socrates, who seeks perfection of the work, the life, the state. And Homer's lies are beyond time and so against time, unlike the "noble" lies Plato assigns to his Socrates. Perhaps Plato (or his Socrates) was the first and last philosopher, even as Jesus was the first and last Christian. We do not have to choose between Plato and Homer, though Plato wants us to choose. If finally we must choose, read Homer. (WW, 63)

The latter part of Bloom's chapter turns instead to a variety of comparisons between the Judaic and Hellenistic traditions, thus revisiting Biblical themes first addressed in the previous chapter. Bloom discerns the critical difference between the traditions in the nature of their respective God or gods. He puts his vision of this difference most succinctly when he states

---

182. Pierre Hadot, *Philosophy as a Way of Life: Spiritual Exercises from Socrates to Foucault*, ed. Arnold Davidson, trans. Michael Chase (Oxford: Blackwell, 1995).

that "Achilles is the son of a goddess, but David is the Son of God" (WW, 71). Zeus makes covenant with no one, and Bloom is "haunted" by W. K. C. Guthrie's assertion that "[w]hat made the gods approach our level was an element of human nature in them, not a hint of the divine in us" (cited, WW, 64). Consequently the nature of the agon faced by human heroes in the two contexts is entirely different: in the Hebraic context the struggle is a struggle to win blessing, whereas in the Greek context the hero inhabits a tragic void halfway between the human and the divine (WW, 70). Yet what exercises Bloom even more than these respective contests is the implicit contest between these two traditions, so irreconcilable and yet both so necessary to the culture we inhabit. What we might call "Bloom's agon" comes from the yoking together of these two traditions, in which the key spokespersons, Homer and the J writer, "have absolutely nothing in common except their uncanny sublimity, and they are sublime in very different modes" (WW, 68). As Bloom goes on to remark, in the Western tradition "cognition goes one way and its spiritual life goes in quite another" (WW, 68). From the perspective of Bloom's own intellectual development what is most provocative about his wisdom book is that in one central regard he undercuts (or perhaps, indeed, outpaces) the Gnostic stance he has previously invoked to brook and then to break a community of cognition and religious impulse, declaring here that "... growing old and ill teaches me that being matters more than knowing" (WW, 97-98), and doubting of wisdom "whether or not it can be identified with the truth which might make us free" (WW, 284). Wisdom literature renounces the Gnostic quest for transcendence, teaching us instead "to accept natural limits" (WW, 4), and what is most surprising in this book is the extent to which Bloom embraces this wisdom, though one intimates an ontological "hypergnosticism" behind Bloom's more exoteric counseling of the wisdom of natural limits. Exoterically, in place of a Gnostic articulation Bloom favors a balancing of the wisdoms of the two traditions. Yet the newfound preference for being over knowing ultimately skews Bloom's presentation in favor of the Biblical tradition, and this makes the incapacity to trust in a covenant with God more pressing than ever. In this sense, we might speak of Bloom as cultivating a "negative Gnosticism," on analogy with negative theology.

In the third installment of the Bloomian foundations we meet next Cervantes and Shakespeare, who together indicate modern strategies for literary transcendence in a world beyond traditional religious covenant. Cervantes' transcendental strategy is located in Quixote's exaltation of the will (WW, 86). To this Bloom contrasts Hamlet's cognitively induced ataraxia, and it is in this comparison of volitional to cognitive outstripping that "[t]he fundamental difference between Cervantes and Shakespeare is exemplified" (WW, 78). In both cases there is a sublime capaciousness which induces in the reader a sense that the literary work dominates any experience of it the reader might have. Cervantes' work is a mirror "held up not to nature but to the reader" (WW, 85), and the quixotic nature of Cervantes' quest reflects a literary absolute in a world crazed by reading (WW, 86). Yet Cervantes' masterpiece does reflect as well the historical reality in which Cervantes composed: in the Knight's quest we find an expression of Cervantes' own experience as "the most battered of eminent writers" (WW, 84). In Cervantes "we feel the burden of the experiential, whereas Shakespeare is uncanny, since nearly all of his experience was theatrical" (WW, 88), yet this dovetails with Bloom's insistence that Shakespeare "did not write the poems of his climate" (WW, 107) but rather "the poetry of all climes and climates, and of all seasons of the soul" (WW, 189).

It is appropriate, then, that Bloom should offer a reading of *Lear* in the context provided by his previous presentation of Ecclesiastes, where he sees the subjective roots of Shakespeare's withering nihilism, and in particular Lear's Emersonian dictum that "nothing begets nothing" (cited, WW, 103). Shakespearean nihilism outstrips the "personal gnosis" of the near-contemporary Giordano Bruno, and speaking of both *Lear* and *Macbeth* Bloom affirms that a "still more negative intuition haunts both of these apocalyptic tragedies" (WW, 108). The paradox of Shakespearean wisdom lies, then, in the fact that it is "so negative when his art is so wealthy beyond wisdom," and Bloom finds himself "puzzled, even bewildered" (WW, 109) in the face of this fact. But what is the relevant value here? Is it the wisdom which Shakespeare delivers, or the art which embodies it? Is the wisdom itself of value, or is it merely the paradoxical carrier of that art which Bloom values above all others?

There is no obvious response to this question beyond pointing out the integral character of wisdom literature as both literary and wise. But Bloom does provide a clue to his own personal balancing of these demands in the trajectory of his discussion from Hamlet to Lear and, finally, to Macbeth, Bloom's personal favorite among Shakespeare's high tragedies.[183] Bloom points out that "Hamlet represents Shakespeare's cognitive power, while Macbeth is Shakespeare's own poetic imagination" (WW, 112); hence Bloom's trajectory moves by implication from the "fascinating bad news" of cognitive drive to the sublime pathos of the imagination. Bloom points out that "*Hamlet* is the ancestral work for all Romanticism" (WW, 110), but in Bloom's canon it is *Macbeth* which most directly points out his own personal investment in the Romantic tradition, grounded in the Romantic conception of imaginative power. Yet the character Macbeth "has force but no inner authority" (WW, 115), and so Bloom's reading suggests that in Shakespeare it is the ambient grounding in traditions of wisdom literature which confirms the legitimacy of the literary imagination. In contrast to

---

183. Harold Bloom, *Shakespeare: The Invention of the Human* (New York: Riverhead, 1998), 545.

Macbeth, Lear "is the image of lost yet legitimate authority" (WW, 115). Perhaps the thoroughly negative character of Shakespeare's wisdom is just what is needed to afford him such a wide literary berth. If so, to recognize this does not diminish the value of the Shakespearean corpus, but only augments the uncanniness of its author. It also leaves it radically unclear in exactly what sense Shakespeare should be called an author of wisdom literature, but such, perhaps, is the nature of Shakespeare's wisdom. I need only add a final word from Goethe, by way of Bloom's paraphrase:

> Goethe credits Shakespeare with the original insight that the function of stage drama is to expand the audience's imaginative and cognitive powers, but only by hindering them. That, according to Goethe, is why there is "no end to Shakespeare." (WW, 181)

THE GREATEST IDEAS ARE THE GREATEST EVENTS

In this section we continue our pilgrimage towards Nietzsche's diagnosis of European nihilism and beyond. As mentioned above, this part of Bloom's book is divided into four chapters, each pairing off two contrasting writers, but Bloom's discussions of these eight writers are not all equally illuminating. By an antithetical maxim, Bloom's commentary on that lineage of "modern wisdom" with which he would find himself most directly allied, circuitously passing from Montaigne through Johnson and Emerson to Freud, is least auspicious; it is in the contrasting figures of Goethe, Nietzsche and Proust that Bloom presents us with the more immediately dazzling insights.[184] This stems not from a lack of real power in Bloom's remarks on the nearer line, but rather from the extent to which his engagement with such direct forbears must, in proper Bloomian fashion, remain occluded. The clue provided by a recurring consideration of the problem of plagiarism and its status is therefore all the more helpful. The discussion of Montaigne is dominated by Montaigne's feigned incapacities, and in particular his claim of poor memory, which supports his appropriation of an entire tradition of wisdom literature into the body of his own text, swallowed whole, as it were. Bloom quotes a passage from Montaigne's essay, "Of Books," in which Montaigne declares, "Let people see in what I borrow whether I have known how to choose what would enhance my theme. For I make others say what I cannot say so well, now through the weakness of my language, now through the weakness of my understanding. I do not count my borrowings, I weigh them" (cited, WW, 121). Montaigne goes on to note that he sometimes deliberately suppresses the authors of these borrowings and confounds them with his own, so that he will "hold in check the temerity of those hasty condemnations that are tossed at all sorts of writings of men still living," thus

---

184. The treatment of Francis Bacon does not mount to this level; in Bacon's particular faceoff, Montaigne is the easy winner.

mixing the reader's battles with Montaigne with those of the reader against Plutarch and Seneca. Ultimately Montaigne excuses these unattributed incorporations to lack of memory, on the one hand, and to their needfulness on the other, acknowledging that "my soil is not at all capable of producing certain too rich flowers that I find sown there" (cited, WW, 122). Relying on his prodigious memory, Bloom renders explicit and indeed theorizes what in Montaigne remains an immanent literary praxis.[185]

Wisdom is passed down through the tradition. But it is the quality of Montaigne's incorporation of this traditional wisdom which distinguishes him: an easy and commanding reception which integrates these gems into its own carpet. Pascal in turn, and by way of contrast, appropriates Montaigne rigidly and in a way which is self-indicting, "since sometimes we hear the pious son castigating the unbelieving father in the father's inescapable accents." Pascal "would be convicted of plagiarism in any American school or university, with their rather literal notions of what constitutes plagiarism" (WW, 127). In his discussion of Samuel Johnson, Bloom considers the Johnsonian Burchfield on the topic of invention as the essence of language. Yet such invention inevitably involves appropriation, and Burchfield "sagely reminds us that plagiarism is a relatively modern legalism" (WW, 161). "It remains true that all strong literature is a kind of theft" (WW, 161), but the more vexing question is what distinguishes strong from weak appropriation, and there is more than a hint that Bloom finds the rigidity of Pascal's appropriation from Montaigne aligned with the sort of legalism that underwrites modern conceptions of plagiarism, and that threatens the vitality of the tradition of Wisdom literature which Bloom seeks to preserve. Against the Pascalophile Eliot, Bloom invokes Emerson: "As men's prayers are a disease of the will, so are their creeds a disease of the intellect" (cited, WW, 191).

Despite his own preternatural powers of memory, Bloom notices that he is often at a loss to locate individual passages from Emerson, which often "blend together in the mind" (WW, 202). There is a deep "overall" effect in the writing of Emerson—which perhaps stands behind what is most American in the tradition of Abstract Expressionism—making Emerson's journals, rather than his essays, the pinnacle of his written expression. Their value is not to be found in the individual entry or aperçu; rather, "[h]uge as they are, they need to be read complete, because Emerson's mind has become the mind of America" (WW, 203). In the face of such capaciousness (and here we must, of course, think also of Bloom) niceties of attribution begin to blur. Such capaciousness expresses a freedom which "is not primarily a formlessness," and is powerfully infectious: "Emerson's power of contamination was unique even in his own century, and even writers who backed away

---

185. Compare Jean Starobinski, *Montaigne in Motion*, esp. 106-20.

from him could not fail to absorb his stance" (WW, 203). Emerson himself expresses this in the gnomic wisdom of the essay, "Self-Reliance": "In every work of genius we recognize our own rejected thoughts: they come back to us with a certain alienated majesty" (cited, WW, 200). Emerson's way to read is "to take back what is your own, wherever you may find it" (WW, 201). Such a conception nullifies the legalistic concern with plagiarism. Emerson is the original American Repo Man, our own Adam Kadmon.

Nietzsche, by way of contrast, "had too many precursors" (WW, 210), and his reading threatens to drown in an ocean of echoes, including most proximately echoes of Emerson. But rather than dwell on these anxieties of influence, Bloom turns to Nietzsche's "wisdom at its most mature," opening a powerful and idiosyncratic avenue into his doctrine of the eternal return. "Nietzsche's deepest teaching," Bloom tells us, "is that authentic meaning is painful, and that the pain itself is the meaning. Between pain and its meaning comes a memory of pain that then becomes a memorable meaning" (WW, 210). Bloom identifies this as a "fiercely Homeric analysis of all significant memory" (WW, 79), all the more troubling to Bloom himself, given that "ever since I was a small boy, I have judged poems on the basis of just how memorable they immediately seemed." Nietzsche teaches that "the poem that has more meaning, or starts more meaning going, is the poem that gives (or commemorates) more pain" (WW, 219).

Nietzsche's vision of aesthetic arrest as a form of pain functions as a masochistic reduction of Goethe's reading of Shakespearean drama as proliferating in meaning through a process of hindrance. Goethe had his own form of this wisdom, which goes by the name of "renunciation." In the second half of his literary career, Goethe gave up the desires associated with his earlier life and thereby achieved in his writing a "freedom from outdated literary conventions." Personal fulfillment is cast out: "The present is renounced, or surrendered to time" (WW, 180). This is an extraordinarily belated version of classical wisdom, which can only be achieved at the expense of an infinitely subtle play of irony and in the context of a classical conception of *Bildung* which Bloom finds to be of a past age: "I am not at all certain that Goethe's wisdom is still available to us, whether we are European or American" (WW, 181). In the late masterpiece of Goethean renunciation, the "Trilogy of Passion" elegies completed in 1824, memorializing the anguish inspired in the seventy-four year old poet by his love for the nineteen year old Ulrike von Levetzow, Goethe anticipates the Freud of "Mourning and Melancholia." Recording his experience of absolute ruin, he laments: "I have lost the whole world, I have lost myself" (cited, WW, 183). The Romantic reaction exemplified by Wordsworth will transmute personal loss into imaginative gain, but Goethe remains closer to the perspective of the ancient Greeks: "Passional loss is not poetic enhancement, whether in Achilles or Goethe, who once had been the genius of "happiness and astonishment'''" (WW, 183). Bloom finds in this old age of Goethe his most significant contribution to wisdom. It is perhaps the canonical version of wisdom closest to the writings of Hans Blumenberg.

Nietzsche's appropriation of the classical tradition retains a visceral character lacking in this late period of Goethe, but at the expense, as we have already seen above, of a massive drive to reduction. Nietzsche's "fiercely Homeric" analysis of the pain of poetry, which "so mingles the ascetic and the aesthetic that we cannot undo their mutual contamination" (WW, 216-17), leaves Nietzsche with "no alterative but to accuse the poet of nihilism," and this moves toward an "antithetical poetics not yet fully formulated, yet lurking in his forebodings of an uncannier nihilism than any yet known" (WW, 216). Here we begin to grasp at least one strand in the provenance of Bloom's "antithetical criticism" and the cognitive burden it must face: that it devolves, at least in this respect, from the fiercest internal response within the classical tradition itself to the resentment of art posed by Plato in his contest with Homer. How are we to reconcile this with Bloom's own fiercely held commitment to the Hebraic tradition? A first response must lie in the recognition that Bloom's antithetical inspiration lies equally, if not indeed more, in the Gnostic tradition, which Bloom will strongly misread in this book as a purification of and return to the earliest traditions of Judaism. We may take it as a maxim for reading Bloom's own writing, sanctioning a distinction between the esoteric and the exoteric, when he remarks of Jesus' pronouncements in the Gnostic Gospel of Thomas: "Many of the hidden sayings are so purely antithetical that they can be interpreted only by our seeing what they severely decline to affirm" (WW, 260). Severely declining to affirm, we may hazard, is Bloom's immanent, negative version of Gnostic wisdom, and represents an ultimate extension of the wisdom of hindrance that passes through Shakespeare, Goethe, Nietzsche and Freud. This "declination" represents not a nihilism at the level of doctrine, but deeper still at the level of assertion itself. It extends the Emersonian "nothing is got for nothing" into the practices of writing and reading, leading on to Beckett and the dilemma of the closing of the Western Canon upon which Bloom has long meditated in such ventures as *Ruin the Sacred Truths* and *The Western Canon*.[186]

Curiously (apparently even to Bloom himself) it is with the Christian Samuel Johnson that Bloom identifies most personally among the wisdom writers discussed here—in an earlier self-description Bloom tagged himself as the "Yiddisher Doctor Johnson."[187] Johnson's struggle with madness was "incessant" and his melancholia, unlike Goethe, "never far away" (WW,

---

186. Harold Bloom, *Ruin the Sacred Truths: Poetry and Belief from the Bible to the Present* (Cambridge: Harvard, 1989); Harold Bloom, *The Western Canon: The Books and School of the Ages* (New York: Harcourt Brace & Company, 1994).

187. Bloom, *Ruin the Sacred Truths*, flyleaf.

168). Thoroughly aware of the dangers of solitude, which Johnson "hated," this solitude nonetheless enhanced his "darker wisdom" as exemplified in his prayers, in which "he endlessly chastises himself for not studying and writing incessantly" (WW, 166). It is to these battles of writing and reading that Bloom's own wisdom tends, and these are inevitably battles in and with solitude. In counterpoint with his prayers, Johnson's response to Boswell that "a man is not obliged to do all that he can" (WW, 166) echoes Bloom's favorite from the aphorisms, already mentioned above, Tarphon's admonition that "[y]ou are not required to complete the work, but neither are you free to desist from it" (cited, WW, 6). Bloom will extend both by speaking of the "interpretive challenge and its prize" as "more life into a time without boundaries" (WW, 259). Reading, for Bloom, is reparative, but neither a vice nor a virtue, and although we read specifically "to repair our solitude ... the better we read, the more solitary we become" (WW, 101). Whitehead's characterization of religion as what humans do with their solitude is not out of place here, and points to the deep association of religion and criticism in Bloom's work, suggesting that if Bloom follows a *poetic* ideal of writing, he nonetheless practices a *religion* of reading. Bloom's reverence for Shakespeare's work may be exemplified most powerfully by the uncanny withdrawal into which its author repairs to write. This absent scene of writing is the solitary locus of a sort of textual branding. The pain with which a literary passage impresses itself is a mark of its own self-defense, and hence marks the costs we face in making it our own.

In the tradition of the modern novel, solitude is thematized in terms of jealousy, and "[s]exual jealousy is the most novelistic of circumstances, just as incest, according to Shelley, is the most poetical" (WW, 235). It is thus not surprising that jealousy and the erotics of isolation stand at the center of Proust's *Remembrance of Things Past*. What renders Proust's treatment of them particularly valuable, however, is the way in which they are made into carriers for the themes of truth and fiction, thus focusing the tradition inaugurated by Cervantes through a privileged, psychological lens. In the process of this most subtle novelistic treatment of human psychology, Proust is able to express the way in which truth and fiction are made issues of burning human interest, and so is able to connect these epistemological themes to the most intimate experiences of temporal duration. The aesthetic search becomes the erotic search, and then in turn the erotic search takes on aesthetic goals, so that "[t]he historicizing aesthete—John Ruskin, say, or Walter Pater—becomes the archetype of the jealous lover, who searches into lost time not for a person but for an epiphany or moment-of-moments, a privileged fiction of duration" (WW, 241). Here we are given a privileged instance of that literary epiphany which takes over the traditional role played by the experience of the divine. This privilege is located in the nature of this experience as simultaneously literary and about the literary, revealed by way of the psychological depths opened up by the derealizing experience of jealousy. "Proust warily, but with the sureness of a great beast descending on its helpless prey, approaches the heart of his vision or [sic] jealousy, his sense that the emotion is akin to what Freud named as the defense of isolation, in which all context is turned away, and a dangerous present replaces all past and future" (WW, 251). Proust's wisdom teaches a transvaluation of time which perches precariously on the edge of a psychological abyss, knowing nothing. In this, it resembles the particular brand of Gnosticism to which Bloom turns in his final section (WW, 267). But even this hope for transvaluation threatens to be undercut by the bitterness of jealousy's dialectic:

> The jealous lover fears that he has been castrated, that his place in life has been taken, that true time is over for him. His only recourse is to search for lost time, in the hopeless hope that the aesthetic recovery of illusion and of experience alike will deceive him in a higher mode than he fears to have been deceived in already. (WW, 256)

CHRISTIAN WISDOM

The clear focus of Bloom's concern in this last section of the book is the Gospel of Thomas, which, despite the hesitancies of scholars, Bloom interprets as a Gnostic text. This, however, is only the first, moderate step in Bloom's reading strategy, for he goes on to see the Gnosticism expounded therein as a belated expression of an earlier Judaic tradition of proto-Kabbalistic wisdom. In this way, Bloom draws the Gospel of Thomas into close dialogue with the Yahweh of the J Writer, freeing it from an agonistic relation with the more orthodox Christian legacy.[188] For this reason, his attempt to counterbalance his reading of Thomas with a chapter on Augustine is largely unsuccessful, for he fails (or refuses?) to remark on Augustine's antignostic orientation in any serious way. At one point in the chapter on the Gospel of Saint Thomas, Bloom even refers to the "surely peculiar ... modern habit of employing "gnosis" or "Gnosticism" as a conservative or institutionalized Christian term of abuse" without recognizing the pedigree of this Christian antignosticism. Even if Bloom's point is that in this modern context Christian antignosticism threatens to become a "peculiar" form of self-hatred, this still does not by itself exempt Augustine from a similar charge, for that would require acknowledging the legitimacy of Augustine's response to gnostic dualism in a way that Bloom seems anything but willing to admit. Something like Blumenberg's diagnosis of the failure of the Church Fathers to synthesize a definitive overcoming of Gnosticism would be needed to repair the gap in Bloom's argument.

---

188. It is at this point that the venture of Bloom's Book of Wisdom opens out most powerfully onto his next volume, *Jesus and Yahweh: The Names Divine* (New York: Riverhead Books, 2005).

It is in a truly peculiar internal dialogue with the J writer that the Jesus of the Gospel of Thomas finds himself. Bloom preaches a "gnostic sermon" whose chief rhetorical figure is the suggestion that the two are convergent in their respective "earlinesses," i.e. their exemption from an otherwise pervasive sense of belatedness. Here, Bloom appeals to the work of Moshe Idel, "the great revisionist scholar of Kabbalah, [who] persuades me that what seem gnostic elements in Kabbalah actually stem from an archaic Jewish religion, anything but normative, of which what we call Gnosticism may be an echo or a parody." Equally, "Christian Gnosticism also may be a belated version of some of the teachings of Jesus" (WW, 262-63). Bloom uses this parallel to couch his hypothesis that the Gospel of Thomas comes from "Q, or from some *ur*-Q, which would mean that there were proto-gnostic elements in the teachings of Jesus" (WW, 262), stressing also the uniform belatedness (both historical and conceptual) of the canonical gospels. In the wisdom of Thomas, "the normative nostalgia for the virtues of the fathers is totally absent:" the gnostic Jesus "has not come to praise famous men" (WW, 264), as in the famous passage from Ecclesiastes which Bloom discussed earlier. We may take it, however, that Bloom's emphasis on the normativity of this nostalgia exempts also the Yahweh of the J Writer as Bloom envisions him, so this provides no relevant distinction between Bloom's J and *ur*-Q.

Instead, what unfolds in Bloom's chapter on Thomas, which he presents as a "gnostic sermon" followed by a "postsermon reflection on the allied strangenesses of Gnosticism, and of Christianity in any of its varieties" (WW, 269), is an elite vision of a purified form of the American religion, potentially available to Jew and Christian alike, in which the central American feature comes in an emphasis on isolation. To the two convictions of *gnosis*, that Creation and Fall are two descriptions of the same event, and that what is best is uncreated, Bloom identifies a third element added by the American Religion, "if our freedom is to be complete." This is that the "ultimate spark of the pre-created light must be alone, or at least alone with Jesus" (WW, 261). These three "convictions" parallel the three "secret sayings" of the Gospel of Thomas as Bloom imagines them in his sermon: that Jesus is identical to the stranger God, not the creator God of Moses and Adam; that the stranger God calls to Thomas; and Thomas' recognition "that he already is in the place of rest, alone with his twin," Jesus (WW, 261).

The Jesus of the Gospel of Thomas is for Bloom not a God, but rather a wandering sage, "unsponsored and free" (WW, 259). Passing by, he teaches us to become passersby; he is "a remarkably Whitmanian Jesus, and there is little in the Gospel of Thomas that would not have been accepted by Emerson, Thoreau, and Whitman" (WW, 260). The passage which this Jesus preaches may perhaps help us to understand how *gnosis* is compatible with Bloom's earlier, personal declaration that as he becomes older, being becomes more valuable than knowing. For "the *gnosis* of who we were, when we were "in the light"" is only what "*begins* to make us free" (WW, 264, my emphasis). From this we pass on to a second step, in which "we bring the axis of vision and the axis of things together again" (WW, 265). Such is the form of *Bloom's* hyperrealistic ambition, a religious cultivation of that earlier "supermimetic" stance I will discuss in the following chapter. Finally, addressing itself to "a subtle elite, those capable of knowing," the Gospel perfects those "who then through knowing can come to see what Jesus insists is plainly visible before them, indeed all around them" (WW, 267). This vision is of a particularly ontological sort, for it lays being bare: not the created being of this world of sorrows, but the uncreated spark of a being which antecedes this veil of tears. "As one who passes by, he urges his seekers to learn to be passersby, to cease hastening to the temporal death of business and busyness that the world miscalls life" (WW, 267). This resembles nothing so much as, and even helps provides a point of entry for, Heidegger's intensive preoccupation in *Contributions to Philosophy* with the Hölderlin-inspired "passing of the last God."[189] Bloom's hyperGnosticism is powerfully negative and heterodoxly ontological.

But throughout Bloom's so-called "gnostic sermon" there are intimations that Gnosticism is a belated, theological version of what Bloom is really after. He refers to the Valentinian scheme which his sermon follows as having "features so broad that by it we can chart most other varieties of gnostic religion" (WW, 268). This is rather reminiscent of a much earlier statement Bloom made about his own scheme of revisionary ratios in the 1979 essay, "The Breaking of Form," where he remarks that the sequence of revisionary ratios "is *there* in the sense that image and trope tend to follow over-determined patterns of evasion."[190] Neither of these passages gives us the final word on how seriously these schemes are to be taken (or indeed how they are to be taken seriously), but each has the shape of a lens. In the current case, what we are ultimately to see is nothing theological at all, but "what I would suggest is an ancient humanism, one that is difficult to reconcile either with late Judaism or early Christianity" (WW, 270-71). This ancient humanism would presumably coincide with the "negative Gnosticism" and "hypergnosticism" I have referred to above.

This last section of Bloom's book casts retrospective light, in particular, on the treatment of Emerson in the book's second part. In one respect, it is a simple continuation of a quandary Bloom himself admits there. That the elite version of Emersonian perfectionism spawns in its historical wake all sorts of pernicious reductions is paralleled here by the relation in which

---

189. Martin Heidegger, *Contributions to Philosophy: From Enowning*, trans. Parvis Emad and Kenneth Maly (Bloomington: Indiana University, 1999), 285-93.

190. Harold Bloom, "The Breaking of Form," in Harold Bloom et al., *Deconstruction and Criticism* (New York: Seabury, 1979), 1-37, here 29.

Bloom's "elite" version of the American religion stands to all those which underwrite the "death-in-life of the dumbing down in which America now leads the world, as in all other matters" (WW, 278). So far as I can see, beyond lamentation Bloom has nothing to say about what should be done in the face of this situation, and his gingerly insistence at various places that Emerson would not personally support the causes promoted in the name of various degenerate forms of Emersonianism amounts to little. This reflects a praxical contradiction in Bloom's own writing: that he would write works which seek out a much wider audience than his more scholarly colleagues is, at least apparently, at odds with the elitism of esoteric gnostic humanism, which Bloom explicitly recognizes as "an affair of intellectuals, or of mystical intellectuals" (WW, 267). But we may hazard that the value of Bloom's work lies in the contradiction itself, for it reflects in inverted form the larger American reality, in which an egalitarian ideology underwrites a society in which economic divisions continue to widen. Here instead we have a recognition that true freedom is rare, and only for a few, and that it is ideological divisiveness which blocks its dissemination. Bloom's book also helps, ambiently, in understanding why even degenerate forms of the American religion have the power they do, for they are indeed bound, albeit in a perverted way, to the true sources of human freedom as Bloom understands them.

In Bloom's Coda on "Nemesis and Wisdom," I read a barely covert meditation on this American condition. Our created world is "Nemesis," and "Goethe and Emerson, themselves not Christian, try to teach us that there is a god in us who can, for a time anyway, hold out against Nemesis" (WW, 284). Bloom reads this pragmatically in terms of William James's dictum that wisdom consists in learning what to overlook. "Is that our only answer now to the query of where shall wisdom be found? At least it does constitute a difference that helps get us through the hard or unlucky days" (WW, 284). (Are these, here at the end of Bloom's book, the dog days of *apophrades*, the last of Bloom's six revisionary ratios?) This, at the end of Bloom's book, is this elder statesman's own version of "hopeless hope."

Against this we must set Emerson's powerful notion of crossing: "Life only avails, not the having lived. Power ceases in the instant of repose; it resides in the moment of transition from a past to a new state, in the shooting of a gulf, the darting of an aim" (cited, WW, 193). As Bloom remarks,

> ... power is always at the crossing. Americans can read Emerson without reading him: that includes everyone in Washington, D.C., now pressing for power in the Persian Gulf (I write this sentence on February 24, 2003). I return to the paradox of Emerson's influence: Peace Marchers and Bushians alike are Emerson's heirs in his dialectics of power. (WW, 198)

The social realities we see are the direct expression of the Emersonian revolution: to borrow Nietzsche's aphorism once again, "the greatest ideas are the greatest events." It is the agon between Emerson and Nietzsche which most critically characterizes Bloom's antithetical conception of wisdom: both are masters of power, but in alternate guises descending from Montaigne and Bacon, respectively. In another book, by another author (who, as Bloom would probably tells us, could only be Southern (WW, 200)), the wisdom of the nineteenth century might have been reflected in a counterpoint between Kierkegaard and Melville, both shadowy presences skirted in Bloom's book.[191] But this would not have been a book on Bloom's wisdom. Rather it would be one which stages the drama of a manifest skepticism about power, and so one which, in failing to embrace power, more overtly embraces the legacy of Hamlet's "fascinating bad news," passing by way of the harrowings of such initiates as Ishmael, Bartleby and Stephen Dedalus. This is not Emerson's way, nor Nietzsche's, and certainly not Harold Bloom's. Emerson teaches us that all action begins at a crossing, and Bloom's wisdom is an agonistic, indeed antagonistic, promotion of the antithetical. For Bloom, as for Emerson, the fork in the road, not the fear of the Lord, is the beginning of Wisdom.

In addition to providing an object lesson in the modern search for wisdom, Harold Bloom helps us to ask the question: in the absence of a theological "repressurization" of modernity, what is the outlook for those more basic human needs that have traditionally been associated with religious traditions? Must we, with respect to these needs, live in an increasingly divided (and divisive) society of the esoteric "haves" and the exoteric "have nots"? Being inherently retardative in its impact, how can wisdom keep pace with the pace of modernity? Bloom's proposal that we find modern wisdom in an unorthodox form of Gnosticism parallels Blumenberg's "theology, insofar as it deserves that name," as I have discussed it above in Chapter One, but in other ways Bloom is more an inverted mirror image than an analogue of Blumenberg. Blumenberg's trajectory moves from modernity to open questions about wisdom, whereas Bloom's moves from wisdom to open questions about modernity. Blumenberg's trajectory is more successful, because even in Bloom's work the issue is that of the status of wisdom *in the modern age*. Notoriously, Bloom has spoken of "Shakespeare's Invention of the Human," but from Blumenberg's perspective this would amount only to a covert route toward the promotion of "Shakespeare as the Invention of the Modern." Angus Fletcher's latest book, discussed in Chapter Three above, helps us to see a sense in which Shakespeare is quintessentially modern, if not the inventor thereof, for Shakespeare's New Poetry capitalizes on motion, the category which underwrites The New Science. Can Bloom acknowledge the specificity of Shakespeare's modernity, and hence Shakespeare's modern "wisdom"?

---

191. In his most recent book, *The Anatomy of Influence*, Bloom affirms his preference for Kierkegaard over Freud on anxiety, and, echoing Kierkegaard, the first of the four major sections of the book is entitled, "The Point of View for my Work as a Critic." But, as he goes on to say, it was Anna Freud who "mapped the mechanisms of defense, and my accounts of influence are indebted to her," AILWL, 14.

Since Bloom's conception of Shakespeare's central wisdom for our modern age lies in the power of Shakespeare's visionary *imagination*, his reading of Shakespeare is a thoroughly (high) romantic one—which should come as a surprise to no one. In the "esoteric humanistic Gnosticism" which he would promote, Bloom attempts to excavate an ancient source for such romantic wisdom, thereby placing himself in the Baconian tradition of the modern magus. But in the early modern period, this conception of an esoteric theology promoted the drive toward a novel worldview, one contributing to the emerging Scientific Revolution in particular. In historical context, Bloom's stance is directed in the opposite direction, not toward the Scientific Revolution, but, we might say, away from the quandaries we face in its aftermath. Such escapism is a high-minded, literary version of what we find in our cinemas, and Fletcher's resolute facing of the scientific context of modern literature is ultimately the "wiser" course.

In the next chapter, I will attempt to synthesize the best in both attitudes by outlining a new modern version of the visionary, combining the "high" romantic insistence on vision with the "low" romantic emphasis on description, and governed by a thorough recognition of modernity's complex pace. But before turning in this direction, I want to say a few words about Bloom's most recent volume, *The Anxiety of Influence: Literature as a Way of Life*.

CODA: WISDOM, LOVE AND OUR EVENING LAND

Harold Bloom ends the "Praeludium" to his most recent work, *The Anatomy of Influence: Literature as a Way of Life*, with the summation: "We all fear loneliness, madness, dying. Shakespeare and Walt Whitman, Leopardi and Hart Crane will not cure those fears. And yet these poets bring us fire and light" (AILWL, x). I take 'fire' and 'light' to point to our need for love and wisdom, respectively, and Bloom's most recent work may be seen, among many other ways, as a dialectical investigation of these two root concerns of poetry. Shelley famously declared in *Prometheus Unbound* that "The wise want love; and those who love want wisdom; / And all best things are thus confused to ill" (I.627-28, cited AILWL, 186). This tragic faceoff echoes that expressed in the two previous lines between good and power, and both are echoed in Shelley's last lament in *The Triumph of Life* that good and the means of good cannot be squared, a dilemma upon which Shelley foundered (AILWL, 142). I cannot hope to trace out the subtle interweaving of the themes of wisdom and love Bloom spins out in this, by his own declaration last major work on influence. Instead, I will tease out only one particular strand, bringing this interplay back to the focus of my own work on the dual issues of modernity and pace.

In tandem with his continued emphasis on gnosis, one of the innovations of Bloom's most recent volume is the extent to which he highlights another tradition of wisdom, stemming from the ancient atomism of Epicurus and Lucretius. In so doing, Bloom returns to the Lucretian roots of his earlier tropology in *The Anxiety of Influence*, which begins with *clinamen*, the Lucretian atomic swerve (AILWL, 335). But arguably the greater impetus for this insistence on Lucretius is the extent to which the specifically modern literary tradition inherits its figures of and capacities for skepticism from this classical source. Bloom's acknowledgment of this skepticism serves as a dialectical balance for any emphasis on a positive gnosis—which, as we have seen, is already complicated by Bloom's particular version of negative or hypergnosticism. This pressure finds a culmination of sorts in Wallace Stevens and Hart Crane, where the ultimate commitment is "to believe in a fiction while knowing that what you believe is not true" (AILWL, 281).

Bloom proceeds directly to the conclusion that "Whitman's America and Crane's bridge are knowing figures, giant images of unfulfilled desire" (AILWL, 281). It is precisely the lack of any straightforward satisfaction that breeds the gigantism of an unrequited longing in which desire and knowledge are fused while remaining at ultimate odds. For Bloom, in the absence of a canonical theological founding—the sort of founding which can be the source of covenant wisdom—love and knowledge must remain at such ultimate odds, to be smelted only at the limits of fiction and figuration. "The structure of Crane's poem and of Brooklyn Bridge hardly can fuse, yet it is Crane's fiction that they do. In that metaphoric interlacing Crane gives us an allegory of American possibilities" (AILWL, 286). By implication Bloom characterizes allegory as a limit of figuration in a way that would apply equally well to the genre of anatomy, and it is no coincidence that these have been respective foci for Fletcher and Bloom, the doppelgänger progeny of Northrop Frye.[192]

As I have already noted in passing, Bloom registers a discomfort with such gigantism which is most explicit in his treatment of Whitman, whose lists he laments in particular (AILWL, 298). So far as figuration is concerned, Bloom's approach remains more traditional than Fletcher's, despite their common acknowledgment of Hollander's notion of troping on

---

192. Bloom registers his immense debt to Fletcher in *The Anatomy of Influence* prodigiously, calling him at one point his "only begetter" in criticism (AILWL, 119) and at another his "critical guide and conscience" (AILWL, ix). See also a more extended appreciation at 24. The title of Bloom's work is obviously modeled on Frye's *Anatomy of Criticism* (as well, of course, as Burton's *Anatomy of Melancholy*, which Bloom says he originally took as a model for his work (AILWL, ix)), but Frye is conspicuously absent from Bloom's book, and Bloom says that he "would not have the patience to reread anything by Frye" (AILWL, ix). See, however, his brilliantly angry introduction to the recent edition of Frye's *Anatomy of Criticism* (Princeton: Princeton, 2000). In a work in which Bloom emphasizes the ultimate power of Shakespearean ellipsis, Bloom's ellipsis of Frye is surely notable. On the other hand, Bloom's powerful obliquity in his approach to Shakespearean topoi seems to be borrowed directly from Burton.

form. In particular, Bloom concentrates on those "masterpieces" in which Whitman's tendency to gigantism is held in exquisite check by a delicacy of balance, and he is manifestly disinterested in Whitman's own insistence that *Leaves of Grass* be read as a whole, itself the gigantic poem of these United States. (Fletcher, by way of contrast, has insisted that the royal road to Whitman is through an inspection of the series of Whitman's successive editions of the work.) But as Eisenstein recognized, it is in such list-driven pieces as Whitman's "Song of the Broad-Axe" that we see the basic principle of Whitmanian "writing-large" itself writ large, as it were. Eisenstein's point might be taken as only pedagogical—that it is in such pieces that we most readily come to learn of Whitman's technical innovations. But Whitman's own commitment to the expansivity of *Leaves of Grass* implies a commitment to such enumerative proliferation (and other allied techniques) which Bloom does not share.

Bloom's powerful reading of Shakespeare in *The Anatomy of Influence*—perhaps, indeed, the center of his entire volume—begins with the insistence that Shakespeare overcame the influence of Marlowe in transforming Marlowe's technique of expansive "cartooning" into a technique of densely dramatic characterization. In so doing, Shakespeare overcomes Marlowe's gigantism and replaces it by the "quickening power" of drama. Here we move from a technique of quantitative scale to one of pace, and in particular the pace of Shakespeare's "cognitive music." To put the point telegraphically, why, then, does Whitmanian gigantism not simply constitute a return to Marlovian ballooning?

Yet, to respond equally telegraphically, there *is* a quickening power in Whitman which Bloom identifies by way of an insight he draws from D. H. Lawrence. Lawrence speaks of a "quick of Time" which is "the *pulsating, carnal self,* mysterious and palpable," and continues:

> Because Whitman put this into his poetry, we fear him and respect him so profoundly. We should not fear him if he sang only of the "old unhappy far-off things," or of the "wings of the morning." It is because his heart beats with the urgent, insurgent Now, which is even upon us all, that we dread him. He is so near the quick. (cited, AILWL, 265)

For Lawrence it is perhaps no exaggeration to say that the fear of Walt is the beginning of wisdom, and Lawrence's insight converges on Bloom's troubled insistence that the power of poetry is the power to cut to the quick.

Whitman's poetry accommodates both such quickening *and* the gigantism of enumerative listing, though Bloom may find the latter to result in tedious, poetic failures. That they are not (always) so can only accrue to a judgment which recognizes a wholesale transformation of the genre of poetry in Whitman, one which absorbs traditional poetic achievements into the balanced quickening of the poetic Now in such masterpieces as "When Lilacs Last in the Dooryard Bloom'd," yet recognizes the gigantism of

Whitman's lists as figurations of this same poetic Now in the *form* of an explosive poetic proliferation.[193] A poem like "Song of the Broad-Axe," or more tellingly the elements of listing in Whitman's "Song of Myself," registers the need for an expansion of the poetic in just those conditions which make the residually traditional evaluation of poetry according to the heretofore canonical model of "masterpieces" outdated. With sufficient creative effort, we may see individual poems such as "Lilacs" as masterpieces according to such previous criteria, but the canonical status of *Leaves of Grass* as a volume must remain inexplicable. The poetic expansion which global innovation registers is analogous to the consequences of that theological condition of "depressurization" I have discussed in Chapter Two above, and both situations lead on to the selfsame problem of acceleration posed by the ongoing modern development. In both instances, we are faced by the central need, already evident in Shelley, for a new reconfiguration of wisdom and love, of light and fire.[194] For this, both Whitman's quickening and his gigantism are requisite to face the new pressures of the "pulsing Now."

Bloom may come closest to addressing this need, at least by example, in his reading of the dedicatory poem which prefaces A. R. Ammons' book-length *Sphere: The Form of a Motion*.[195] The dedicatory poem, which bears as title only its dedication, "For Harold Bloom," is deemed by Bloom "Ammons's summa," and he goes on to remark, "he could not surpass this nor did he need to, for even Ashbery has nothing this exalted" (AILWL, 311). In Ammons' poem, "'Longing' ebbs to an image for '*longing*'" just as "in Whitman, 'adhesiveness' ebbs with the ocean of life, and the love of comrades generalizes yet further into the wound-dresser's dirge for all the veterans" (AILWL, 311).

"In this, my final statement on the subject," Bloom remarks, "I define influence simply as *literary love, tempered by defense*" (AILWL, 8). Tempering by defense, it seems, is achieved through the alchemical admixture of wisdom as an agent which fastens love into artful configuration. The poet's wisdom commemorates the fading of love into literature, of longing into the poetic figure of *longing*, so that voice becomes Ammons' central trope, just

---

193. There are, of course, apparent literary precedents for Whitman's technical gigantism: one thinks of Rabelais and Sterne in particular. A more extensive investigation would require an identification of what distinguishes Whitman's technical innovations from these seeming anticipations.

194. This novelty is historically relative, of course; Bloom identifies an earlier stratum in Francis Bacon's essay "Of Love," where Bacon declares, "*That it is impossible to love and be wise*" (cited, AILWL, 86). This crux, which represents a larger Renaissance tradition of preoccupation with folly, is taken by Bloom as a "fit motto for Shakespeare's Sonnets," which are thus by implication (and not, I think, wrongly) identifiable as a source for the later Shelleyan predicament.

195. A. R. Ammons, *Sphere: The Form of a Motion* (New York: Norton, 1974).

as Whitman's tally, in its amplitude of evocative registration, is central both for Whitman and for almost all American poetry that follows (AILWL, 311).

Yet it is the amplitude which remains problematic. The poem *Sphere* "divides its critics, except for the dedicatory chant, which many consider his finest short poem" (AILWL, 314). Bloom judges it "an overtly agonistic work, the context being with the meditative Stevens upon a ground that Ammons fails to usurp," noting that "*Sphere* aims too high, some say" (AILWL, 314). But the problem is a more general one of not yet having critical standards by which to judge such works. The point here is not to argue for any specific reevaluation of this particular poem by Ammons—in my estimation it is likely bested by Ammons' later book-length *Garbage*,[196] which meets the contemporary American (and American poetic) condition more frontally. Bloom's romantic conception of the poetic transformation of love into wisdom is already exploded by the canonically romantic Shelley, and poets such as Whitman, Ammons and Ashbery, especially in their global ambitions, are not best served by this orientation. If we remain in the wake of this romantic explosion the most we can seek is belief in an unbelievable fiction.

What is needed, instead, is a vocabulary for the coordination of the various dimensions of pacing—qualitative, quantitative and motive—in the outer reaches of these poets' ambitions. In the final chapter, I will turn to a first attempt at such evaluation, but, before that, a more proximate step is required by way of a comparative consideration of the critical practices of Harold Bloom and Angus Fletcher. For now, I leave the final word to Ammons, whose confrontation with Stevens, whatever the case in *Sphere*, I judge in *Garbage* to be definitive, and on just the point at issue here. Referring back to the "dispositional axis" of the pre-Socratics already mentioned in the poem's second installment, Ammon's ends the fifth by declaring: "the dispositional axis is not supreme (how tedious) / and not a fiction (how clever) but plain (greatness / flows through the lowly) and a fact (like as not)"[197]

---

196. A. R. Ammons, *Garbage* (New York: Norton, 1993).

197. Ammons, *Garbage*, 39 (no end punctuation). Compare Ammons, *Sphere* §57, 35-36, and §135, 70-71.

7

Visionary Design: Mathematical Analogues for The Reading Of Poetry

> Your argument, Francesco,
> Had begun to grow stale as no answer
> Or answers were forthcoming. If it dissolves now
> Into dust, that only means its time had come
> Some time ago, but look now, and listen:
> It may be that another life is stocked there
> In recesses no one knew of; that it,
> Not we, are the change; that we are in fact it
> If we could get back to it, relive some of the way
> It looked, turn our faces to the globe as it sets
> And still be coming out all right:
> Nerves normal, breath normal.
> —John Ashbery, "Self-Portrait in a Convex Mirror"

INVITATION TO THE DANCE

Eisenstein remarked on a potential "numbing" that may accrue to repetition, and Fletcher has pointed to the tendency of a diurnal rhythm to become similarly numbing, but complexity of argumentation also brings its own form of tedium and staleness. What is required to relieve this particular form of psychic debilitation is not a monument, or even an intermission, but, as Ashbery intimates, a shift in perspective. Thomas Kuhn is best known for his description of the "gestalt shifts" which are responsible for revolutionary developments in science, and a thoroughgoing romanticism has built itself up around such spectacular escapes from normality of argument. In the passage from "Self-Portrait in a Convex Mirror" I cite above, Ashbery identifies a shift from 'we' to 'it', our life draining out while 'it''s life is as full as a well stocked quarry. It seems like the right sort of epigraph for that turn in a book where the author moves from his analysis of received wisdom to proposals of his own. But Harold Bloom, ever the reader as skeptic, rightly cautions that such figures of "earliness" are the stuff of psychological belatedness, and always designed to mislead. The globe to which Ashbery refers in the above passage is at once convex mirror and world as globe—could it perhaps even hint at Shakespeare's theater?!—and enters into a type of complex figuration of Copernican reversal to which Ashbery seems particularly drawn. I will defer further discussion of these Copernican figurations and reversals until my final chapter, and appreciate here only the consistent capacity Ashbery possesses to provide us with the most thought-provoking of complex figures.

In this chapter, I begin to present my own approach to the pace of modernity in terms of a "topological dynamics" for reading modernity at the pace of poetry, which presents a crucial exemplification of the pace of modernity "writ large" in the literature of the imagination. As a first step, I build an argument around a methodological contrast I identify between Bloom's "high" and Fletcher's "low" romanticism, seeing in their respective outlooks a classical (if anomalous) and a modern orientation respectively. My own proposal will function, I hope, as a third alternative, breaking the stalemate of the low versus high romantic debate by finding an escape hatch.

The argument is straightforward enough, but complex in the number of pieces it is required to assemble, and so I begin here by enumerating the major points of concern, then erecting a scaffolding upon which to situate them before delving into the details. In what follows, I propose an analogical movement back and forth between mathematical and poetic concerns. In order to focus the argument, I take as my main poetic example John Ashbery's "Self-Portrait in a Convex Mirror."[198] In contrast to the exercise I will conduct in the final chapter, here I am not intent on establishing a reading of the poem, but intend rather to point out two ways in which the poem *might* be read. These two options will correspond to two different types of mathematical structure: on the one hand poetic *ratios*, which draw their inspiration from the mathematical notion of a fraction, and on the other what we might call poetic *potentials*. These latter are most visibly mapped in terms of *threshold* values, which suggests that there is something like the notion of a function in the background. Mathematically, I want to talk about the differences and crossovers between fractions and functions and use this as a wedge for prizing apart two different ways of reading poetry.

---

198. In John Ashbery, *Self-Portrait in a Convex Mirror* (Penguin, 1976), 68-83; the passage in the epigraph is at 76.

In his 1979 essay, "The Breaking of Form,"[199] Harold Bloom offered a reading of "Self-Portrait in a Convex Mirror" in terms of the structure of his six revisionary ratios; this will provide us with a "fractional" reading of the poem. But Bloom locates the roots of his thinking in Angus Fletcher's work on the poetics of thresholds, taking the notion of crossing to point to the bar which must be traversed in passing from the numerator to the denominator of a poetic fraction. In so doing, Bloom creatively misreads Fletcher's notion of liminal crossing, and we may understand the revision which Bloom's revisionary ratios require in terms of the devolution from a functional approach to a fractional one. It is here, in particular, that the mathematical analogy which underpins the structural distinction between these two approaches becomes productive in its application. Specifically, it points to what a "functional" reading of Ashbery's poem would look like, which I sketch on the basis of Fletcher's liminal poetics. It is to the task of charting this course that I now turn.

FROM LIMINAL POETICS TO REVISIONARY RATIOS

Wesley Trimpi has remarked at length on the background of Hellenistic literary theory in rhetoric, mathematics, and what he calls "moral dialectic."[200] His point, in particular, is that the analysis of literary experience, as opposed to the production of literature, only forms late in the classical tradition and on the basis of other models of analysis. Here, of course, I will want to focus on the background which mathematical analysis provides.

Harold Bloom has also recognized a Hellenistic literary context for his scheme of revisionary ratios. In the battle between the schools of Alexandria and Pergamon, influenced by Aristotle and the Stoics respectively, two competing stances toward criticism developed in terms of the cultivation of opposing attitudes toward "ratio," or proportion.[201] The Alexandrians championed *analogy* or "equality of ratios," while their rivals in Pergamon favored *anomaly* as a "disproportion of ratios."[202] Bloom aligns himself with this latter school, which sees the literary text as "an interplay of differences," from which meaning arises.[203] This provides Bloom with a model of ratio-criticism which is specifically *revisionary*: literary production is seen as a struggle on the part of a poet to swerve away from the figural proportion in which his text threatens to be captured vis-a-vis a precursor

---

199. In Bloom et al., *Deconstruction and Criticism*, 1-37.
200. Wesley Trimpi, *Muses of One Mind: The Literary Analysis of Experience and Its Continuity* (Princeton, 1983); for a summary statement of the thesis, see 73-79.
201. See also F. H. Colson, "The Analogist and Anomalist Controversy," *The Classical Quarterly* **13** 1 (January 1919) 24-36.
202. Bloom, "Breaking," 13.
203. idem, 13-14.

poem. The first of Bloom's revisionary ratios will be the Lucretian *clinamen*, or atomic swerve.

The tone of Bloom's criticism is "uncanny" or "antithetical," as he denominates the stance of the second century anomalist Crates of Mallos, Librarian of Pergamon, but in any case it is grounded in a structure of (dis)proportions. This leads almost immediately to what has perhaps been most roundly criticized in Bloom's approach: his application of the revisionary ratios as a general template for the reading of poems across a wide variety of historical and literary contexts. But if Trimpi is correct, and the roots of literary analysis are to be found, among a small number of disciplines, in the analysis of mathematical structure, then it seems likely that Bloom is only being overt about a feature of literary analysis which is more frequently, and perniciously, relied upon tacitly and so without explicit control. However this may be, Bloom's approach is helpful for my concerns precisely because it wears its (ir)rational structure so explicitly on its sleeve. And Bloom's approach seems to me powerfully helpful (and hurtful) in the guiding hands of his often masterful analyses.

Bloom himself has responded to the critical concern with the omnipresence of his revisionary ratios, remarking that

> I have experienced my own defensive emotions concerning the sequence of revisionary ratios that I find recurrent in so many poems, quite aside from the defensive reactions I have aroused in others. But the sequence is *there* in the sense that image and trope tend to follow over-determined patterns of evasion.[204]

I take this to mean that there is a *psychological* basis for the prevalence of the revisionary ratios in poetic production. This prevalence is the result of a pattern of defensive evasion among the producers of these poems. The pattern results, specifically, from the overdetermination of the psychological mechanism of evasion: its need to accomplish multiple psychic feats conceptually in one and the same poetic gesture. This conceptual multiplicity is knotted together in the image or corresponding trope and generates the particular *power* of the poetic production. On this construal, the poetic pattern is the reflection of a patterned psychic defense mechanism, but the residue which is left in the poem tends, in fact, to occlude the particular circumstances of its psychical production—in keeping with its psychically defensive function. There is, then, a relative disjunction between the psychological and tropological levels, and the scheme of revisionary ratios helps us to identify the

---

204. idem, 29. Most recently, in *The Anatomy of Influence*, Bloom reads Shakespeare's dramatic development along his career in terms of the six ratios (AILWL, 68), but then later remarks that "in the labyrinth of this book" the revisionary ratios cannot provide a wished-for thread, since only Shakespeare and Whitman can do that for me," now regarding the "esoteric sixfold" as "a purely personal dialectical dance, part of the Kabbalah of Harold Bloom" (AILWL, 195).

reflected pattern of (dis)proportions we encounter in the poem, always in the ambient context provided by the identification of precursor poems. As a template this may serve as a sort of "shorthand" for carrying along the structure of the generative psychic mechanisms without having to carry the psychological context of poetic production along explicitly. As such, the tropology figures a detachment of the critical reading from the writing of poetry. Indeed, given the overdetermination associated with defense mechanisms, this psychological context is actually occluded and we are left with no alternative but to rest content with the vestigial pattern of tropological revision. Thus the Freudian notion of defense underwrites a peculiar sort of critical literary formalism, in which the proper subject of literary analysis is the figurative structure of poetic language.

Given the formal nature of this analysis, the specific mathematical model in terms of which it is couched becomes particularly important, for it is in the appeal to mathematical structure that each variety of literary formalism will make its pedigree most explicit. Here, once again, Bloom has done us the service of being as explicit as is conceivably possible by isolating, not just the ratio-model underlying his analytic procedure, but indeed the particular *sort* of ratio criticism he supports. Yet in this regard it is quite ironic that Bloom locates the roots of his procedure in reflections on Angus Fletcher's work on liminal poetics, for Fletcher's approach is best associated with quite a different mathematical attitude. Further, I claim, Bloom's creative misreading of Fletcher's work is most apparent precisely in the way he adapts it to the sort of structural conditions which his ratio-driven approach requires.

Although Bloom refers to Fletcher's studies of "Spenser, Milton, Coleridge, and Crane,"[205] it is particularly Fletcher's essay, "Threshold, Sequence and Personification in Coleridge"[206] which exercises him, and so I will focus on this instance of Fletcher's threshold poetics here. In this essay, Fletcher is at particular pains to understand the development of a purified poetry of the threshold in such later Coleridgean efforts as "Limbo" and "Ne Plus Ultra." The latter poem takes as its model George Herbert's "Prayer," and in general Fletcher sees the intensification of Coleridge's liminal poetics as associated with his growing estimation of seventeenth century poetry later in life. The genealogy Fletcher supplies manages to bind Coleridge in a way which reaches even further back, redeeming Coleridge's bardolatry in the process. At the heart of this bardolatry Fletcher finds Coleridge's preoccupation with a Shakespearean "readiness" which exemplifies the threshold stance. This liminal poise is reflected by a balance between movement and methodical order, "since 'without continuous transition there can be no method,' while 'without a preconception there can be no transition with

---

205. idem, 23.

206. Reprinted in Angus Fletcher, *Colors of the Mind: Conjectures on Thinking in Literature* (Harvard, 1991), 166-88. All citations are to this version of the essay.

continuity'."[207] In this way, Fletcher sees Coleridge as the genuine inheritor of Shakespearean literary power.

Such an organization is inherently dramatic, or at least proto-dramatic, and so ordered according to the progression of time, and it is here that we find the transition from the topological threshold to the temporal sequence. Since lyric poetry more narrowly, and Romantic poetry more generally, are not typically dramatic in form, the carrier of sequence will be the prophetic voice which marks the apprehension of the threshold. "Here both sight and sound tend to create a sense of time, and time is enigmatic."[208] But how is prophetic voicing to carry a temporal tone? In the *Critique of Pure Reason*, Kant remarks that we must always represent time in terms of space.[209] "In itself" time is a kind of nothingness, whose elusive slipperiness is registered in Augustine's remark that "we cannot rightly say that time *is*, except by reason of its impending state of *not* being."[210] Yet without literally contradicting it, in an important sense the poem manages to invert Kant's dictum, beginning on a spatial note and ending with a temporal description. For the poem clothes space in the language of development, and development is temporal. Structurally, this is most easily seen in the paradigmatic instance of sequence, the counting numbers. "In themselves," these numbers are "atemporal," and we can mark out equidistant points on a spatial continuum to represent them. But in the human act of counting, these numbers follow each other in temporal order, according to an ongoing "this, and then this, and then this," and so on, indefinitely. As Fletcher puts it, under a phenomenological analysis "our phrase 'next door' would have to be replaced by 'and then' or simply by afterwards."[211] It is this underlying "poetics of number" which we may take as a starting point for understanding Fletcher's analysis of Coleridge. Although from a "numerological" perspective we may think of number sequences as static and timeless, "[y]et the *poetics* of number accept, and do not, under pressure from logic, reject man's time-bound duration.... Poets use spatial terms to control changes in time. They spend their lives measuring lines of poetry .... We may conclude that the poetic pursuit of the logos demands a measuring and time-feeling poetic activity."[212] The emphasis on poetic activity contrasts tellingly against a denuded ontology of number.

---

207. Fletcher, *Colors*, 177.

208. idem, 170.

209. Kant, *Critique of Pure Reason*, trans. Werner Pluhar with an introduction by Patricia Kitcher (Hackett, 1996): "For as regards time, which after all is not an object of outer intuition [i.e. space] at all, we cannot present it to ourselves except under the image of a line insofar as we draw that line ..." (194 = B 156). See also B 50 and B 154.

210. Cited, Fletcher, *Colors*, 171.

211. idem, 173-74.

212. idem, 174.

Without being in direct contradiction to it, Bloom's scheme of revisionary ratios washes out the critical, temporal dimension of Fletcher's poetic. Just as Fletcher's insistence on the temporal dimension does not contradict the Kantian dictum that time can only be *represented* indirectly, so too Bloom's divergence from Fletcher results from a difference in emphasis. In Bloom's case the emphasis falls on the fiction of duration, rather than on what we might call in Fletcher's case the duration of fiction. In the poetics of number, Fletcher emphasizes the temporal embodiment of the numerical; in the revisionary ratios Bloom abstracts the structure of number to provide a tropological scheme for the representation of the temporal. Of course, in Fletcher's case, poetry must not just *be* temporal but must also be capable of describing temporal progression, and this leads to further complications associated with the *language* of development, as mentioned above. However, in Bloom's reading the status of the revisionary ratios is most important in how it sets up the possibility of crossing from one ratio to another. Thus there is no intrinsic need to focus on the temporal progression of the ratio-structure within a poem. Bloom's scheme provides us with a numerical poetics rather than the poetry of number which Fletcher describes.

To be sure, in the reading of post-Miltonic poetry, Bloom faces the problem that the belated poet is rarely able to maintain a threshold stance, achieving the Shakespearean "readiness" that Fletcher would ascribe, as ideal, to Coleridge. Unlike Coleridge, Bloom understands sequence not as continuous transition, but rather as a "mode of survival," and so as the "fiction of duration"[213] I have already mentioned. The psychological provenance of his insistence on poetry as an agonistic battle between dialectic and representation is motivated by this agonistic struggle for survival, and is reflected in the fundamental dichotomy "between irony and synechdoche" with which Bloom inaugurates his sixfold tropology.[214] This produces a model of poetry in which poetic power involves countertroping, or troping on trope, leveling the field between poetry and criticism, since this latter is also a troping of tropes. Poetry and criticism are joined in the activity of *"the poet in the reader* (any reader, at least potentially)"[215] in a belated democratization of poetry; already in *The Anxiety of Influence* Bloom had recognized that his stance required that "all criticism is prose poetry."[216]

Yet this expansion of the poetic field also requires the late-Freudian recognition that this poetic activity may be at its most powerful in the prolongation of anxiety,[217] which in turn necessitates a de-idealizing depiction of

---

213. Bloom, "Breaking," 29.
214. idem, 11.
215. idem, 8.
216. Harold Bloom, *The Anxiety of Influence* (Oxford, 1973), 95; see also Harold Bloom, *A Map of Misreading* (Oxford, 1975), 3.
217. Bloom, "Breaking," 18.

reading. Synecdochic troping "begins a process that leads to an *un-naming*," which "hints at the vicissitudes that are disorders of psychic drives," exemplified by sado-masochism, which is "synecdochic, in a very dark sense."[218] It is this tropological function which ties the linguistic artifact down into the mazes of the psyche, and suggests, equally darkly, that Bloom's scheme has taken over Fletcher's dialectic of temple and labyrinth, not to the end of accounting for the poetry, but rather for *dis*counting it, aggressively displacing the poems and Fletcher's precedent simultaneously. Consequently, Bloom's insistence later in this essay that "Ashbery's reading of his tradition of utterance, and my reading of Ashbery, are gestures of restitution"[219] is a weak self-misreading of Bloom's own procedure (pointing to a problem attending the sixth and final stage of Bloom's rational scheme, to which I return below). Here Bloom is guilty of the same misrepresentation for which he indicts Hölderlin in a letter to Schiller earlier in the essay, and to the same end: his self-attested weakness becomes a means for undoing his precursor. Beyond the poems of our climate, Bloom sets out to write the climate of our poems, or even, beyond meteorology, a star chart of our influences. Ultimately the magnitude of the ambition may warrant, if not legitimate, Bloom's act of aggression.

What this reflects in the underlying commitment to ratio structures is the possibility for the construction of fractions upon fractions upon fractions. At one point in his essay, Bloom ascends to a third level of tropes, referring at this point to a "bewildering triple intertropicality at work that makes a mockery of most attempts at reading."[220] Indeed, there is no conceptual reason to stop there, and once the work of criticism displaces the poem it reads we will necessarily need to add at least one more level, and perhaps three. In principle, we could add such levels indefinitely: unlike Dedekind's construction of the mathematical continuum,[221] in which we are done once the real numbers are constructed from the rational fractions, there is no reason for the tiered levels of revisionary ratios to "bottom out." Instead, we are faced with something more like the continuum of non-standard analysis, in which disproportions can be modeled by appealing to infinitesimals, and there is no end to the orders of infinitesimals to which we may appeal—this is all an anticipation which I will clear up in the section below. By taking the route of *anomalous* criticism, Bloom embarks on a ratio structure "without reserve," to borrow George Bataille's suggestive term.

By way of contrast, Fletcher's poetics is single-tiered, since time is taken as an *independent* variable fixing a measure for the duration of fiction, rather than being absorbed, as Bloom effectively does, into the "fiction of

---

218. idem, 11.

219. idem, 37.

220. idem, 16.

221. Richard Dedekind, *Essays on the Theory of Numbers*, trans. Wooster Woodruff Beman (repr. Dover, 1963).

duration." In contrast to Bloom, Fletcher's approach suggests a mathematical functionalism, in which time is the independent, or input, variable, and the output is a dynamically evolving sequence of spatial topoi, whose signature is the transition occurring at a "threshold value," when a crossing occurs between the vertical topos of "temple" and the horizontal "labyrinth" or vice versa.[222] In the next section, I sketch a comparison of these two mathematical paradigms. Bloom's strongest counter to this dialectic would be to charge that it "reverts" to a dichotomy between metaphor (vertical) and metonymy (horizontal). In so doing, the dialectic will be in no position to account for the psychic "prolongation of anxiety" which the strong poem may afford. Indeed, I believe that if the battle between these two methods is to be fought exclusively on the field of tropes, then Bloom's method inevitably triumphs. In this regard, Fletcher's turn to the domain of tropes at the end of his essay on Coleridge tends to weaken the force of his poetic dramatism.

FRACTIONS AND FUNCTIONS

Now it is requisite that I paint a kind of cartoon backdrop depicting certain episodes from the history of mathematics. In keeping with the literary and philosophical nature of this essay, my approach will be quite fanciful by mathematical standards. But the goal is to establish a scaffolding of concepts which may be brought into analogy with the reading of poetry, and I allow this to set the tone. Reader, please bear with me: a backdrop is only meant to be seen in the vaguest of outlines. It depicts a city of great interest, but doing it justice would require an opera of its own.

I begin with a constellation of problems with the foundational status of Leibniz's mathematics, less investigated than it should be by historians of both philosophical and mathematical domains.[223]

Following the geometrical presentations of the ancients, Leibniz begins with the presentation of proportions of line segments, which is to say that he begins with a geometric system of ratios or "fractions." But in order to solve the mathematical problems he faces, Leibniz must analyze these ratios with greater and greater precision, and this ultimately leads him to a

---

222. Angus Fletcher, "Basic Definitions of *Threshold* for a Theory of Labyrinths," in Richard Milazzo, ed. *Beauty and Critique* (New York: TSL, 1982), 142-52.

223. The canonical reference remains H. J. M. Bos, "Differentials, Higher-Order Differentials and the Derivative in the Leibnizian Calculus," *Archive for History of Exact Science* **14** 1-90, 55. The single most important manuscript source is Leibniz's 1676 *De quadratura circuli ellipseos et hyperbolae cujus corollarium est trigonometria sine tabulis*, ed. E. Knobloch (Vandenhoeck & Ruprecht, 1993). No English translation of this manuscript is available, but there is a French translation with commentary in G. W. Leibniz, *quadrature arithmétique du cercle, de l'ellipse et de l'hyperbole*, introduction, trans. and notes Marc Parmentier (Vrin, 2004).

kind of foundational crux, in which two divergent options present themselves. On the one hand, Leibniz may introduce the notion of an infinitely small line segment, so that, we may say, he may extend his analysis of proportions into the domain of "disproportions," i.e., proportions between line segments which stand in no *finite* proportion. Such "anomalous" ratios allow Leibniz the analytic precision he requires, but they are *fictive*, stories we tell with no metaphysical legitimation. Unlike finite magnitudes, which may be *represented* by geometrical line segments, infinitely small magnitudes, or infinitesimals, have no such representation. Equally, we cannot represent the notion of an infinitely large magnitude by a geometric segment, for such a line would need to be infinitely long but terminate at both ends, and Leibniz finds this impossible. Leibniz is only able to resolve this problem by pragmatically positing whimsical, inconceivable magnitudes, infinitely small and large, which allow him to talk about anomalous *dis*proportions as if they were in fact proportions.[224] The analogy with Bloom's "anomalous ratio criticism" stands ready.

There is another option, which Leibniz briefly explores, and which is developed much more fully later in the history of mathematics. As Husserl's student Dietrich Mahnke first showed, Leibniz was in fact the first mathematician to capture the notion of mathematical function, in which one "dependent" variable—the "output"—is understood to vary as a function of another "independent" variable—the "input."[225] This approach, which would only really be canonized in a thoroughly foundational way in the 19th century by the French mathematician Augustin Cauchy, would have allowed Leibniz to define the quantities he needed, and in particular the derivative of a function, to resolve his problems with foundational precision.[226] But in Leibniz's early context the functional approach lacked the pragmatic advantages of the approach by way of anomalous infinitesimal ratios. There is one school of thought, whose most distinguished contemporary representative is Roger Penrose, which would argue that even the functional approach may be "demeaned" by a pedantic insistence on the rigor which accompanies the development of mathematics following from Cauchy's "rigorous" definition of the derivative of a function. Ultimately, even more than the divide between fractionalists and functionalists, it was the divide between "loose" infinitarists and "tight" rigorists which dominated later attitudes to the foundations of mathematics.

---

224. I discuss this at more length in "An Enticing (Im)Possibility: Infinitesimals, Differentials, and the Leibnizian Calculus," in *Infinitesimal Differences: Controversies between Leibniz and his Contemporaries*, ed. Ursula Goldenbaum and Douglas Jesseph (Berlin: Walter de Gruyter, 2008), 135-151.

225. Dietrich Mahnke, "Die Entstehung des Funktionsbegriffes," *Kantstudien* 31 (1926), 426-28.

226. See Judith Grabiner, *The Origins of Cauchy's Rigorous Calculus* (MIT, 1981).

Rigorous standards of proof were also the pride and joy of ancient mathematics, which shuddered at any loose play with the "infinite," for from an ancient perspective the infinite was "bad news," even if fascinating, amounting only to a sort of indefinite morass. Among the ancients, only Archimedes experimented with infinitely small quantities, and this only in work he suppressed, and which was only rediscovered at the beginning of the 20th century! It was not until the 17th century that mathematicians were really willing to play "fast and loose" with the infinite, and then still often only with considerable mathematical and theological trepidation. Such play, among practitioners such as Galileo and Leibniz, needed to be cloaked in all sorts of provisos about its fictional or conjectural status. This was not, however, merely a theological precaution: it bespoke as well a recognition that the grounding for such infinite play was radically unclear. So, despite their apparent inconceivability, Leibniz devoted considerable effort to finding the right way to describe the status of infinitesimals and infinitely large quantities, and his discussion of these subjects bears an uncanny resemblance to his discussions of the ontological proof for the existence of God.[227]

Until the middle of the 20th century, the battle between loose lips and tight ships continued to favor the rigorous elimination of infinitesimals, but in the 1960's Abraham Robinson showed how "non-standard" infinitesimals and infinitely large quantities could also be put on a firm footing.[228] Coming so late in the historical game, the "standard" fractional *and* functional rigorists have maintained their superiority in the mathematical academy over the infinitesimal rigorists, but philosophically the battle has been once again set wide open. There is a web of extraordinary complexity at issue, which extends well beyond the bounds of my cartoon backdrop. Here what is most important is the early modern conceptual faultline between fraction and function and the geography of strategies for dealing with the infinite which surround this rift.

There is an episode of capital importance stretching across the 18th and 19th century middle-ground of the history of modern mathematics which needs to be seen against this backdrop: the development of complex analysis. It registers the same sort of shock that Parmigianino's self-portrait in a convex mirror registered with respect to the artistic development of perspective in the renaissance, for it introduces an analogous "twist." Archimedes was executed by the soldiers whom he advised not to disturb his circles, but Parmigianino so shocked the soldiers who broke into his studio that, as Ashbery tells us, they spared his life. The birth of complex analysis registers an analogous shock, from which the history of mathematics is still reeling.

---

227. Paolo Mancosu, *Philosophy of Mathematics and Mathematical Practice in the Seventeenth Century* (New York: Oxford, 1996).

228. Abraham Robinson, *Non-standard Analysis* 2nd ed. (Princeton, 1996).

THE INFINITE AND THE IMAGINARY: TWO COMPLICATIONS OF QUANTITY

Above, I have described how incommensurability and disproportion were handled from a fractional perspective: append to the domain of finite magnitudes fictional, infinitely large and small ones and allow these also to enter into "anomalous" fractional combination. Failing a completely rigorous approach to functions, which was only to develop much later, is there a similar sort of "trick" that could be used to make functions as pragmatically useful as fractions were in the infinitesimal calculus? Yes, there is, and the idea is even more bizarre than the idea of appending infinitely large or small quantities: append instead the square root of negative one! The square of a number is what you get by multiplying it by itself, and if you multiply a positive number by itself you get a positive number. But if you multiply a negative number by itself you *also* get a positive number: minus two times minus two equals *positive* four. That means that all squares are positive. Since a "square root" of a number y is a number x, such that, when you multiply x by itself, you get y, a negative number cannot have a square root. In complex analysis, we insist, nevertheless, that it can. What could redeem such mathematical insanity? The best short answer is: the pragmatic usefulness of this extraordinary insistence.

Fortunately, it is not so difficult to explain why this is so, at least in very rough outline. There are, potentially, all sorts of different functions. Anything which associates a unique "output" with each "input" is a function. Mathematically, the world of functions is wide open. But, unlike fractions, which can all be expressed as ratios, there is no single way all functions can be expressed in advance. Already in the 17th century, even before mathematicians were comfortable with the idea of function, there were tremendous debates about what should count as curves, and the debate about curves leads directly into the debate about functions. The only obvious way to address this dilemma is to find a simple description which generates a collection of functions which do mathematically interesting and useful things.

The most obvious candidate is the collection of polynomial functions. These are familiar to all of us from high-school algebra: they are functions like $y = 4x + 7$, which (before programming calculators, anyway) we learned to graph on the coordinate plane. But, if you restrict yourself to "ordinary" numbers, these sorts of functions are very limited. The extraordinary power of complex analysis comes from what you can do with functions like these (the so-called "analytic" functions) when you allow the inputs and outputs to include "complex" numbers like $1 + 3i$ or $7 - 3i$, where 'i' designates the (positive) square root of negative one.[229] Why this voyage into the realm of complex numbers discloses a treasure-trove of mathematical discoveries is

---

229. - i (negative i) is also a square root of -1.

one of the truly great adventure stories in the history of mathematics, told to perfection by Roger Penrose in the early chapters of his recent book, "The Road to Reality."[230] I will focus on only one small part of this story, which you may read about in greater detail there.

In order to have a collection of functions comparable in power to Leibniz's fractions, you need to take "fractions" of functions: $y(x) = f(x) / g(x)$, where $f(x)$ and $g(x)$ are simple examples of the polynomial functions mentioned above.[231] Here x is the input, and since when we plug it into the functions f and g we get outputs $f(x)$ and $g(x)$, we can associate x with the output $f(x)/g(x)$, i.e $f(x)$ divided by $g(x)$: this is how the function $y(x)$ works. This gives us the so-called Möbius functions. Then whenever $g(x) = 0$, we will produce "anomalous behavior," since anything divided by zero is strictly speaking undefined.

We now have a collection of functions replete with anomalous behavior, and so it gives us something of the power of the anomalous ratios made possible by the Leibnizian infinitesimals and infinite numbers described above. But it gives us quite a lot more as well, for the coupling of complex numbers and such anomalous behavior introduces, almost literally, a new "twist," with many striking geometric consequences. In particular, the Möbius functions stand in a very tight and dramatic relation to hyperbolic geometry. Hyperbolic geometry is not as scary as it might sound, and in fact it will lead us back with surprising directness to the poetic issues at hand. Before proceeding, though, let me stress one final time in summary what we have achieved with the Möbius functions: we have a *functional* model which captures the same sort of anomalous power as *fractional* models were able to capture by introducing fictional infinitesimals and infinite numbers into the fractions.

Now, on to the geometry.[232] Hyperbolic geometry is the geometry you get if parallel lines are pinched closer together the closer they come to the focal point of vision. Take a line and draw a single point not lying on that line. In traditional, Euclidean plane geometry you could only draw *one* line through this single point which was parallel to the original line. In the hyperbolic case you can produce *lots* of lines through the latter point which are parallel to the former line: they all start off going through that point, and as they move away from the point they peel farther and farther away from each other.

This geometry can be represented by shrinking all of the plane down onto a circle. As we move out toward the horizon of the circle, the figures

---

230. Roger Penrose, *The Road to Reality* (London: Jonathan Cape, 2004).

231. Namely, $f(x)$ and $g(x)$ are first order polynomials with real coefficients, i.e. of the form $f(x) = ax + b$ and $g(x) = cx + d$, where a, b, c, d are real numbers, subject to the special condition that $ad - bc > 0$.

232. My discussion of hyperbolic geometry is little more than a promissory note. The reader is strongly encouraged to consult the beautiful presentation—with striking illustrations—in Penrose's *The Road to Reality*, 33-50.

become rapidly smaller. We may think of this as representing the entire plane squeezed down into a circle with only the center of the circle photographically "unreduced." As you move away from the center of the circle, the figures start shrinking, but we may think of this as a representational necessity associated with the limited radius of the circle. On the plane, the figures would all be the same size; on the circle they must shrink down as we move outward. In the hyperbolic geometry which this circle represents, "lines" are the circular arcs which intersect the boundary of the circle at right angles; this also includes diameters of the circle drawn through its center as a limiting case. Since we have squeezed the whole plane down into a circle, you can see the lines represented all the way out to "infinity," i.e. the edge of the circle. When you draw a triangle on this circle, the interior angles of the triangle are "pinched together," and so are "constricted" as you move toward the apex, i.e the point of the triangle where two of its sides meet.

This hyperbolic disc has a very close relation to the Möbius functions which I will not attempt to describe here. For our purposes, suffice it to say that this representation makes "visible" an architectonic design of great aesthetic beauty. The infinity of the complex hyperbolic plane is reflected in the shrinking of the figures "to infinity" at the boundary of the disc. Further, the "pinching" together of parallel lines and the constriction of the interior of hyperbolic triangles hints at a peculiar "twisting" of complex geometry which is related to the more intuitive torsions we will encounter in visual art below.

There is another (partial) manner of representing the hyperbolic plane on a disc which we should compare before proceeding: this is the manner of representation you get if you map the points on the plane down onto the disc without "pinching" or "constraining" the way a hyperbolic representation does. This representation is called *projective* and in this case the angles of triangles don't get pinched together—which means that the angles don't respect the shrinking process from the plane to the circle. In this figure, in general, shapes don't shrink down as quickly, so that much more of the disc is taken up by the shapes close to the center. If you look at such a projective circle it will convey much more of the illusion of a sphere than the hyperbolic representation does. As a competition between geometric accuracy and perspectival illusion, the tension between these two representations is at the heart of convex portraiture, to which I now turn.

CONVEX PORTRAITURE

Fletcher alerts us to two precedents for understanding the way in which the geometry of convexity impinges on the mechanics of poetic representation: mapmaking and what we might call frontispiecing. The former embodies a practical fact which lies at the root of all geometric translation back and forth from the sphere to the plane: "As cosmographers have known since the Renaissance, one can accurately project either the size of the sphere or the shape of the topographic area upon the sphere, but one cannot accurately project both size and shape at once."[233] Fletcher identifies projection as the mechanism underlying the poetics of the "metaphysical conceit," which, "while projecting an appearance of logical sequence, disperses its thought through devices we might imagine derived from the new science of mapmaking."[234] Donne embodies the method of "conceiting" itself into a conceit, by likening his body to a map, which "tortures the sphere, to make it projectively flat."[235] The key to this divisive straddling between sphere and plane is the semantic register of torsion and twisting, and the great mathematical advantage (and challenge) of imaginary over infinitary techniques is its introduction of such a twist. Although Fletcher concludes that "[t]he Metaphysicals could think about the unthinkable," this is a particular variety of the unthinkable fitted to the writhing of topographic distortion.

Fletcher extends this meditation upon torsion in his thoughts about the central role played by the vortical convex diadem in Vico's frontispiece to the *Nuovo Scienza*. In this frontispiece the figure of a winged metaphysics is situated at the point of reflection of a ray of light which extends from the eye of God and then is reflected downward onto the poet Homer. The ray of light is reflected off a mirrored jewel adorning the breast of metaphysics, but as Vico remarks, the jewel is "convex, thus reflecting and scattering the ray abroad, to show that metaphysic should know God's providence in public moral institutions or civil customs, by which the nations have come into being and maintain themselves in the world." Were the mirror flat, the divine light would instead have its end solely in "metaphysic taking private illumination from intellectual institutions and thence regulating merely her own moral institutions, as hitherto philosophers have done."[236] For Vico, the transition from flat Euclidean space to the convexity of the sphere mirrors the transition from the private to the public domain.

As Fletcher points out, such convex dispersion is in line with the overall mannerist treatment of space in Vico's frontispiece, which does not establish a fixed perspective but instead hovers about multiple centers of spatial reference. These spatial regions swirl like vortices about the symbolic domains represented in the engraving, and are linked by a snakelike torsion which connects the three central icons associated with the three planes of vision: divine, metaphysical and "poetic." The various S-shaped zigzags which the picture enacts "suggest not only a line of beauty, but, more strongly, the

---

233. Fletcher, *Colors*, 62.
234. idem, 61.
235. idem, 61-62.
236. Giambattista Vico, *New Science*, trans. David Marsh (London: Penguin, 1999), 5.

flame-like freedom of the living forms of natural growth."[237] For Fletcher, the perspectival distortions "correspond to the turbulence of actual, 'relative' rather than 'absolute' human history,"[238] and so are the spatial analogue of that "poetics of number" which Fletcher contrasted in his essay on Coleridge with number's denuded ontology. Vico understands this embodiment particularly in terms of the *public* nature of the attitude which his *New Science* promotes.

Just as sequence always extends vectorially in the direction of its consecutive progression, the convexity of Vico's method permits a certain "excessiveness" which is appropriate to the prophetic dimension of his frontispiece as visionary threshold. Again in analogy to the poetics of number, which cannot remain "constrained by logic," Vico's method does not confine itself narrowly to the domain of "positive proof," but instead proliferates out into the larger, necessarily more flexible, domain of the public, whose amplitude can only be captured by the principles of a prophetic, visionary design.[239] This amplitude is required to accommodate the two extremes which any science of Vico's sort must include: a depth of research which must attend to the smallest of factual details, and a breadth of historical vision which is "unprecedented" in its global ambition. These competing requisites lead to what Fletcher calls Vico's "syncretism," and this syncretism is reflected in the frontispiece by the multiplicity of its spatial designs, which are not capable of being subsumed under one perspectival rubric.[240] Unlike Dürer's *Melencholia I*, whose vanishing point coincides with the "distant sun," Vico's frontispiece conforms to no single vanishing point. In so doing it substitutes for the aesthetic power of Dürer's unified vision a Mannerist complexity in a move which is essential "if the increasing awareness of relativism is to find its method of ordering."[241] Such a stance, it seems, is the most appropriate response to the burgeoning complexity of the world in which we find ourselves. At a minimum, it reflects the assimilation demands we face in an increasingly complex modern society.

Both the figural proliferation in Bloom's poetics and the torsional vision which Fletcher depicts point in the direct of a common preoccupation with the unbounded. In Bloom's case, this unboundedness takes the form of that synecdochic "undoing" which is psychologically associated with the death drive's "prolongation of anxiety." In Fletcher, the unboundedness of the "syncretism of excess" finds its closest "methodological" expression in Shakespeare's "readiness," Vico's syncretism, and Coleridge's "dramatic vision." Neither type of vision seems capable of doing justice to the other, so

---

237. Fletcher, *Colors*, 156.
238. ibid.
239. idem, 161.
240. idem, 163.
241. ibid.

how are we to compare them? We can begin by focusing on the unboundedness associated with each, what I have called the parafinite, or the "logically large as you please." The unbounded, or even more accurately the parafinite, expresses the common denominator of Bloom's and Fletcher's respective approaches, explored in divergent ways. A more adequate approach would put this concern front and center, yielding a vision of the parafinite.

READING THE SHIELD OF A GREETING

The operation I need to perform upon *Self-Portrait in a Convex Mirror* requires the violence of incisions, for I intend to take the poem as an example and look at how it might be read. It might be well to keep in mind the image of a reputed person undergoing a surgical procedure. Or, to extend the analogy further, we might even think of a team of medical specialists evaluating various surgical options to perform upon this eminent individual, for I want to look at various possible ways of reading the poem, and (to switch back again), my concern is ultimately with the team of operating specialists rather than the patient lying etherized upon the table. Such is the requisite (and sometimes offensive) diagnostic remove of our advanced medical age.

Let me begin by sketching the contours of what is most relevant for my purposes in Bloom's reading of the poem. Bloom takes his sixfold trope of tropes as a guide for his reading, along the lines of the procedure he sets out in *A Map of Misreading*. It is worth noting that in the earlier volume, *The Anxiety of Influence*, Bloom does not yet suggest that individual poems should be read in terms of a sequential progression through the six revisionary ratios he lists. But in the later volume, Bloom conjectures that the strongest poems will follow out the sequence of ratios rather strictly, and develops this conjecture in conjunction with a division of the ratios into two sets: those of limitation and those of representation. In the order of these ratios each trope of limitation is followed by a trope of representation, and the transition from the one to the other is an instance of what Bloom calls a poetic crossing. This notion of crossing is particularly indebted to Fletcher's "liminal poetics," and each such transition registers a minimal move in the sequence of three crossings which go together to make up the sequential progression through the revisionary ratios. Although it is governed by a sixfold pattern, Bloom's poetics follows the astronomical rule of three, according to which all data can be broken up into a threefold pattern of two peaks—here the first and third crossings—and one trough—here the middle crossing.[242] The three crossings then generate one "supercrossing," or crossing of crossings, and so exemplify that redoubling which Bloom also locates critically in the last of his six revisionary ratios, metalepsis, which is a "figure of figure."

---

242. See Bloom, *Map*, 96.

Although in this summary I have gone beyond what Bloom says explicitly, the extension I propose is naturally supported by the psychoanalytic analogy Bloom uses to motivate his sequential presentation of the ratios:

> Ferenczi, in *Thalassa*, says that "one might quite properly speak of a condensed recapitulation of sexual development as taking place in each individual sex act." Similarly one might speak of all the revisionary ratios (defenses or tropes or the phenomenal maskings of both in images) following one another in truly central, very strong poems. Ferenczi sees the sex act as an attempt to "return to the state of rest enjoyed before birth." Analogously, we can see the poem as an attempt to return to pure anteriority at the same time that it ambivalently tropes against anteriority.[243]

Bloom's scheme is one which is heavily indebted to the genetic conjecture (whether fallacy or not) that ontogeny recapitulates phylogeny, and in the context of poetry this means that every strong poem recapitulates the development of the poetic tradition from which it stems—we may take this simply as a broader perspective for understanding the notion of influence. As such, it is naturally suited, in particular, to the sort of meditative extension of the lyric tradition which we find exemplified in such late canonical poems as Browning's "Childe Roland to the Dark Tower Came," which Bloom uses to test his "map" in *A Map of Misreading*, and Ashbery's "Self-Portrait in a Convex Mirror," which takes as its ostensible object an autobiographical meditation both displaced into and distended within the field of vision. Ashbery's swerve away from the poetic and into the tradition of the visually aesthetic is itself figured in the *clinamen* or swerve with which Ashbery begins his poem: "As Parmigianino did it ..." But the displacement into another tradition, figured linguistically by the introductory 'as', registers both that the beginning of poetry is always an evasion (on Bloom's view) and also, incipiently, that in a deeply figural sense poetry is always anteceded by a figurally "visionary" super-poem, or design, of which the written poem itself can stand as at most a projected shadow. The bold violence of Bloom's revisionary scheme is only made manifest if we recognize that Bloom has claimed to isolate just this visionary design in his sixfold scheme of influence, not just as the design behind an individual poem but indeed as *the* design, the "superpoem," behind the strongest poems in our tradition. As I have already insisted above, Bloom's ambition is not so much to write the poems of our climate as the climate of our poems, and any insistence that "what matters is not the exact order of ratios, but the principle of substitution," or that "the map of misprision is no bed of Procrustes"[244] is only superficially defensive, and at a much deeper level an instance of the sort of kenotic, "undoing" aggression which Bloom himself diagnoses in the

---

243. idem, 91.
244. idem, 105. Compare AILWL, 195.

case of the strongest of lyric poets, Hölderlin. As it is for Hölderlin, so for Ashbery *kenosis* is also the prevalent ratio.[245]

Ashbery's poem itself divides into "six verse-paragraphs, a happy division which I shall exploit, naming them by my apotropaic litany of evasions or revisionary ratios,"[246] and like the sixfold *Meditations* of Descartes, Ashbery's are rather equally weighted until the final, sixth, where again in the Cartesian tradition and following Bloom's diagnosis of the governing trope as the redoubled metalepsis, there is a systematic recapitulation of the trajectory of the first five sections, thus embedding the genetic scheme according to which the poem itself is structured. For my purposes, the details of Bloom's itinerary through Ashbery's poem, sketchily indicated as they are (a full appreciation would require extensive filling out of the pointers Bloom provides), are less important than the "origin and goal" of Bloom's evocation. This is most powerfully reflected, and most problematically, in the last section of Ashbery's poem, which Bloom calls "the giant *metalepsis* or ratio of *apophrades* that concludes and is the glory of his poem."[247] In reading this last section, Bloom "digresses" first upon Fletcher's "theories of threshold, sequence and personification, as they were my starting-point for thinking about transumption,"[248] the latter being a name for the strategy which operates metaleptically according to the psychic defenses of introjection and projection, or impersonating and "expersonating," as we might say. Fletcher's meditations on personification occur more obviously in the context of daemonization, which Bloom associates with his fourth rhetorical figure, hyperbole. Hyperbole is the figure of "representation" preceding metalepsis; these are the two figures which Bloom must append to the classical fourfold of irony, synechdoche, metonymy and metaphor to round out his six. There is thus already a strong connection between Bloom's fourth and sixth stages, and we may think of the sixth and final stage as a reversing of the negative valence associated with the second crossing into hyperbolic representation. This repolarization occurs in the catastrophe where hyperbole, already a figure of overreaching extension, is itself stretched to a kind of limit, and drawing on Fletcher, Bloom notes that "[c]omplete projection or introjection is paranoia, which means, as Fletcher says, that 'madness is complete personification'. But most strong poets avoid this generative void, though all pause upon its threshold."[249] It is the instability associated with the conjunctive need both to proceed to the limit and to evade its totalizing implication which faces the poet in his struggle with this most ambitious of

---

245. Bloom, "Breaking," 30. See also Ashbery, *Other Traditions* (Cambridge: Harvard, 2000), 5, and *Where Shall I Wander* (New York: Harper Collins, 2005), 17-22.
246. idem, 23.
247. idem, 33.
248. idem, 33-34.
249. idem, 34.

rhetorical tropes. We may see a parallel philosophical struggle in the context of Husserl's belated *Cartesian Meditations* and his incapacity to complete the sixth, and final, one.[250] I hope in the context of this essay the reader will feel some intimation that the poetic difficulties which are brought to a head in this sixth region are mutually reflected in and illuminated by the difficulties in the foundations of mathematics sketched above.

In his reading of this last stanza of Ashbery's poem, Bloom next digresses yet further into John Hollander's work on the transumptive power of echo strategies in Milton's allusive use of simile, in which Hollander identifies a parallel between the multitudinousness of the satanic legions and the accumulation of autumn leaves. This Miltonic allusiveness itself induces in turn a "crowding of the imagination" which Angus Fletcher has demonstrated magnificently and in depth in his magisterial work on Milton's *Comus, The Transcendental Masque*.[251] Here it is a figural version of the "poetics of number" which is at issue, and the capacity of the poet to enact this through figural techniques of proliferation. This background illuminates Ashbery's initiation of this sixth stanza with a "surprised sense of achieved identification" depicted in terms of a "breeze whose simile is a page's turning."[252] This breeze is in turn transumed by a wind upon which we find a "diagram still sketched," "returning the self-portrait to an introjected earliness, an identification of poet and painter."[253] This achieves an "earliness" which defends against death, as for Bloom all poems must in both origin and aim.

But Bloom identifies the greatest power of metaleptic introjection in a passage which exposes Ashbery in all of his problematic greatness, or so I will argue. In a "metaleptic reversal of the poem's ironic opening," Ashbery openly evokes the sense that "we are a little early, that / Today has that special, lapidary / Todayness that the sunlight reproduces / Faithfully in casting twig-shadows on blithe / Sidewalks," and continues on with a description of the perspectival uniqueness of the everyday "as one / Is always cresting into one's present."[254] This is followed, as Bloom sees it, by a gradual rejection of the "paradise of art, but with enormous nostalgias coloring farewell," climaxing in a "sublime pun, fulfilling Fletcher's vision of threshold rhetoric," when Ashbery, addressing Parmigianino, bids him to "withdraw

---

250. Edmund Husserl, *Cartesian Meditations, An Introduction to Phenomenology*, tr. Dorion Cairns (The Hague: Martinus Nijhoff, 1960). The task of drafting the *Sixth Cartesian Meditation* was delegated by Husserl to Eugen Fink; see Eugen Fink, *Sixth Cartesian Meditation: The Idea of a Transcendental Theory of Method*, with textual notations by Edmund Husserl, tr. Ronald Bruzina (Bloomington: Indiana, 1995).

251. Angus Fletcher, *The Transcendental Masque: An Essay on Milton's* Comus (Cornell, 1971).

252. Bloom, "Breaking," 34.

253. idem, 35. For Ashbery's use of 'diagram', compare the beginning of his *Flow Chart* (New York: Knopf, 1991), 3, and Fletcher's discussion, *New Theory*, 210 and 219-20.

254. Cited, Bloom, "Breaking," 36.

that hand, Offer it no longer as shield or greeting, / The shield of a greeting, Francesco: / There is room for one bullet in the chamber ..."[255] Bloom reads off Ashbery's punning ambiguity as referring both to the problematic "room as moment of attention for the soul not a soul" and as "the suicide (or Russian roulette?) of a self-regarding art."[256] Dialectically, the poetic meditation can be accomplished only under conditions which literally do it in, and so figural earliness can only be achieved in literal ending.

However, beyond what Bloom has laid out, I want to underscore the extent to which Ashbery's pun is (like Whitman's lists) aesthetically defective by any traditional canons, and that this aesthetic defectiveness is part and parcel of his aesthetic strategy of defense. In terms of image and semantic register, the bullet in the chamber is not prepared in the poem in any way which the reader can easily identify, and so is assaultive—in just the way that a bullet is designed to be![257] The aesthetic dislocation which such an image registers finds a dialectical counterpart in the sense that the earliness Ashbery attempts to recuperate in a poem such as "The Recital," the last of his *Three Poems*,[258] is achieved too easily and so fails to be achieved at all. But in the context of Ashbery's poetry, one must always be wary of such effects and take seriously the possibility that they redouble powerfully and positively at a higher level. Is the "plastic sturgeon" of Ashbery's recent "Wolf Ridge" over the top, or is it driving something home?[259] Or is it driving something home by being over the top? Or is there any fact of the matter?[260] We have reached a point at which historical canonization procedures must ultimately dictate, and only time will tell. My point is rather that we must identify the potential for poetic suicide which Ashbery's gambits necessarily leave open. There is always room for one bullet in the chamber.

The point at which comparison between Bloom's and Fletcher's strategies for reading such a poem as Ashbery's "Self-Portrait" becomes most natural is in Ashbery's admonishing Parmagianino no longer to offer his self-portrait as "shield or greeting, / the shield of a greeting." Bloom glosses this by recognizing Ashbery's poem also as "the shield of a greeting, its defensive and communicative functions inextricably mixed,"[261] thus as an intrinsically

---

255. Cited, ibid.

256. idem, 37.

257. For a more tractable example, one might compare the "comb" that pops up in the last lines of Ashbery's recent poem, "Counterpane," in John Ashbery, *Where Shall I Wander*, 65-66.

258. John Ashbery, *Three Poems* (Penguin, 1977), 107-18.

259. Ashbery, *Where Shall I Wander*, 36.

260. On an allied front, and one which ultimately connects to the debates in mathematical foundations described above see Hartry Field, *Truth and the Absence of Fact* (Oxford: Clarendon, 2001), esp. 263-69.

261. Bloom, "Breaking," 37.

antithetical construction along the lines according to which the poem can only be a figural success at its literal expense. On this reading Ashbery's admonishment to Parmigianino becomes an act of figurative faith, and so an exemplification of the "nostalgias coloring farewell" at the end of this staged colloquy. "Achieved dearth of meaning is exposed as an oxymoron, where the 'achieved' outweighs the 'dearth',"[262] and so Ashbery's invocation exemplifies Bloom's faith, as well, that "the antithetical critic, following after the poem of his moment and his climate, must oppose to the abysses of Deconstruction's ironies a supermimesis achieved by an art that will not abandon the self to language."[263]

This is fine enough, but it does little to tell us specifically about the specifically *visual* function of shielding, and it is here that Fletcher's approach can help tremendously, not in a way which contradicts Bloom's insistencies, but which trains the spotlight on another dimension. Bloom's sixfold scheme may be taken as one candidate for a categorical sketch of the structure of visionary design, derived from a mixture of empirical sources and theoretical precedents, and applicable to the most canonical poems of the tradition which it orients. Such an attitude deliberately abstracts from the question of whether and, if so, how the nature of visionary design is related to the sensible capacity to see, and it abstracts as well from the tradition of visual art as it stands in relation to the poetic tradition: *ut pictura poesis*. Thus, in his gloss upon Parmigianino's portrait as shield Bloom focuses on the paradoxical communicative response which such "shielding" elicits in *both* painting and poem.[264] But this speaks not at all to the *convexity* of either particular shield nor, indeed, even to their generally anamorphic potential. What can Fletcher's "poetics of convexity" tell us in this regard?

We may begin by noticing that Parmigianino's self-portrait is a kind of inverse of Donne's conceit of the body as flat map, and that from the perspective of Donne's conceit the "distortions" of Parmigianino's convex self-representation would in fact constitute a restitution of the full-bodied spheral man which Donne's body flattens out.

But there is an inevitable ambiguity associated with such "restitution," as is exemplified by the projective and hyperbolic representations of the plane on a disk, one of which "looks" like a sphere, the other of which faithfully encodes the local representation of angles. Any analysis of Parmigianino's

---

262. ibid.

263. ibid.

264. On shields, compare Murray Krieger, *Ekphrasis: The Illusion of the Natural Sign* (Baltimore: Johns Hopkins, 1992), "Foreword: Of Shields," xiii-xvii. Krieger's larger discussion of ekphrasis is also relevant to the issues at hand, and Wesley Trimpi's *Muses of One Mind* discusses the related issue of decorum at length. See also, Wesley Trimpi, "The Meaning of Horace's Ut Pictura Poesis," *JWCI* **36** (1973), 1-34, and Wesley Trimpi, "Horace's 'Ut Pictura Poesis': The Argument for Stylistic Decorum," *Traditio* **34** (1978), 29-73.

self-portrait is further complicated by the fact that not all parts of the self-portrait derive from the same plane: Parmigianino's hand extends out from the rest of his body to the reflecting surface of the mirrored sphere, and so the focal point of the representation is displaced downward from the middle of the sphere to a point close to the bottom of it. Behind Parmigianino himself we see reflected the room in which he sits. Roughly, then, there are three planes reflected off the surface of the sphere: the plane of the hand, the plane of the rest of Parmigianino (in which the visual focus is on the artist's face) and the plane of the surrounding room in which Parmigianino sits. Since these three planes are reflected in a convex mirror, the difference between their distances to the reflecting surface is exaggerated, and we have a dwarfing of the middle-ground by the foreground, with the dramatic recession of the background being pushed off to the edges of the sphere on the sides and top. The overall effect of this visual constellation—at least as I experience it—is one of irreconcilable tension, indeed of a higher-order tension between tension and lack of tension, for the depiction of Parmigianino's visage at the center of the portrait is surprisingly calm and undistorted. The depiction of Parmigianino's hand breaks the illusion in multiple ways: because of the convex distortion with which it is reflected, but also because it seems to begin to step out from the portrait itself, to cross the threshold between what is depicted and what inhabits the space on "this side" of the portrait. It is as if the hand extends out of the mirror itself to greet us, or at least tries to do so. Yet in so doing, it inevitably can only emphasize the ultimate boundary between depiction, depicted, and those to whom it is depicted. Visually, it is in this sense that the hand serves as "shield of a greeting," "as though to protect / what it advertises."[265] It is the hand, in such proximity to the convex mirror which reflectively depicts it, which keeps the viewer at arm's length, and in so doing establishes a convex pictorial "shielding" of Parmigianino, "sequestering" his visage.[266] We are meant to feel the lengths to which Ashbery shields himself as well.[267]

But perhaps even more significantly, the distention of the hand described at the beginning of the poem—which is itself a pictorial swerve or clinamen from Euclidean perspectival accuracy, while perhaps remaining an accurate depiction of this convex reflection—announces the fractiousness of the project of self-portraiture in general. Locating this in what he (wrongly) takes to be the first artistic self-portrait,[268] Ashbery traces this fractiousness

---

265. Ashbery, *Self-Portrait*, 68.

266. ibid.

267. Compare Larry Rivers' fine *Poem and Portrait of John Ashbery* (1977) in Larry Rivers, with Carol Brightman, *Drawings and Digressions*, with a foreword by John Ashbery (New York: Clarkson N. Potter, 1979), 238.

268. Dürer's 1484 sketch "copied from myself in a mirror" provides a counterexample; see Fletcher, *Colors*, 160, citing John Pope-Hennessy's *The Portrait in the Renaissance* (New York, 1966), 126.

back to the roots of self-reflection in a way which suggests tremors not only in the notion of pictorial representation but in poetic representation and philosophical reflection as well. The fact that Parmigianino's self-portrait enlists techniques already developed in the Renaissance to move into the terrain aggressively explored by the Mannerist disunification of perspectival representation prophesies the splintering of visionary design that we find in poetry, visual art, mathematics and philosophy in the modern age. In so doing, it announces a global predicament of representational modernity, reflected not only in Parmigianino's self-portrait, but inversely in Donne's bodily map, in the metaphysical "flattening" associated with Cartesian extension and the philosophical labyrinth of the mind-body argument in Descartes' sixth meditation, as well as in the triumph of Cartesian coordinate representation over the nascent tradition of projective geometry.

None of this yet speaks to Ashbery's handling of Parmigianino's self-portrait in his poem, but his choice of focus already establishes a choice of historical frame which Fletcher's meditations on the poetics of projection help us to see better. It also provides a historical context for locating the tradition of "disjointure" which pervades Ashbery's poem and makes it aesthetically challenging directly by way of its consistent refusal of any consistent standard of evaluation. Bloom attempts to square this circle by offering us an "anomalous" benchmark against which to grade Ashbery's poem. Particularly in this context the extent to which Bloom's sixfold scheme remains a merely formal device is probably a saving grace, but to recognize this is at once to recognize its grave limitations. Neither can a "poetics of projection" deliver a recipe for deciphering Ashbery's work, which is not intended as a puzzle to be "solved." But it can attune us to Ashbery's use of pictorial precedent as a way for meditating on what is most uncanny and problematic about his poetry, and so give us a more immediate context for understanding the daring in Ashbery's evasion of poetry by way of the pictorial. This hard fact is the most difficult to grapple with in reading not just this poem, but Ashbery's work in general. Ashbery is not just absent from this poem, or just from his poetry, but from all poetry, and the meditation of "Self-Portrait," which is about the quasi-absence of the soul, or at most its uneasy location in a bodily housing, is indirectly about poetic absence, about the impossibility of "poetry" inhabiting the poem. In this regard, the notion of visionary design is the hidden analogue of the more overt soul: it is what Ashbery's poem doubts and actively seeks to eliminate even as it takes painting as its thematic focus. This twist registers an antithetical movement which it is beyond the bounds of Bloom's categorial scheme to illuminate or ultimately even to frame, and which can only be addressed by situating Ashbery's poem concretely in the context of the art and poetic history which it actively explodes. If I may be forgiven a pun, an Ashbery poem "dispaces" its context. Fletcher's poetic meditations on convexity point in this direction, giving us a way to talk about the discursive appropriation of pictorial design, as in his analysis of Vico's frontispiece. In a world of fractions upon fractions upon fractions, there are no pictures. Pictorial design, even if it anomalously refuses a fixed center of perspectival reference, must lie within a common manifold of presentation, usually the visual plane, and so ultimately always corresponds to the fixing of one "independent" variable.

VISION: A COMMON FIELD OF POETRY AND MATHEMATICS

What effectively *defines* the specific depth at which the notion of visionary design must reside is its projected capacity to illuminate such various fields of endeavor as art, mathematics and philosophy. What I have not been able to say about it here would fill books. In particular, beyond some primitive consideration of the mechanics of pictorial representation, I have said nothing about what links the notion of visionary design specifically to vision among our five senses, and most pressingly what distinguishes the role of vision from the role of hearing. For now, I will maintain silence on these difficult points. Perhaps we all have some "intuitive" conception of this connection between vision and the notion of an intuitive scheme, an "urplan" that lies behind and coordinates individual manifestations of artistic, mathematical or philosophical intent. The fact that my use of the term 'intuitive' redoubles here is certainly part of the challenge, and so part of the point. Perhaps, in some sense, "metaphysics" is, or should be, nothing other than the attempt to articulate such ground plans explicitly, doomed always from the start since it is in the nature of such plans to require vagueness of articulation for their flexible implementation.

In this essay, I have attempted to move back and forth between the notion of such a plan in the mathematical and the poetic domain. A common, and joining, thread has been the link both domains share to the techniques of perspectival representation. But the real agenda behind the sort of work I have adumbrated here is more aggressive: it is the suggestion that it is *only* in the coordinate exploration of the way that such visionary design works in manifold areas of human investigation that we can come to recognize the full power of the notion of a visionary scheme. Even if this stronger thesis is not granted, the coordination of architectonic plans in various areas can, I insist, serve as a marvelously rich heuristic ground for extending our capacity to probe the organizing principles of such complex ideational artifacts as bodies of poetry and mathematical research programs. Bloom himself has insisted that the chief benefit of his tropological scheme lies in its heuristic power to alert us to interesting connections we would otherwise overlook, and he recognizes as well that these conjectured tropological connections must always be tested by bringing them back into connection with the more immediately imagistic structures of the poems at issue. In this, he has provided a kind of template for visionary design, but one which is curiously nonvisual. Although he has roundly criticized deconstructive theorists for their tendency to view language as a prison house, Bloom's own approach remains fundamentally linguistic. If we are to remain sensitive to the long foreground of language in perception, we need to cultivate other methods, like the one Fletcher suggests. Beyond this, we need the sorts of cross-connections I have begun to suggest in this chapter.

There is one regard in which the tack I have chosen in this chapter is special, and so not readily generalizable to broader connections between poetry and mathematics. I have chosen to focus on an example in which there is an overt common bond between the two enterprises by way of the respective links to pictorial representation. Although this *is* a privileged example, naturally supplying as it does the connection between the visionary and the visual, it is ultimately only one example among many. The connections between poetry and mathematics (or the connections between poetry and painting, or the connections between painting and mathematics, or ...) are manifold and subtle. As a practitioner of both, I have myself developed a shorthand vocabulary, under the rubric "topological dynamics," which I use as a kind of "private language" to attend to these connections, and this chapter publicizes only a very small corner of this idiolect. In the public presentation of the poetic and the mathematical there will, of course, always remain a world of linguistic difference: none of the connections I have identified bears directly on the local, verbal texture of poetic or mathematical production. This local texture of poetic and mathematical production must be respected, and understanding the great extent of the local divergencies in these two cases, largely responsible for the traditional distinction between the arts and the sciences, must begin with an investigation of the public demands of poetic and mathematical communication, respectively.[269] I cannot argue for it here, but I believe that issues surrounding the status of so-called "private languages," more accurately denoted as something like cognitive idiolects or ways of thinking, are philosophically coeval with the issue of visionary design. Let me end, then, with a gnomic apothegm from the historian Paul Veyne, drawn from his work on the poetry of his friend, René Char: *Problème: une langue parlée par un seul individu peut-elle être belle? Oui, puisque toute langue s'apprend.*[270] Overcoming the boundaries between disciplines is a *pedagogical* concern, and a pressing one, which can teach us what we might otherwise overlook about how we think, at our most personal and most inspired.

---

269. In conversation, Edward Halper has suggested that some commonality of local texture between poetry and mathematics could be understood in terms of the notions of recursion and iteration. This is an interesting suggestion which deserves to be explored.

270. Paul Veyne, *René Char en ses Poèmes* (Gallimard, 1990), 174.

8

The Outlook for Legitimacy and The Pace of Modernity

In the earlier chapter on Blumenberg I have characterized his conception of the legitimacy of the modern age in terms of modernity's definitive overcoming of the Gnostic challenge. Indeed, Blumenberg himself characterizes his notion of modernity's legitimation in just these terms (LMA, 126). However, I also suggested that Blumenberg's notion of the legitimation of modernity is itself beset with problems by virtue of the fact that this very act of legitimation itself comes to resemble a Gnostic theology. In the absence of any defensible notion of legitimation, Blumenberg would be forced to retreat to the project of promoting modernity in the absence of any legitimating defense, and this would open him to just the sort of decisionism he seeks to overcome. This would effectively annul the rational core of Blumenberg's project.

In this chapter, I develop and extend Blumenberg's notion of legitimation, drawing on discussions from *The Legitimacy of the Modern Age*, in ways which deepen the characterization of modernity associated with Blumenberg's project. These dimensions of the legitimacy of the modern age are rooted in Blumenberg's work itself, but suggest ways in which Blumenberg's argument for the legitimacy of the modern age can be made less dependent on the success or failure of an ultimate overcoming of the Gnostic challenge. In particular, I will argue that we may extract a notion of legitimation from Blumenberg's work which is fully consistent with Leszek Kolakowski's notion that modernity is "on endless trial," so that the work of legitimating the modern age is seen to be an ongoing task.[272] Again, I do not mean to suggest that this characterization of legitimation is at odds with Blumenberg's work,

---

272. Leszek Kolakowski, *Modernity on Endless Trial* (Chicago: University of Chicago Press, 1990).

only with an overly narrow understanding of what would count as a definitive overcoming of the Gnostic challenge. Instead of understanding such an overcoming in philosophically argumentative terms, we should recognize the way that, as in the case of Harold Bloom's gnostic proposal, such initiatives are at least currently subsumed by larger modern agendas. This notion of legitimation is more sensitive to the ongoing "theological depressurization" of modernity and would also accommodate notions of "repressurization" to the extent that they should become needful and meaningful. In general, it is a notion of legitimation much more keyed to the features of what I have referred to previously as the "promotion of modernity," but with the advantage that it supplies an underlying structure of justification for "modernity's ongoing task." The key to this transformation of Blumenberg's notion of legitimacy will be to focus on issues of modern pacing.

A key to Blumenberg's own conception of the legitimacy of the modern age is provided by his description of the elder Husserl in the introduction to the third part of *The Legitimacy of the Modern Age*: "The 'Trial' of Theoretical Curiosity." While Blumenberg rejects the strategy of recovery which underlies the narrative of Husserl's *The Crisis of the European Sciences*, nonetheless, in contrast to the Heideggerean turn to the notion of 'care' as a defamation of theory under the guise of a return to the primacy of existential orientation, the Husserl of the 1930's emerges as an unequivocal hero of persistence in the modern theoretical attitude:

> Scarcely a decade after theory, as mere gaping at what is 'present at hand,' had been, if not yet despised, still portrayed as a stale recapitulation of the content of living involvements, it was the greatness of the solitary, aged Edmund Husserl, academically exiled and silenced, that he held fast to the resolution to engage in theory as the initial act of European humanity and as a corrective for its most terrible deviation, and that he required of it a rigorous consistency, which is still, or once again, felt to be objectionable. Hermann Lübbe has described as the characteristic mark of this philosophizing, especially in the late works, the "rationalism of theory's interest in what is without interest": "The existential problem of a scholar who in his old age was forbidden to set foot in the place where he carried on his research and teaching never shows through, and even the back of the official notice that informed him of this prohibition was covered by Husserl with philosophical notes. That is a case of 'carrying on' whose dignity equals that of the sentence, 'Noli turbare circulos meos'." (LMA, 236)

The comparison with Archimedes helps to register two points. The first is that Husserl's particular version of persistence is itself closely aligned with his reading of the European tradition in terms of a primordial commitment to theory. But such a commitment is clearly evident in a (late) ancient context in the case of Archimedes, and so this commitment to the priority of theory cannot be used in isolation to identify the characterizing mark of modernity. This leads to the second point, which is that the valorization of Husserl, alongside Archimedes, in the passage quoting from Hermann Lübbe, is intended to exemplify a *vigilance* which is not itself exclusively a function of the commitment to theory.

In this latter regard, a passage toward the end of the third part of *The Legitimacy of the Modern Age* is critical. Blumenberg discusses Freud's psychoanalytic theory and the peculiar difficulties that attend it as a consequence of the fact that the psychoanalyst's act of theoretical curiosity, hence investigation, is, in addition to its theoretical value, expected to serve a therapeutic and resolutive purpose for the patient. In an attempt to elucidate the consequences for the psychoanalyst of this alignment of theory and therapy, Blumenberg turns to Freud's discussion of Leonardo da Vinci's "pathology," in which, along the lines of Leonardo's own deathbed report, his curiosity is understood to have affected his artistic endeavors "pathologically." In his characterization of Leonardo's, as well as Freud's, curiosity, Blumenberg provides us with a powerful necessary criterion for characterizing the sort of curiosity which must underlie the modern condition of theoretical investigation:

> The curiosity that, in both Leonardo and his analyst, has become an instrument rests on a powerful energetic basis of acquired autarky. The artist, in any case, with his commitment to his work, seems, judging by the analysis of his resignations, to be on a wrong path rather than a detour. (LMA, 452)

With characteristically acerbic irony, Blumenberg situates the "failure" of da Vinci as an artist in line with the success of Freud as a theorist. Here again a problematic earlier figure (Archimedes/da Vinci) is aligned with a powerful later one (Husserl/Freud), setting the terms for a presentation of the difficult, because contextual, transition which is required for modernity to become legitimate and, hence, sustainable, in ways that the enterprises of Archimedes and (according to Freud) da Vinci were not in their respective endeavors and historical locations. The necessary (but not, I will argue, sufficient) criterion which Blumenberg embeds in his discussion of Freud's analysis of da Vinci has two parts: both a powerful energetic basis and the acquisition, on this basis, of an autarchic status for theoretical curiosity.

It is the "powerful energetic basis" which is (largely) lacking in antiquity, with the example of Archimedes serving as a threshold case, and it is only after the intensification of cognitive affect associated with the development of late, medieval nominalism that such an energetic basis is systematically available for the enterprise of theoretical investigation: theologically in the medieval tradition, and in a this-worldly setting in the modern age. What Blumenberg calls the *absolutism* of focus embodies such a "powerful energetic basis" and allows for it to be sustained in a systematic way:

> Because theology meant to defend God's absolute interest, it allowed and caused man's interest in himself and his concern for himself to become absolute. The position of his openness to theology's claims forced his self-concern to reoccupy it. (LMA, 197)

The deeper characterization of what is required for Blumenberg to defend the modern age as legitimate is therefore that the modern age be defensible as the **systematic** context for theoretical investigation undertaken with a powerful energetic basis. By 'systematic', I intend that this context must be provided in such a way that it is available not merely for isolated, exceptional individuals (Archimedes), but in a way which is stable and widely culturally available. In turn, it is this "powerful energetic basis," freed from the medieval theological context, which will lead to the specific dynamics of modern pacing. Conversely, the pace of modernity supplies us with a leading clue for the articulation of this underlying energetic basis. The systematic context of this energetic basis must not only promote and sustain theoretical autarchy but also **regulate** its pacing and the pacing of its consequences. The pace of modernity is therefore intimately tied to the pace of theoretical endeavor. Blumenberg himself emphasized the need for a systematic context for theoretical investigation; the only novelty I propose here is to extend the implications of this systematic context for issues of modern pacing. In this way, however, I hope to stabilize Blumenberg's conception of legitimation by extending it to issues of pacing. This constitutes a minimal conceptual extension of Blumenberg's enterprise, but it leads to radically novel insights. In particular, I will claim, it allows us (but also forces us) to view the epochal transition to the modern age as a dramatic transition in scale, a "dis-pacing," because an irreducible and irreversible outpacing, of the previous age. Defending this thesis would require an extensive historical reconstruction, but the rudiments of such a presentation are already visible in the treatment of the man → Man transition as discussed in the work of Arendt and Blumenberg above. Elizabeth Brient's work on the transmission, unacknowledged by Blumenberg, of the medieval theological conception of the intensive infinite to the modern age in the form of a worldly intensive infinity would also support such a reconstruction.[273]

The brunt of Blumenberg's work in providing a defense of modernity's legitimacy lies in *describing* modernity in such a way that its support for intensive theoretical investigation can be seen as systematically rational: thus the normative defense of modernity depends, in turn, on a descriptive, historical characterization of the modern tradition, and it is first here that attention to modern pacing becomes critical. To be sure, this descriptive, historical characterization is allowed to be markedly "reconstructive": we are engaged in what the detractors of Imre Lakatos would call "potted"

---

273. Elizabeth Brient, *The Immanence of the Infinite: Hans Blumenberg and the Threshold to Modernity* (Washington, D.C.: Catholic University, 2002).

history.[274] Nonetheless, such a notion of rational reconstruction must be distinguished from other strictly, and more narrowly, conceived approaches to normative defense, since it both allows and requires that history, as an object of description, has or may be taken to have a systematic underlying rational basis which permits such reconstructive effort. This is to say that there is an ineliminably historical dimension in Blumenberg's (and indeed Lakatos') legitimation of theory, potted though it may be. Surprisingly, such a historical dimension must be insisted upon, since Blumenberg indicates that the historical dimension of his defense must also necessarily remain quite weak.

Key to his rational reconstruction of modern history is Blumenberg's positing of a principle of sufficient rationality as a minimal, "emergency consolidation" requisite to support the notion of self-assertion which underlies his conception of the relation between knowledge and action in the modern age. This principle is justified *pragmatically* as a psychological requisite for the tenability of a minimally stable conception of the human condition in a world which has been "abandoned" by God, for

> the modern age began, not indeed as the epoch of the death of God, but as the epoch of the hidden God, the *deus absconditus*—and a hidden God is *pragmatically* as good as dead. The nominalist theology induces a human relation to the world whose implicit content could have been formulated in the postulate that man had to behave as though God were dead. This induces a restless taking stock of the world, which can be designated as the motive power of the age of science. (LMA, 346)

In the absence of a foundational appeal to God—and in this regard Blumenberg sees the Cartesian enterprise as recidivist in comparison to other early modern efforts such as Bacon's and Bruno's—an alternative source of rational stability must be identified, and Blumenberg locates this in the above-mentioned principle of sufficient rationality:

---

274. Lakatos himself finessed the problem of rational reconstruction, as is evident from a perusal of the second volume of his philosophical papers, *Mathematics, science and epistemology*, ed. John Worral and Gregory Currie (Cambridge, 1978). In the unpublished "Cauchy and the continuum: the significance of non-standard analysis for the history and philosophy of mathematics," ed. J. P. Cleave, a section on "Rational Reconstruction versus History" is promised (44) but silently omitted; in the essay, "The Method of Analysis-Synthesis," Lakatos brackets the larger question and contents himself with the assertion that "history can only be rationally understood in the light of such [rational] reconstructions" (87). Perhaps his fullest response to the problem of the relation of history to its rational reconstructions comes in a footnote to the essay, "Changes in the Problem of Inductive Logic," where he asserts that

> [m]ethodology is wedded to history, since methodology is nothing but a rational reconstruction of history, of the growth of knowledge. Because of the imperfection of the scientists, some of the actual history is a caricature of its rational reconstruction; because of the imperfection of the methodologists, some methodologies are caricatures of actual history. (And, one may add, because of the imperfection of historians, some histories of science are caricatures both of actual history and of its rational reconstruction.) (178)

> ... this book's concept of rationality is neither that of an agency of salvation nor that of a creative originality either. On the analogy of the principle of sufficient reason, I would like to entitle this concept that of a sufficient rationality. It is just enough to accomplish the postmedieval self-assertion and to bear the consequences of this emergency self-consolidation. The concept of the legitimacy of the modern age is not derived from the accomplishments of reason but rather from the necessity of those accomplishments. (LMA, 99)

What is 'necessary' is a sense of the human condition as something cognitively sustainable—and not just for exceptional, isolated individuals. Hence, we may formulate the legitimacy of the *intensification* of theoretical investigation described above as follows: the intensification of theoretical investigation, understood as the conducting of autarchic theoretical investigation on the basis of a powerful energetic basis, is itself a *requisite* for the sustenance of *any* cognitive orientation in the historical context provided by the collapse of late, medieval nominalist theology. Yet this sustainability requires a further *systematic* context for the assimilative regulation of the accelerative pacing which it implies.

Blumenberg immediately proceeds to insist that his legitimation is not in any sense reliant upon an appeal to the novelty of the solution proposed by the modern age. Indeed, whatever novelty this solution possesses is effectively forced upon it by the failure of previous "solutions" to the problem of the human cognitive condition. It is in this context that Blumenberg's proposed description of a modern "solution" must be understood as historical, yet only in the weak sense that its emergence is historically conditioned. Blumenberg admits that "in part II of this book an attempt is made at presenting a 'historical' justification accomplished by other means than appeal to quantity of time and to continuity," i.e. the justification of the modern solution is not seen as acquiring legitimacy from the historical period over which it developed or from its continuity with solution-strategies previously historically available. Nonetheless,

> [i]f it turned out to be possible to produce historical arguments as well for the rationality of the rationalism of the modern age, this would, in view of the whole structure of the argument, not amount to a demonstration of any competence beyond that required by the modest finding of self-assertion. (LMA, 99)

I will take issue with this claim in the following section, but for my current purpose it is sufficient to note that in opposition to the traditionalism of his critic, Carl Schmitt, Blumenberg rightly insists upon the *lack* of the appeal to historical *categories* (tradition, renaissance, revolution) in the justification of the modern age. As Blumenberg points out elsewhere, and I believe rightly, such a criticism also identifies a core of irrationalism in Thomas Kuhn's approach to the structure of scientific revolutions.[275] Blumenberg's justification is a pragmatically rational justification, bearing significant comparison both to Lakatos' conception of rational reconstruction and to Lakatos' critique of traditional forms of justificationism in the philosophy of science. Yet Blumenberg stops short of addressing questions about the requisite framework to accommodate modernity's accelerative pacing, which require a demonstration of the "rationality of modern rationalism" along the lines Blumenberg dismisses above.

How, then, are we to understand this characterization of Blumenberg's notion of the legitimacy of the modern age as a function of the justification of intense, theoretical investigation in terms of Blumenberg's more explicit characterization of the modern age as the second and definitive overcoming of Gnosticism? I would supply the following step, which does not appear explicitly in Blumenberg's argument: Gnosticism is not itself *systematically* sustainable as a solution to the human cognitive condition. On this supplied reconstruction, Blumenberg's argument would be that, in the absence of the modern solution, the collapse of late, medieval nominalism as a sustainable worldview threatened to produce resurgent Gnosticism as an (untenable) countersolution, and the modern solution successfully avoided this consequence. As an excusable simplification, we might say that in the modern age Gnosticism is privately, but not publicly, sustainable. But this is not yet enough to explain why the modern solution should be construed as "definitive": in order to argue for this Blumenberg must show, at a minimum, that the modern solution is not susceptible to the sort of problems posed by the solution attempted by the synthesis of the Church Fathers which, as Blumenberg understands it, ultimately degenerated into the untenable stance of late, medieval nominalism. What is required is precisely to show that the sort of gnostic proposals mounted by Harold Bloom (and perhaps, ultimately, even Blumenberg's own methodology) can be adequately assimilated into the fabric of modernity. Key to this demonstration is the recognition that such proposals factor into modernity's overall pacing in terms of their thematization of a retardative desire not *theoretically* compatible with

---

275. While Blumenberg insists that he is "not making a belated plunge into the dispute about Thomas Kuhn's *The Structure of Scientific Revolutions*," he remarks also that "this is not necessary, when what is at stake is only the type of theory of the history of science that it represents, insofar as it presents a process form of singular significance" (LMA, 464). Here what is significant is that Kuhn's approach cannot serve (any more than could Schmitt's) the sort of legitimating function which Blumenberg takes his account to provide, since "'[s]cientific revolutions,' if one were to choose to take their radicalness literally, simply cannot be the ultimate concept of a rational conception of history; otherwise that conception would have denied to its object the very same rationality it wanted to assert for itself" (LMA, 465). Blumenberg must establish a procedure for describing the "epochal threshold" between the medieval and modern ages which is rational in its recognition of the lack of such a radical discontinuity.

the dynamic conception of rationality resulting from the "emergency consolidation" Blumenberg identifies. In a modern context, then, such "recidivism" is only successful insofar as it *practically* enlists that ideal of human self-assertion which it attempts *theoretically* to negate. It is thus not *rational* in the requisite sense, and so not capable of public legitimation. As long as the dynamics of modern pacing can absorb such retardative initiatives—which indeed go some distance in "humanizing" modernity's pace, and so even contribute to its stabilization—modernity retains its *dynamic* legitimacy. This new conception of legitimacy, dependent on the explicit recognition of the pacing of modernity, extends but is consistent with the new reading of Blumenberg's legitimacy which I have proposed. It does point out, however, that Blumenberg's own attempt to legitimate modernity stops short of what is fully required. Below, I will identify this as a weakness of his entirely *pragmatic* understanding of the adoption of a principle of sufficient rationality as an emergency consolidation of reason in the turn to the modern age, but first some observations about Blumenberg's pragmatism are needed.

What I call Blumenberg's "pragmatism" reflects his larger methodological commitment to assuming the weakest possible orientation capable of establishing the functional adequacy of modern rationality to its historical condition. The weakness of Blumenberg's direct appeal to history in his attempted justification functions in a similar way. The weakness of this appeal to history serves as a considerable strength of Blumenberg's proposal, for to argue in *historical* terms that a solution is definitive requires just the sort of foreordination which, in the absence of an appeal to God as foundational authority, the modern solution cannot guarantee. Blumenberg's methodological pragmatism reflects not just a commitment to parsimony, but more deeply the commitment to such minimalism being a rational requisite for the sort of justification proposed. On Blumenberg's behalf, I suggest that in line with his methodological minimalism, we understand modernity's overcoming of Gnosticism in the following way: as an unstable solution, Gnosticism fails in the presence of any solution which provides similar strengths in the absence of such instability as Gnosticism evinces. Since the modern solution effectively accomplishes this task, it must register as a definitive overcoming of Gnosticism. The success of this reconstruction, however, is still dependent on the resolution of any issues of pacing which Blumenberg does not formally acknowledge.

Once supplied with this reconstruction, a hefty task still besets Blumenberg. Yet, it is unclear to me how Blumenberg may accomplish his intended aim in any less demanding way. On this reconstruction, Blumenberg, or more realistically his representative, is saddled with the task of showing that the modern solution is a solution with all of the positive features of the Gnostic pseudo-solution yet lacking its disadvantageous instability. The suggestion I have made that modernity is capable of *absorbing* and indeed even profiting from gnostic impulses and proposals goes some distance toward responding to this concern.

As I discussed in the earlier chapter on Blumenberg, at the beginning of the second part of *The Legitimacy of the Modern Age* Blumenberg remarks that while it is inappropriate to consider the modern age as a relapse into paganism following an era governed by Christian theology, "[m]ore on target ... is [the accusation] of a relapse into Gnosticism" (LMA, 126). Appropriately, the title of the first chapter of this part is "The Failure of the First Attempt at Warding Off Gnosticism Ensures Its Return" (LMA, 127). In this chapter Blumenberg tells us both what was successful and what was unsuccessful in the Christian attempt to ward off the "Gnostic challenge":

> The Gnostic dualism had been eliminated as far as the metaphysical world principle was concerned, but it lived on in the bosom of mankind and its history as the absolute separation of the elect from the rejected. (LMA, 135)

It was the ultimate psychological untenability of this latter dualism which ushered in the return of full-blown Gnosticism. But this indicates that there is something (ultimately) psychologically preferable about Gnostic dualism in comparison to what we might refer to as the soteriological dualism of Christian theology, particularly in its late, nominalist varieties.

As Blumenberg makes clear, whether we consciously do so or not, we are all forced to value the impact of the modern affirmation of intensively undertaken theoretical investigation. In a passage of eloquent directness, Blumenberg outlines the level at which the stakes of the decision for modernity are set:

> Most of the people whose lives today depend on science would not even be alive, or would no longer be alive, if science had not made their lives possible and prolonged them. When one puts it that way, it sounds laudable. On the other hand, this means at the same time that the overpopulation of our world is also an excess produced by science. Are there unambiguous conclusions that can be drawn from this statement? One should avoid too easy answers to this question. To a large extent, science has broken the brutal mechanism of the "survival of the fittest": it gives more life to people who are less 'fit' for life and keeps them alive longer. Is this a humane achievement? Here again it would be frivolous to say that we have an answer to the question. But to pose it is to make as clear as possible the significance of what one is dealing with when one not only focuses on the dependence of our reality on science but also defines that dependence as problematic. (LMA, 230)

In this passage Blumenberg discusses the most basic demographics of what we might call *human* pacing in the modern age: the term of life and the quantity of population, both closely tied to the natality thematized by Arendt, but conditioned by modern science. Blumenberg's defense of the legitimacy of the modern age needs to be recognized as one which is predicated upon avoiding "too easy answers to this question;" indeed, it does not supply any definitive answer at all, but only opens up paths for the consideration of the question. In this respect, the legitimacy of the modern age is not so much something that first needs to be *defended* as its "questionable legitimacy" is something to be described. Yet this is a only first step; a thicker criterion of legitimacy based on pacing is a second. In particular,

> [t]he existence, and even the mere dimensions of the existence, of science are not things over which we have the power of disposition as long as we do not feel entitled to answer in the affirmative the question whether the nonexistence of existing persons or the discontinued existence of people whose existence has at any time been in danger would have been a more humane alternative. (LMA, 230)

Blumenberg chronicles the frighteningly absurd consequences of the "too easy answers" to such questions provided by Maupertuis during the Age of Enlightenment. Peter Singer's program for the "desanctification of life" would perhaps supply us with a parallel contemporary exemplification, which at least has the advantage, which Maupertuis' more innocent historical context did not provide him, of offering us a *reductio* of the current state of moral philosophy in the absence of decisive answers to Blumenberg's questions and faced with the relevant historical evidence. All of these may be viewed as proto-gnostic challenges to modernity, which modernity is required to assimilate into its dynamic pace.

What is required for a legitimation of modernity, in this regard at least, is a rational framework for orientation. In a discussion of Kant's essay, "What Does It Mean to Orient Oneself in Thought," Blumenberg points out a footnote in which Kant appeals to the logical structure of the categorical imperative to establish the "Maxims of the Self-Preservation of Reason": to assume something as reason for an action amounts to it being possible to universalize it as a principle for reason. Kant takes such universalizability as a consistency condition for reason itself, as is clear when he goes on to comment that "[i]f enlightenment is nothing other than this very self-preservation of reason, then the freedom of cognition that it demands is not an arbitrary but a lawful freedom" (LMA, 432). On this model, reasons are motives for action that are self-consistent with the general provision of motives for action. Such consistency is necessary and sufficient for rational orientation, and so although it is evaluated relative to needs, it is separate from specific needs in its legitimation. As Blumenberg remarks, "need sets in motion, but it does not orient; it is legitimate, but it does not legitimize" (LMA, 432). Although Blumenberg will substitute a pragmatic justification of the principle of sufficient rationality for Kant's universalization of reason as principle, in each case the goal is to provide a legitimating framework for the orientation of legitimate needs.

It is important to point out another regard in which one may mistake Blumenberg's legitimation for something more ambitious than Blumenberg's aim: it is not an attempt to argue for reason from an antecedent standpoint neutral between rationality and irrationality. Rather, it is by appeal to reason that we argue for reason, and it is perhaps in these terms that the "threat" of Gnosticism is best understood. For Blumenberg, the point is not to evaluate whether Gnosticism or modern rationality better serves the historical need-context bequeathed to modernity by the fall of nominalistic theology, nor indeed need we assume that the historical need-context of "modernity" is constant or even persistent in any particular regard, beyond recognizing the entirely contingent fact that what Blumenberg calls "assertion needs" change at variable rates, with some assertion needs persisting longer than others. In this latter regard, as Blumenberg states, "[i]t is enough that the reference-frame conditions have greater inertia for consciousness than do the contents associated with them, that is, that the questions are relatively constant in comparison to the answers" (LMA, 466).

For Blumenberg, the "overcoming" of Gnosticism is successful to the extent that a rationally *consistent* alternative to the Gnostic orientation may be provided which is historically and culturally cogent in principle. In the presence of such a consistent alternative, the praxical contradiction in the Gnostic orientation will, one may at least hope, be capable of being "floated along" in the dynamics of modern pacing. Presumably we would never practically be in a position to evaluate such a rationally consistent alternative without appealing to the evidence supplied by the historical development of some version of it (just as, albeit in a much more limited way, Kant's enterprise must appeal to the particular nature of human cognition in order to provide a rational critique),[276] but there is sufficient evidence in Blumenberg's work that he means to distinguish between the "context of justification" and the "context of inquiry." Because we are dealing with the modern age, itself a historical entity, history necessarily enters into both contexts, but in different ways: in the first case it supplies a domain of imperfect implementation with respect to which justification may be evaluated; in the latter context it supplies a source for heuristic motivation, and hence for understanding. At this scale, Blumenberg's project stands in the same basic Enlightenment frame as does Kant's critical project. Necessarily, Blumenberg's project shifts uneasily beneath the weight which is set by such goals; in particular, the question of the relation between Gnostic theology and Blumenberg's own methodology becomes one about the extent of our capacity to maintain a rational approach in the promotion of the legitimation of rationality itself. This capacity is particularly challenged when it addresses *legitimate* human needs which are not (because they *cannot* be) legitimating in a modern context.

---

276. Kant, *Critique of Pure Reason*, B585.

Before the success or failure of Blumenberg's enterprise in this, or any other, regard may be assessed, the project must first be properly construed. My remarks in this section have been largely intended to serve this propadeutic aim. On my construal of Blumenberg's project of legitimation, many of the problems associated with previous evaluations of Blumenberg's project require reconsideration. More pressing still than such reconsideration is the task of considering the potential problems which face Blumenberg on my construal of his position. On this construal, the position from which Blumenberg provides a legitimation of the modern age requires an "outlook" on the problem of legitimation and hence must satisfy a certain criterion of surveyability.

Although my proposal offers a route for addressing questions of theology in the modern age, it requires in turn a breadth of *human* vision in order to bring forth the requisite legitimation. In this section I have begun to touch upon this set of concerns, in particular, in the remarks concerning the rational reconstruction of history. Such a reconstruction must be consolidated from a perspective which has at its disposal both a repository of the relevant historical evidence and a firm grasp of the rationality which is required to enlist this evidence in the provision of a non-historically grounded defense of the relevant historical development. Hence, the chief problem that continues to beset Blumenberg's project, even should all other challenges be met, is the practical problem of mastering both the relevant (historical) evidential base and rational methodology.

This, at least, is an appropriately philosophical, as opposed to theological, challenge, yet that it is so points to the fact that Blumenberg's project tacitly, and at points even explicitly, enlists a particular conception of philosophical grounding appropriate to such a set of concerns. The conceptual distinction between lifetime and worldtime embedded in the title of Blumenberg's later volume begins to provide tools for the evaluation of the requisite conditions of surveyability, and the work Blumenberg does there shows how, indeed, those conditions themselves become part of the modern predicament which must repeatedly be addressed. In his discussion of the bankruptcy of historicism, Blumenberg points to the man → Man transition, as I have already discussed above; the fundamental question is whether Blumenberg's own project also requires a version of it— as I think it does in order to address the dynamics of modern pacing. The full accountability for "modernity" remains involved in the very process of modernizing the methodology of the historical attitude, and this leads directly into those issues of pacing I will consider in the next section. However, on the reconstruction of Blumenberg's position which I have supplied, we are free to see the basic project of *legitimating* modernity as one which antecedes a more historically "substantial" sense of *accounting for* it. Further, the more ambitious task of accounting for modernity must be an ongoing endeavor according to the very criteria provided by this antecedent legitimation. Indeed, on the reading I have proposed, Blumenberg's corpus of work must be seen as both a description of this ongoing project of historical modernity and as itself a contribution to it. Yet it remains an open question whether Blumenberg's work remains prolegomena to any future philosophy or elegiac portrait of the philosophical tradition's collapse under the weight of its methodological prerequisites. Ultimately, we must suspect that neither of these dramatic extremes is more than a simplification of the current state of philosophy, but their juxtaposition does pose a question which, from an antithetical poetic orientation, will come to dominate the final chapter. First, I want to outline further in the next section a philosophical context for considering these questions, one that relies on an explicit introduction of the issue of modernity's pace.

PUSHING FURTHER WITH PACE

In the previous section I have attempted to indicate how Blumenberg's own conception of legitimacy may be re-envisioned in order to face potential problems arising from the proximity of his own methodology to Gnostic theology. Retrospectively, this proximity should not be entirely surprising, given that the project of legitimating the modern condition may serve a retardative function with respect to modernity's pacing in some (but far from all) ways similar to that which a Gnostic theology would seek to achieve in a modern context. Much more consideration would ultimately be required to evaluate my proposal, but in this section I want to focus instead on the extension of Blumenberg's legitimation by way of the appeal to modernity's pace.

To pursue this extension we require some basic notion of dynamic stability, for my thesis is that the legitimacy of the modern age can only be evaluated contextually in terms of its dynamic pacing and whether this provides a stable context for the emergency consolidation Blumenberg identifies as a legitimation of human self-assertion. To put matters another way: the capacity to assert ourselves is only legitimate for as long as the modifications in our condition which this produces preserve the stability requisite to our ongoing human needs. I understand by such stability a condition which is both dynamic and non-catastrophic; a minimum of such stability consists in the ongoing legitimation of human self-assertion. Such a legitimacy may be called into question, as by Gnosticism, but were this contention to disrupt the fundamental structural role which this legitimation plays, then modernity's stable promotion of human self-assertion would be defeated. The problem is complicated by the fact that our needs are themselves a function of the ongoing modification of our condition, and so are also not constant. Yet this also offers a crucial degree of flexibility, since our needs may also adapt in ways which help to preserve the underlying stability they require. The need for adaptation is the proximal source of those assimilation needs of which I have spoken in the Introduction.

It seems clear that our ability to predict or even judge our capacities for adaptation prior to testing them is quite minimal, and this is a strong reason to believe that the project of legitimation envisioned must, in this concern for stability, be ongoing. At best, we will be in a position to legitimate our condition with respect to some current parameters of acceptable stability, which may change dramatically over time.[277] Even so, the criteria for evaluating the viability of our current situation will require that we rely on certain relatively fixed, widely accepted desiderata. Just as Blumenberg's project of legitimation requires the recognition that such a legitimation must always be accomplished against the background of *relatively* fixed assumptions, so here there will be a need to appeal to such points of tacit agreement. However, if we are to extend the evaluation of modernity's legitimation by considering its pace, a second layer of assumptions will be requisite in order to evaluate the *current* pacing of modernity's ongoing dynamic development. Most pressingly, a methodological context is needed for such consideration.

I have remarked above on the "minimal pragmatism" Blumenberg's methodology dictates, and I have also remarked on the structural analogies between his defense of the principle of sufficient rationality, on the one hand, and Kant's defense of the inherent consistency of rationality, on the other. In both regards, Blumenberg's methodology may be compared to C. S. Peirce's as exemplified in the 1903 Harvard Lectures, *Pragmatism as a Principle and Method of Right Thinking*.[278] In Peirce's lectures, his argument for the pragmatic principle plays an analogous role to that played by the transcendental deduction in Kant's *First Critique*. As in Blumenberg's case, Peirce's strategy is to argue for a weaker principle (in his case, the pragmatic principle) than the system of principles required by Kant's stronger conception of rationality, with a commitment to weaker means of argumentation being sufficient (and, because they are weaker, also available) to argue for the weaker principle. In both Peirce's case and Blumenberg's we may safely characterize these means as pragmatic, and I do not take issue with this methodological "retreat" per se. However, in both Peirce's and Blumenberg's case, what is lacking in comparison with the Kantian project is any articulation of the systematic *context* for the application of their respective pragmatic principles of rationality. This systematic context must come in the form of a structure

---

277. I would view initiatives in environmental philosophy as one attempt to do this in a circumscribed way. Analogous remarks to those I have made above both about the fruitfulness and also the limitations of Fletcher's notion of 'environment-poem' could be made about environmental philosophy.

278. C. S. Peirce, *Pragmatism as a Principle and Method of Right Thinking: the 1903 Havard Lectures on Pragmatism*, ed. Patricia Ann Turisi (Albany: State University of New York, 1997).

for the application of a principle of pure rationality to the domain of experience, and in Kant's critical project, this is what is provided by the Table of Categories requiring a transcendental deduction.[279]

If the specific contribution of pacing to the issues which beset the legitimation of modernity indicates that precisely such a context of rational application is required—as I have suggested above—then this defect in projects such as Peirce's and Blumenberg's must be repaired. In the absence of a Kantian transcendental deduction, I believe this requires that we "produce historical arguments as well for the rationality of the rationalism of the modern age" (LMA, 99), precisely those arguments which we have seen Blumenberg insist above are superfluous and thus can have no bearing on the project of legitimating modernity. To demonstrate that modern rationality is stable in the face of *ongoing* Gnostic challenges requires historical arguments that modern rationality is "rational" in ways that go beyond its simply offering an emergency consolidation in the face of the psychological untenability of the late medieval condition. At a minimum—though personally I remain dubious that this is at all sufficient—we might argue that the *minimality* of this emergency consolidation is itself responsible for an emerging stability in the pace of theoretical investigation and—again, perhaps—by implication the pace of modernity. There are several important 'ifs' here, and even if these concerns could be discharged, it would still remain the case that we were making some argument about modern rationality over and above what is required to defend it as an emergency, i.e. immediate, consolidation. If, as I have tried to do, we take sufficiently seriously the residual theological pressurization of the early modern age and the developing theological depressurization we find as modernity progresses, we should remain even more dubious about the *long-term* stability of such an emergency consolidation absent some further argument. What we need is some rational understanding of the stability of modernity's dynamic pace.

In Blumenberg's project, as we have seen, there is an apparent incompatibility between the pragmatic justification of this emergency consolidation and his insistence that modernity constitutes a *definitive* overcoming of Gnosticism. I have suggested a way to finesse this issue as far as possible within the methodological parameters of Blumenberg's own project, but ultimately we must acknowledge that the overcoming of Gnosticism relies not just on Gnosticism's praxical rational inconsistency, but also on the extent to which modernity remains capable of *absorbing* such initiatives. It is in this latter regard that a "systemic context" is required for justification, and this requires (something like) an account of modern rationality not just in terms of its consistency but also in terms of its capacity systematically to be extended

---

279. In Peirce's case, it may be that his proposed "metaphysics of continuity" could ultimately provide such a context, but such a proposal faces many challenges that Peirce's work is far from resolving.

from historical context to context. That such an argument must remain minimally historical can be seen from the fact that not only are such contexts themselves historical, but the identification and specification of such contexts is an intrinsically historical business.

The delimitation of the relevant contexts also depends on the circumscribing identification of those contexts in which we could reasonably expect human rationality to respond successfully. To take a limiting example, in the case of a successfully implemented all-out nuclear strike, rational response comes to the scene too late, and so becomes a non-issue. But less extreme cases are equally methodologically pertinent. Should we expect human rationality to be able to respond in the face of massive economic or environmental catastrophe? The answer to this question is, of course, "hopefully, yes," but the more important methodological point is that our capacity to respond will be a function of the stability and flexibility of application of human rationality across variation in context. In our contemporary historical condition, this functional relation is perhaps the most basic issue of the *pacing* of modern rationality. I would suggest that it is the deeper, structural condition which underlies the contemporary philosophical preoccupation with cultural relativism.

In the wake of a recent economic "crisis," we may call on this particular context to specify the sorts of concerns which are at issue here. Relevant questions would be: how much of a "crisis" was this? What role did economic bailout play in "averting the crisis"? To what extent is recent economic history (over, say, the years 2005-2009) an indication that the economic system is *fundamentally* unstable? How successful can we expect our economic "tools" to be in responding to other potential economic "crises"? Similar questions could be raised about an impending crisis resulting from global warming. The point of extending the legitimation of modernity by including issues of pacing is not, of course, to generate direct answers to these questions. It is, rather, to provide a theoretical context within which we may ask historically more general questions *about* these questions, such as, why do we ask them, and why do we expect the range of responses to be delimited in the ways that we do? These anterior, more general questions may, however, serve as potent heuristic sources for indicating *possible* answers to the more specific questions at issue. Why do certain issues (such as, I suggest, the environment) prove more intractable to rational address than others (such as, I suggest, more straightforwardly economic ones)? (The first answer, I suggest, is that we can address the latter in terms of a more limited, therefore tractable, conception of rationality.) Again, the point is not to provide *understanding* regarding these questions directly, or even to provide a fixed context for such understanding. Most fundamentally, the point instead is to provide some legitimation for the sense that it is reasonable to ask such questions and expect some answers—rather than, for example, simply throwing up our hands or burying our heads. We are dealing with a more general, rational version of what is typically referred to as "confidence in the economy." It is the generality of the rationality in which we require confidence which poses the focal philosophical difficulty.

In his later work, Blumenberg also moves in a direction which would help with these issues, but not specifically by extending his notion of the legitimation of the modern age. Instead, Blumenberg devotes considerable attention to the status of attempts—and most extensively, Husserl's—to develop a philosophical anthropology, which is to say, a philosophical account of human nature. It is nearly obvious how such a venture would help with the questions which are at issue here, for it would circumscribe in particular those contexts which are "compatible" in some fundamental sense with our experience of the human condition. The psychological pressure associated with late medieval nominalism becomes, in the relevant sense, "inhuman," and this serves as a psychic trigger for the emergency consolidation Blumenberg describes. Here again, the historical documentation provided by Jean Delumeau is extensive and convincing, but it demonstrates not only how this fear contributed to the downfall of the medieval worldview but also to the emergence of a "western guilt culture" that would play an integral pressurizing role in the early modern period.[280] Such historical investigations may yield ways to understand the dynamic stabilization of the modern condition in terms of ongoing forms of (non-theological) "re-pressurization." A further dimension of philosophical anthropology could aid in determining the range of pacing which is humanly sustainable, and would go some way, for example, to providing a general philosophical context for articulating the intolerability of totalitarian conditions, for example. Hannah Arendt's *The Human Condition* would count as a large first step in this direction.[281] Although these concerns would naturally lead into questions of morality and prudentiality, conceptually speaking they antecede them, as they are more directly associated with the rational sustainability of human action itself.

Blumenberg's meditations on philosophical anthropology are extensive and labyrinthine. At a minimum, one would have to consider the entirety

---

280. Jean Delumeau, *Sin and Fear: The Emergence of a Western Guilt Culture 13th- 18th Centuries*, trans. Eric Nicholson (New York: St. Martin's Press, 1990).

281. Hannah Arendt, *The Human Condition* (Chicago: University of Chicago, 1958). I thank Elizabeth Brient for reiterating that Arendt's ambition in this volume was not to provide a general philosophical anthropology, but only an account of the *vita activa*. This would be complemented by her later work on the *vita contemplativa* in LM. What is required from philosophical anthropology for the proposed legitimation of the modern condition lies at the intersection of these two classically distinct concerns in an account of the structure of human action specifically in its relation to independent theoretical investigation. For Arendt's own quandaries with her appeal to this traditional distinction between *vita activa* and *contemplativa*, see Elisabeth Young-Bruehl, *Hannah Arendt: For Love of the World* (New Haven: Yale, 1982), 449-50.

of the volumes *Lebenszeit und Weltzeit* and the posthumous *Beschreibung des Menschen*.[282] My venture here must necessarily be at once more modest and also more independent. What I suggest is that we attend to the implications of modern pacing for human rationality. On the one hand, the fact that human nature is capable of assimilating accelerations in modern pacing, at all levels from the perceptual and cognitive to the more broadly interactional and sociocultural, discloses a dimension of flexibility in human nature that historically remained previously unrevealed. On the other hand, it is clear that there are limits to this assimilation, as Arendt already made clear in the historical-philosophical description of the totalitarian condition discussed at the beginning of this volume.

Short of providing a historical-transcendental deduction of the rational conditions for the stability of pacing in modern culture—a tremendous project which must await (indefinitely!) another time—what can be provided as evidence for the way in which pacing contributes to the dynamic viability of modernity is the exemplification of the sort of intellectual ventures I have considered in this volume. These chapters of appreciation have been offered as witness both to the dynamic pacing of intellectual endeavor within the modern intellectual enterprise and to the attention to the fundamental categories of modern pacing which these enterprises disclose. Their range and breadth exemplifies just those aspects of pacing which I have identified as integral to the modern condition: a conviction of the worth of intense theoretical investigation, carried on with willful acceleration at a high clip. Over and above any insight I have been able to provide into these enterprises, it is the strong fact of their *presence* which provides a first descriptive exemplification of the legitimacy of modernity's pace. Were analogous endeavors to prove unsustainable in the contemporary or future intellectual climate, this in and of itself would count as a strong mark against the intellectual stability of modern pacing. Given that the legitimation of modernity is deeply involved in the promotion of independent intellectual investigation, the stability of pacing of such intellectual pursuit is closely correlated with the stability of modernity's overall pacing, understood as the pacing of the consequent *implications* of independent and systematically conducted theoretical investigation. Here we find the deepest historical significance of ongoing intellectual endeavor in the modern age. It argues at once for intellectual work carried out in the most independent spirit, and yet also for its deep historical relevance to the ongoing project of modernity.

---

282. Hans Blumenberg, *Beschreibung des Menschen,* Aus dem Nachlaß herausgegeben von Manfred Sommer (Frankfurt am Main: Suhrkamp, 2006). The first half book is devoted focally to Husserl.

9

Convexity and Complexity: Trading Places With John Ashbery

> What did matter now was getting down to business, or back to the business of day-to-day living with all the tiresome mechanical problems that this implies. And it was just here that philosophy broke down completely and was of no use. How to deal with the new situations that arise each day in bunches or clusters, and which resist categorization to the point where any rational attempt to deal with them is doomed from the start?
> —John Ashbery, "The System"

READING THE COMPLICATIONS OF A FIGURE

With a consideration of Blumenberg's notion of legitimation now behind us, this chapter presents a preliminary object-lesson in the reading of modernity's pace. My epigraph serves as an antithetical introduction, asserting as boldly as possibly the rights of poetry and "particulars," not just alongside but specifically in the breakdown of philosophical approaches to modern rationality. We should never take a passage from Ashbery's poetry entirely at face value, however.

I begin by placing several passages from Ashbery's *Three Poems* on the table for consideration. In order, Ashbery's three prose poems are "The New Spirit," "The System," and "The Recital." "The New Spirit" ends in a division between the narrative voice of the poem and the absent voice of the "you" to whom the poem is addressed.[283] The voice of the poem orbits around the dark matter of this second voice and "the major question that revolves around you, your being here" (TP, 51). This passage looks ahead to a later passage in "The Recital": "This single source of so much pleasure and pain is therefore a thing that one can never cease wondering upon. On the one hand, such boundless happiness for so many" (TP, 115). Happiness is a concern in all three of these poems, as is its polar opposite: "On the other hand, so much pain concentrated in the heart of one" (TP, 115).

In "The System," interposed between, we find a distinction drawn between a few people who suffer terribly and the rest who don't. This dichotomy between the one and the many runs in tandem with the dichotomy between the one and the you. Each of us is a multitude as well as an isolated individual, a composite as well as a prime number. As individuals, the isolated suffer and grow; the multitude as multitude does not. At the same time, we experience the energy and beauty of the others as a miraculous manna from heaven, our eyes turned inward to the dark matter within. 'One' is associated with suffering and growth, and a negation of both of those with 'many', so that by implication a kind of lightness and fullness is associated with the many without. Throughout the three poems we find passages where the narrator reflexively insists that "this is all happening within." Where is the boundary between inside and outside in this poetic phenomenology? The specter of solipsism crops up towards the end of "The System": "I know too that my solipsistic approach is totally wrongheaded and foolish, that the universe isn't listening to me any more than the sea can be heard inside conch shells" (TP, 94).[284]

The end of "The New Spirit," with which I began, inaugurates an undertaking: "It was obvious that a new journey would have to be undertaken ..." (TP, 51). This journey is " ... perhaps not the last but certainly an unavoidable one, into an area of an easier life" (TP, 51). The stage is set for the dialectic of the one and the many, the inner one which is difficult, the outer many which is easy in some sense, " ... 'where the lemons bloom,' so that the last trials could be administered in an ambience of relaxed understanding" (TP, 51). Despite this ominous atmosphere, you welcome these trials at the beginning of your journey, "an opportunity of definitively clearing your name, but are no less enthusiastic about the carefree, even frivolous atmosphere in which it all takes place ... " (TP, 51). The obsessive dialectical

---

283. Compare Helen Vendler, *Invisible Listeners: Lyric Intimacy in Herbert, Whitman, and Ashbery* (Princeton: Princeton University, 2005).

284. Compare Wittgenstein: "Someone who, dreaming, says "I am dreaming", even if he speaks audibly in doing so, is no more right than if he said in his dream "it is raining", while it was in fact raining. Even if his dream were actually connected with the noise of the rain." *On Certainty*, ed. G. E. M. Anscombe and G. H. von Wright (New York: Harper and Row, 1972), 90e. This is the final remark in Wittgenstein's last extended manuscript.

opposition continues as we approach "the major question that revolves around you, your being here." (TP, 51)

The existential question is not the question of the "I," but of the "you." Of course, this flips back and forth throughout the poem, but the central rotation is about the dark matter of the "you." And in just this regard the major question is the question of "being here," not "being there."[285] But where is "here"? Where are "you"? Ashbery's *Three Poems* is an exercise in trading places.

In the cosmological sense, you are here on earth. A question that revolves around you is a question in a pre-Copernican universe. In a quintessentially modern irony, Kant's conception of his own "Copernican revolution" is a subject-centered maneuver, a maneuver which puts the conditions of our experience first.[286] But the subject at the center of Ashbery's poem is the reader, not the poet, just as one would expect in the sort of environment-poem which Angus Fletcher has identified specifically with an eye to Ashbery. Somehow, the reader and the poet have traded places. Our Copernican revolution has grown complicated in this post-Kantian atmosphere, further so and driven home when we find the major question "again affirmed in the stars" (TP, 51). Ashbery ratchets up the complication of his figure: we have a question which is revolving around you, and now this rotation is affirmed in the stars—the stars which you, in turn, see revolving around, from your vantage here on earth. Ashbery has thrown you back onto the stars:

> And this is again affirmed in the stars: just their presence, mild and unquestioning, is proof that you have got to begin in the way of choosing some one of the forms of answering that question, since if they were not there the question would not exist to be answered, but only as a rhetorical question in the impassive grammar of cosmic unravelings of all kinds, to be proposed, but never formulated. (TP, 51)

The fact that the question is a major question, the question revolving around you, is affirmed by the stars, which are themselves mild and unquestioning. In the absence of the stars, the question would only be rhetorical.

---

285. Robert Penn Warren, *Being Here: Poems 1977-1980* (New York: Random House, 1980).

286. Hans Blumenberg discusses this issue in *The Genesis of the Copernican World* (Cambridge: MIT, 1987), trans. Robert M. Wallace, 611-12. While sympathizing to a point with Russell's characterization of Kant as a Ptolemaic counterrevolutionary, Blumenberg ultimately defends Kant. Blumenberg's charge that Russell was "guided by something he has never read" is at least figurally, and perhaps even literally, accurate, but his defense of Kant's Copernicanism ("Kant, with his rhetorical figure, keeps completely within the framework of the equivalence that Copernicus developed between motions of the outmost sphere and of the Earth" (610) is, to my mind at least, more questionable. I am more sympathetic to the view of Frank Pierobon in *Kant et la fondation architectonique de la métaphysique* (Grenoble: Jérôme Millon, 1990); see esp. 61ff.

Our exercise in reading must pace along Ashbery's labyrinth, make it our own, in unpacking the complications of a rhetorical figure.

A THOUGHT EXPERIMENT

We will find an Ariadne's thread to guide us along our labyrinth in a thought experiment that was originally proposed by Henri Poincaré, which Hans Blumenberg discusses at the beginning of *The Genesis of the Copernican World*:

> A thought experiment that the French mathematician Henri Poincaré suggested at the beginning of this [i.e. twentieth] century has acquired a peculiarly new valence for us. He started from the question whether there would ever have been a Copernicus if our earth were continually surrounded by an impenetrable and always unbroken blanket of clouds. Put another way, the problem ran: would we know that the earth turned on its axis and went around the sun if we had never been able to practice astronomy? Poincaré did not yet know anything of the technical possibilities of piercing even a blanket of clouds of this sort with flying machines and rockets, nor did he know anything of a non-optical astronomy such as has arisen in the form of radio astronomy. How could a mankind located inside an atmospheric cave ever have learned that the earth belongs to a planetary system, and ultimately to a universe made up of worlds and that it moves in this universe in multiple ways? Without the view of the daily rotation of the heaven of the fixed stars, would not any conjecture that was directed against the overwhelming evidence that the ground on which we stand and live is at rest have been impossible?[287]

Poincaré believed that humans would have eventually discovered the motion of the earth, but the unavailability of the fixed stars would have drastically slowed the pace of their investigation. Ashbery has located the major question that revolves around you in a mild and unquestioning astronomical context. What if there were no such context? In fact, toward the end of "The System" you and the narrator switch places again: you are "there" and the narrator is "here," and your role becomes that of a protective cloud cover:

> You are still there, far above me like the polestar and enclosing me like the dome of the heavens; your singularity has become oneness, that is your various traits and distinguishing marks have flattened out into a cloudlike protective covering whose irregularities are all functions of its uniformity, and which constitutes an arbitrary but definitive boundary line between the new informal, almost haphazard way of life that is to be mine permanently and the monolithic sameness of the world that exists to be shut out. (TP, 101-02)

---

287. Hans Blumenberg, *The Genesis of the Copernican World*, trans. Robert M. Wallace (Cambridge: MIT, 1987), 4.

When Parmigianino paints his portrait in a convex mirror, the viewer stares in and sees his own reflection displaced by that of Parmigianino, but a Parmigianino distorted by the convexity of the mirror. Call this the displacement of convexity: indeed, early on in "The System" "an attractive partner" identified as "*the* heaven sent one" is characterized as "the convex one" with whom the individual will who sallies forth "has had the urge to mate all these seasons without realizing it," while we are counseled by Pascal to "stay in our room" (TP, 57). Call this displacement of the astronomical context, anticipated by Pascal's counsel, the displacement of complexity. Then we are dealing with a meta-displacement, a figural analogue of Bloom's metacrossing or Fletcher's hyperlabyrinth: trading a convex displacement for a complex one.

Much later in the volume, Blumenberg returns to Poincaré's thought experiment in a discussion of Averroes' consideration of Plato's allegory of the cave in the *Republic*. In Averroes we find a reduction in "the importance that antiquity ascribed to the intuition of the public phenomenon of the moving heavens."[288] According to Blumenberg, our situation in the cosmos is actually not particularly important for the methodological orientation of pre-modern physics: Ptolemaic and scholastic physics do not take this cosmological context into account in any significant way, precisely because they don't take into account what forces us to come to the conclusion that the earth is moving. Among the scholastics, this diminution of man as *contemplator caeli*

> ... comes out most clearly in Averroes in his reference to Plato's allegory of the cave. Time exists not only for those for whom intuition of the heavens is always possible, but also for those who are blind, or for whom the view of the heavens is blocked.[289]

In Averroes and in Scholasticism, we find a position which is immanent to the perspective of the cave. The allegory of the cave no longer serves primarily to present and to lead one on the path out of the cave, but rather to probe the possibility of life in the cave. Now there is no light shining into the cave from above: the cave scene has become a pivot around which the philosophical status of immanence has been intensified.[290]

The figure from "The Recital" is in a strong sense the opposite of Averroes' picture of life in the cave: there the question is only a real one because of the ultimate reference outward to the fixed stars. But at the end of "The System," this figure has been inverted into one resembling Averroes': you are no longer the center around which the question revolves but the

---

288. Blumenberg, *Genesis*, 472.
289. ibid.
290. Blumenberg's reading of the reception history of Plato's allegory of the cave, including further discussion of Averroes, is given in his final masterwork, *Höhlenausgänge*.

cloud cover whose uniformity blocks out the "monolithic" world which has been rendered irrelevant in the narrator's now haphazard way of life, which seems to inherit its irregularities somehow from the irregular effects of the uniform cloud cover. In effect, you are the cave.

Averroes' allegory of the cave strikes one as an early form of Poincaré's thought experiment with the heavens that are permanently hidden, but without an interest in the revolution of the earth. In elementary reflections of this sort, man's way of possessing the world begins to disconnect itself from intuition. What would it be like to live in a cave, from which there were no exit? We couldn't rely on our intuition, because in this case there is no reflection of our intuition in the condition of the stars. There would be no motivation for us to answer our questions coming from outside, from a larger cosmological context. There is no Platonic "ladder," as we find it in the *Symposium*, which moves us in the direction of our intuition of the forms, no obvious way to get from our condition in the cave "back" to the condition of intuition. Plato insists that there is such a ladder, and with that the Platonic tradition begins. In the Platonic tradition we pursue philosophy to get outside of the cave and see what the sun looks like; then we descend back down. What if we were never in a position to leave the cave; what would philosophy be like then?

It would resemble precisely the tradition which culminates in the disconnection of the scientific worldview from our human experience (you can read Musil's *The Man Without Qualities* as exemplary for this turn). From this perspective the idea that we could find a reflection of our existential condition in the stars is a kind of antiquated philosophical solace; it's a classical sop that we're throwing to ourselves. And it's a sop that Ashbery is throwing, in a way that may or may not be ironic, at the end of this first poem, but which has been drastically retracted by the end of "The System." There it seems almost that the narrator is better off without a capacity to pierce the uniformity of your cloud cover, living haphazardly in the irregularity of his cave.

Given the challenge faced by appeals to intuition in the unique methodological intensification associated with the advent of modernity, it becomes all the more ironic and interesting that the last section of "The New Spirit" can be interpreted in terms of a kind of return to intuition. I have discussed earlier Asbhery's troubling penchant for ending weakly. In *Three Poems*, the third poem "The Recital" is scant by comparison with the other two, and in isolation it is the weakest of the three poems. The most apparent way to read the end of the first poem is as a gesture of reconciliation, and one which also strikes me as terribly weak and unearned (a chalking of this weakness up to simple irony will not help). It may very well be that Ashbery's greatest strength lies in his self-confidence to end weakly. But whether an uncanny self-confidence lies behind it or not, it happens with an unsettling consistency. With Harold Bloom and Paul Bray, we might try to account for this by saying that Ashbery is a romantic.[291]

But turning to the passages in *Three Poems* which elicit the figure of the cave and the exit from the cave provides us with a different view of matters. Directly preceding the figure from the end of "The System" which I've laid out above, we find this:

> If you need a certain vitality, you can only supply it yourself. Or there comes a point anyway when no one's actions but your own seem dramatically convincing and justifiable in the plot that the number of your days concocts. I have been watching this film, therefore, and now I have seen enough. As I leave the theater I am surprised to find it is still daylight outside. The darkness of the film as well as its specks of light were so intense I am forced to squint. In this way I gradually get an idea of where I am. (TP, 105)

This metaphor of watching the film of yourself is the thought-experiment that Wittgenstein engaged in in his refutation of the possibility of a phenomenological language, and there are also resonances with Wittgenstein in other passages of *Three Poems*.[292] But Ashbery's passage continues by undercutting the straightforward sense in which there is an emergence from the filmic cave. In some sense you could now read the emergence from the filmic cave as the emergence from a kind of phenomenological, philosophical condition, one grounded in an appeal to intuition. Only this world, the world into which I emerge, is not as light as the other one! While on exiting the narrator is forced to squint, actually it's the specks of light in the film that are most intense. The world outside of the marquis "is not as light as the other one. It is made gray as with shadows like cobwebs that deepen as the memory of the film begins to fade" (TP, 105-6).

To frame the figure of the filmic cave from the other side, I turn to a passage that steps over the bridge into the second paragraph of "The Recital," which discusses the nastiness of childhood. Literally, this second paragraph begins with the sentence, "That this is true of course is beyond argument." But many Ashbery paragraphs begin in the second sentence, as is the case here.

---

291. Paul Bray, "The Time of Happiness: Tone and Tradition in Ashbery," *Annals of Scholarship* **15** 2-3 29-49.

292. On Wittgenstein's rejection of a phenomenological language, see David G. Stern, *Wittgenstein on Mind and Language* (New York: Oxford University Press, 1995), esp. 136-40. The most overtly "Wittgensteinian" passage in *Three Poems* occurs at 78 in "The System": "... we have only to step forward to be in the right path, we are all walking in it and we always have been, only we never knew it." This motif, of course, extends well beyond Wittgenstein. Compare also Mark Strand, "The Story of Our Lives" in *Selected Poems* (New York: Atheneum: 1980), 97-103.

> But we ought to look into the nature of that childishness a little more, try to figure out where it came from and how, if at all, we can uproot it. And when we first start to examine it, biased as we are, it seems as though we are not entirely to blame. We have all or most of us had unhappy childhoods. Later on we tried to patch things up; as we entered the years of adulthood it was a relief for a while that everything was succeeding. We had finally left that long, suffocating tunnel and emerged into an open place. (TP, 108)

Here is another kind of exit, one which recalls leaving the birth canal. What is this experience of exit? Is there really an exit? It seems better for a while, Ashbery goes on to tell us, but our condition quickly passes over into a retrospective one in which "all our energies are being absorbed by the task of trying to revive those memories, make them real, as if to live again were the only reality …" (TP, 109). Are we then engaged *à la recherche du temps perdu*? Rather I think Ashbery is attempting to uncover, as he does throughout the poem, a condition of oscillation, a back and forth between alternatives, each in isolation appearing utterly unsatisfactory. So far from being a freestanding poem, "The Recital" is an afterimage of the ping-pong match between "The New Spirit" and "The System." In fact, this oscillation is something we must *perform* in reading the poem. Our two figures, the first from the end of "The New Spirit," the other from the end of "The System," together establish a hyper-figure of this oscillation. We oscillate back and forth from the displacement of convexity to the displacement of complexity, trading between traded places.

THE TEMPO OF THINKING

In response to his discussion of Ashbery in *A New Theory For American Poetry*, Angus Fletcher reports that Ashbery said to him, quite simply, "I like the fact that you say I'm meditating." One of the ways in which Ashbery is meditative is that his poems are often about reading. It's extremely difficult to talk about the experience of reading a poem, and in some sense you can't, of course. In some sense there's no substitute for reading the poem. One way to try to address this issue is Fletcher's idea of the environment-poem, in which the reader becomes the subject of the poem. Preparing for a lecture, "Ashbery and the Electronic Subscriber," Fletcher remarked to me, "Somehow I feel like saying, just read the stuff." And that is a point I equally want to insist on. A reading can only be an improvisation.

In his most recent book, Fletcher remarks: "Imagine any great miming: the hysterical drives of impersonation, and hence of acting a part, enhance the prime effect of theater—a lively sense that the story told is a story moving faster than its commentary, moving free of any allegorical gloss."[293]

---

293. Fletcher, *Time, Space and Motion*, 124.

Fletcher identifies this dramatic form of mimetic outpacing as quintessential for The New Poetry. Analogously, we might suggest that the pace specific to modernity is one that outstrips any commentary we would care to provide upon it, so that any such commentary becomes simultaneously a commentary on its own ultimate absence of meaning (it is "retarded"). As Arendt diagnoses in her readings of Nietzsche and Heidegger in *The Life of the Mind*, this absence of meaning is the dark shadow of nihilism, which casts itself across the modern historical continent.

But the absence of meaning and the default of traditional philosophical projects—and here 'traditional' in its modern sense means first and foremost following in the wake of Descartes—are the negative reflection of modernity's dynamic livelihood, its realistic outstripping of any proposed conceptual scheme. Modernity is inevitably out ahead on the road, waiting for you. But who are you?

The tack that I have advocated in this book is a variation on the theme of trading places. Reading is an asymmetric exercise in trading places,[294] for in reading you put yourself in my place. And as Fletcher insists, crucial for the modern cultivation of dramatic mimesis is your peculiar human capacity to do just that, speaking of "a somewhat mysterious capability we humans possess, namely to participate in the other, whether that other be an actual other human, or an idea abstracted from human existence."[295]

This might sound like a call, reactionary at this late hour, for yet another revival of hermeneutics. It is not, because although reading involves understanding, it is not *about* understanding. It *is* about re-presenting, but not in the way usually considered. Rather, it is re-presenting as *performing*: the dimension of individual human activity is most fundamental. In this regard, Gadamer does a massive injustice to the passage from Rilke which he uses as an epigraph for *Truth and Method*.[296] Rilke writes of catching what one has thrown oneself versus catching what has been thrown by "an eternal partner;" in this latter case, catching becomes a "power—/ Not yours, a world's."[297] Understanding is a function of acting, rather than vice versa, and it is so in Rilke's poem. To take this passage as an epigraph to a work on *hermeneutics* makes it sound the other way around. Further, understanding is always, at best, a partial function of action, for action outstrips understanding, and we are always left with the question, "but what is action?" It is only in action that we get down to the business of particulars. In the act of reading, in my solitude, I get down to your business and make it my own. Blumenberg: "It simply cannot be hermeneutics if the

---

294. Thanks to Tess Varner for insisting on this asymmetry.

295. ibid.

296. Hans-Georg Gadamer, *Truth and Method*, trans. edited by Garrett Barden and John Cumming from the 2nd (1965) edition (New York: Crossroad, 1985).

297. Rilke, cited in Gadamer, *Truth and Method*, v.

author must be understood against himself—as against his hermeneuts."²⁹⁸ Fletcher: "The excitement of the lively reader reading is the true definition of treasure."²⁹⁹

For my part, I began this volume with an epigraph from John Ashbery, and it is unlikely that I have done any more justice to it than Gadamer did to his epigraph from Rilke. But I would wish to make amends for one possible lacuna, which is a function of the curtailment of Ashbery's text. After speaking of "the outer rhythm more and more accelerate, past the ideal rhythm of the spheres that seemed to dictate you," and that now "is to be transcended," Ashbery goes on immediately following the ellipsis in his own text to insist that "[t]he pace is softening now, we can see why it had to be." Of this softening pace he continues: "Our older relatives told of this. It happened a long time ago but it had to happen, which is why we are here now telling about it" (TP, 6). It may seem in the absence of this continuation that my epigraph paints a picture unfaithful to the intentions of its original poetic location.

But in placing the epigraph at the beginning of this book, arresting it as I have, I intend the book itself not as a version of the story of this softening pace that "we are here now telling about," but rather as the sort of *quickening* Montaigne promotes in the passage from "Of experience" I have cited already at the start of this volume.³⁰⁰ This ambition follows the traditional admonition to seek "more life into a time without boundaries" (WW, 259), but without Bloom's nostalgias coloring farewell. Addressing the pace of modernity is a first step in redressing the acceleration which such a quickening must displace (/"dis-pace"), extending and revising but not *altogether* incompatible with traditional sources of wisdom.

Thought, like understanding, is a function of action, yet we might think of our various actions as "thought experiments."³⁰¹ An experiment is valuable precisely insofar as it outstrips our understanding: we hope to learn from it. Yet this, too, is only a limited way of coming to grips with the human capacity for action: it files this capacity back into line with the faculty of thinking. As Arendt understood him, Kant thought of judgment as a faculty for bringing thought and action together. Whether or not Kant himself meant so to yoke thought and action under a common faculty, a question we may leave undecided here, to do so would be mistaken. It would fall into the productive but misguided attempt to slacken not just the pace of reading

---

298. *Es muß nicht gleich ›Hermeneutik‹ sein, wenn der Autor gegen ihn selbst verstanden werden muß–wie gegen seine Hermeneuten.* (Blumenberg, LW, 17).

299. Angus Fletcher, Introduction to Robert Louis Stevenson, *Treasure Island* (New York: Barnes and Noble, 2005), xxxix.

300. Montaigne, *Complete Works*, 853, cited in Starobinski, *Montaigne in Motion*, 237.

301. Compare Thomas Kuhn, "A Function for Thought Experiments," in *The Essential Tension: Selected Studies in Scientific Tradition and Change* (Chicago: University of Chicago, 1977), 240-65.

but the pace of human action in general, to bring it back into a premodern (now: postmodern) philosophical fold. Judgments are *acts* of "reading," and the labyrinthine philosophical avoidances of this acknowledgment are blinding.[302] Husserl, 2 August 1917: "Duty demands that I bring to completion and to publication my labors of many years, especially since they provide the scientific foundations for a reconciliation between the naturalistic world-view that dominated the epoch just expired and the teleological world-view. But the teleological world-view is the definitively true one."[303] It is apparently part of the vocation of the philosopher to attempt foreclosure of modernity over and over again.

If modernity is to be distinguished historically by its peculiar dynamism, all such philosophical foreclosures are ultimately misguided, no matter how otherwise productive. Yet equally mistaken are those decisionisms which sever the connection between action and thought. Instead, we should approach our historical condition in terms of its pace. Hans Blumenberg ends *The Legitimacy of the Modern Age* by asserting that "history knows no repetitions of the same; 'renaissances' are its contradiction."[304] What we may seek—and all we may finally seek—in pacing is a dynamic vocabulary which would allow us to push forward our entanglement in the domain of action—human or otherwise.[305]

---

302. Stanley Cavell, "Between Acknowledgment and Avoidance," in *The Claim of Reason*, new edition (New York: Oxford, 1999), 329-496.

303. Cited in John Scanlon's "Forward" to Edmund Husserl, *Ideas Pertaining to a Pure Phenomenology and to a Phenomenological Philosophy*, second book, trans. R. Rojcewicz and A. Schuwer (Dordrecht: Kluwer, 1989), XIX. See Karl Schumann, *Husserl-Chronik: Denk- und Lebensweg Edmund Husserls* (The Hague: Nijhoff, 1977), 212-13. The passage is drawn from a letter to Albrecht. Husserl's own later recognition of such undeserved optimism is recorded in a note of Summer, 1935; see Blumenberg, *Beschreibung des Menschen*, 225.

304. Blumenberg, *Legitimacy*, 596.

305. Ammons, *Garbage*, 54-55.

Bibliography

Ammons, A. R. *Brink Road* (New York: Norton, 1996).
Ammons, A. R. *Garbage* (New York: Norton, 1993).
Ammons, A. R. *Sphere: The Form of a Motion* (New York: Norton, 1974).
Arendt, Hannah, *Between Past and Future* (New York: Penguin, 1977).
Arendt, Hannah, *The Human Condition* (Chicago: University of Chicago, 1958).
Arendt, Hannah, *Lectures on Kant's Political Philosophy*, ed. with an interpretative essay, Ronald Beiner (Chicago: University of Chicago, 1992).
Arendt, Hannah, *The Life of the Mind* (San Diego: Harcourt, 1978).
Arendt, Hannah, *Men in Dark Times* (San Diego: Harcourt Brace Jovanovich, 1968).
Arendt, Hannah, *The Origins of Totalitarianism*, new edition with added prefaces (San Diego: Harvest, 1968).
Ashbery, John, *Flow Chart* (New York: Knopf, 1991).
Ashbery, John, *Other Traditions*, (Cambridge: Harvard, 2000).
Ashbery, John, *Self-Portrait in a Convex Mirror* (Penguin, 1976).
Ashbery, John, *Three Poems* (Penguin, 1977).
Ashbery, John, *Where Shall I Wander* (New York: Harper Collins, 2005).
Auerbach, Erich, *Mimesis: The Representation of Reality in Western Literature*, trans. Willard Trask (Princeton: Princeton, 1953).
Bacon, Francis, *Novum Organum*, trans. and ed. Peter Urbach and John Gibson (Chicago: Open Court, 1994).
Bacon, Francis, *The Works of Francis Bacon*, ed. James Spedding, Robert L. Ellis, and Douglas D. Heath (London: Longman, 1857-74).
Bassler, O. Bradley, "An Enticing (Im)Possibility: Infinitesimals, Differentials, and the Leibnizian Calculus, in *Infinitesimal Differences: Controversies between Leibniz and his Contemporaries*, ed. Ursula Goldenbaum and Douglas Jesseph (Berlin: Walter de Gruyter, 2008), 135-151.
Bertaux, Pierre, *Hölderlin* (Frankfurt am Main: Suhrkamp, 1981).
Bloom, Harold, *Agon: Towards a Theory of Revisionism* (New York: Oxford University, 1982).
Bloom, Harold. *The Anatomy of Influence: Literature as a Way of Life* (New Haven:

Yale, 2011).
Bloom, Harold, *The Anxiety of Influence* (New York: Oxford, 1973).
Bloom, Harold, ed., *Deconstruction and Criticism* (New York: Seabury, 1979).
Bloom, Harold, *A Map of Misreading* (New York: Oxford, 1975).
Bloom, Harold, *Ruin the Sacred Truths: Poetry and Belief from the Bible to the Present* (Cambridge: Harvard, 1989).
Bloom, Harold, *Shakespeare: The Invention of the Human* (New York: Riverhead, 1998).
Bloom, Harold, *Wallace Stevens: The Poems of Our Climate* (Ithaca: Cornell University, 1977).
Bloom, Harold, *The Western Canon: The Books and School of the Ages* (New York: Harcourt Brace & Company, 1994).
Bloom, Harold, *Where Shall Wisdom Be Found?* (New York: Riverhead, 2004).
Bloomer, Jennifer, *Architecture and the Text: The (S)crypts of Joyce and Piranesi* (New Haven: Yale, 1993).
Blumenberg, Hans, *Beschreibung des Menschen*, Aus dem Nachlaß, hrsg. von Manfred Sommer (Frankfurt am Main: Suhrkamp, 2006).
Blumenberg, Hans, *The Genesis of the Copernican World*, trans. Robert Wallace (Cambridge: MIT, 1987).
Blumenberg, Hans, *Lebenszeit und Weltzeit*, 2nd ed. (Frankfurt am Main: Suhrkamp, 1986).
Blumenberg, Hans, *The Legitimacy of the Modern Age*, trans. Robert Wallace (Cambridge: MIT, 1985).
Blumenberg, Hans, *Matthäuspassion* (Frankfurt am Main: Bibliothek Suhrkamp, 1988).
Blumenberg, Hans, *Paradigmen zu einer Metaphorologie*, 2nd ed. (Frankfurt am Main: Suhrkamp, 1999).
Blumenberg, Hans, *Paradigms for a Metaphorology*, trans. with an afterword [sic] Robert Savage (Ithaca: Cornell, 2010).
Blumenberg, Hans, *Shipwreck with Spectator: Paradigms for a Metaphor of Existence*, trans. Stephen Rendall (Cambridge: MIT, 1997).
Blumenberg, Hans, *Die Vollzähligkeit der Sterne* (Frankfurt am Main: Suhrkamp, 1997).
Blumenberg, Hans, *Work on Myth*, trans. Robert Wallace (Cambridge: MIT Press, 1985).
Bohm, D., and Hiley, B.J., *The Undivided Universe: An ontological interpretation of quantum theory* (London: Routledge, 1993).
Bos, H.J.M., "Differentials, Higher-Order Differentials and the Derivative in the Leibnizian Calculus," *Archive for History of Exact Science* **14** 1-90.
Bossy, John, *Giordano Bruno and the Embassy Affair* (New Haven: Yale, 1991).
Bray, Paul, "The Time of Happiness: Tone and Tradition in Ashbery," *Annals of Scholarship* **15** 2-3 29-49.
Brient, Elizabeth, *The Immanence of the Infinite: Hans Blumenberg and the Threshold*

to Modernity (Washington, D.C.: Catholic University, 2002).
Briggs, John, *Francis Bacon and the Rhetoric of Nature* (Cambridge: Harvard University Press, 1989).
Brouwer, L.E.J., *Collected Works* (Amsterdam: North Holland, 1975), 2 vols.
Bruno, Giordano, *The Heroic Frenzies*, trans. Paul Eugene Memmo (Chapel Hill: University of North Carolina, 1964).
Burke, Kenneth, *Language as Symbolic Action: Essays on Life, Literature, and Method* (Berkeley: California, 1966).
Burton, Robert, *The Anatomy of Melancholy*, ed. Floyd Dell and Paul Jordan-Smith (New York: Tudor Publishing, 1927).
Carter, Elliott, *Symphonia: Sum Fluxae Pretium Spei*, recording available on Deutsche Grammophon 459 660-2, liner notes by Bayan Northcott.
Cavell, Stanley, *The Claim of Reason*, new edition (New York: Oxford, 1999).
Colson, F. H. "The Analogist and Anomalist Controversy," *The Classical Quarterly* **13** 1 (January 1919) 24-36.
Connes, Alain, "On the fine structure of spacetime," in *On Space and Time*, ed. Shahn Majid (Cambridge: Cambridge University Press, 2008), 196-237.
Davenport, Guy, "The Dawn in Erewhon," in *Tatlin!* (New York: Charles Scribner's Sons, 1974).
Dedekind, Richard, *Essays on the Theory of Numbers*, trans. Wooster Woodruff Beman (repr. Dover, 1963).
Delumeau, Jean, *Sin and Fear: The Emergence of a Western Guilt Culture 13th- 18th Centuries*, trans. Eric Nicholson (New York: St. Martin's Press, 1990).
Derrida, Jacques, *Of Grammatology*, trans. Gayatry Chakravorty Spivak (Baltimore: Johns Hopkins, 1976).
Dijksterhuis, E. J., *Archimedes*, with a new bibliographic essay by Wilbur R. Knorr (Princeton: Princeton, 1987).
Dupré, Louis, *Passage to Modernity: An Essay in the Hermeneutics of Nature and Culture* (New Haven: Yale University Press, 1993).
Eisenstein, Sergei M., *Immoral Memories: An Autobiography*, trans. Herbert Marshall (Boston: Houghton Mifflin, 1983).
Eisenstein, Sergei M., *Nonindifferent Nature*, trans. Herbert Marshall (Cambridge: Cambridge University Press, 1987).
Eisenstein, Sergei M., *Selected Works*, Volume 2: *Towards a Theory of Montage*, ed. Michael Glenny and Richard Taylor, trans. Michael Glenny (London: British Film Institute, 1991).
Eisenstein, Sergei M., *Selected Works*, Volume 3, ed. Richard Taylor, trans. William Powell (London: British Film Institute, 1996).
Empson, William, *Seven Types of Ambiguity: A Study of its Effects in English Verse*, revised edition (New York: New Directions, 1947).
Empson, William, *The Structure of Complex Words* (Cambridge: Harvard University, 1989).

Field, Hartry. *Truth and the Absence of Fact* (Oxford: Clarendon, 2001).
Fink, Eugen. *Sixth Cartesian Meditation: The Idea of a Transcendental Theory of Method*, with textual notations by Edmund Husserl, tr. Ronald Bruzina (Bloomington: Indiana, 1995).
Finkelstein, David, *Quantum Relativity: A Synthesis of the Ideas of Einstein and Heisenberg* (Berlin: Springer, 1997).
Firewall, Village Broadshow Pictures DVD Video 59410.
Fletcher, Angus, *Allegory: The Theory of a Symbolic Mode* (Ithaca: Cornell, 1964).
Fletcher, Angus, "Allegory Without Ideas," *boundary 2* **33** 1 (2006), 77-98.
Fletcher, Angus, "Basic Definitions of *Threshold* for a Theory of Labyrinths," in Richard Milazzo, ed. *Beauty and Critique* (New York: TSL, 1982), 142-52.
Fletcher, Angus, *Colors of the Mind: Conjectures on Thinking in Literature* (Harvard, 1991).
Fletcher, Angus, "Imagining Earth," *Annals of Scholarship* **19** 1 (2009), 1-20.
Fletcher, Angus, "Introduction," to Robert Louis Stevenson, *Treasure Island* (New York: Barnes and Noble, 2005).
Fletcher, Angus, *A New Theory For American Poetry: Democracy, the Environment, and the Future of the Imagination* (Cambridge: Harvard, 2004).
Fletcher, Angus, *Time, Space and Motion in the Age of Shakespeare* (Cambridge: Harvard, 2007).
Fletcher, Angus, *The Transcendental Masque: An Essay on Milton's* **Comus** (Cornell, 1971).
de Fontenelle, Bernard le Bovier, *Conversations on the Plurality of Worlds*, trans. H.A. Hargreaves (Berkeley: University of California, 1990).
Frye, Northrop, *Anatomy of Criticism*, with a foreword by Harold Bloom (Princeton: Princeton, 2000).
Gadamer, Hans-Georg, *Truth and Method*, trans. edited by Garrett Barden and John Cumming from the 2nd (1965) edition (New York: Crossroad, 1985).
Di Giampaolo, Mario, *Parmigianino* (Florence: Cantini, 1991).
Gordon, John, *Finnegans Wake: A Plot Summary* (Syracuse: Syracuse University Press, 1986).
Grabiner, Judith, *The Origins of Cauchy's Rigorous Calculus* (Cambridge: MIT, 1981).
Hadot, Pierre, *Philosophy as a Way of Life: Spiritual Exercises from Socrates to Foucault*, ed. Arnold Davidson, trans. Michael Chase (Oxford: Blackwell, 1995).
Heidegger, Martin, *Contributions to Philosophy: From Enowning*, trans. Parvis Emad and Kenneth Maly (Bloomington: Indiana University, 1999).
Heidegger, Martin, *An Introduction to Metaphysics*, trans. Ralph Manheim (New Haven: Yale University, 1959).
Heller, Michael, "Where physics meets metaphysics," in *On Space and Time*,

ed. Shahn Majid (Cambridge: Cambridge University Press, 2008), 238-277.
Hersh, Burton, *The Old Boys: The American Elite and the Origins of the CIA* (New York: Charles Scribner's Sons, 1992).
Hollander, John, *Powers of Thirteen* (New York: Atheneum, 1983).
Husserl, Edmund, *Cartesian Meditations, An Introduction to Phenomenology*, tr. Dorion Cairns (The Hague: Martinus Nijhoff, 1960).
Husserl, Edmund, *The Crisis of the European Sciences and Transcendental Phenomenology*, trans. David Carr (Evanston: Northwestern University Press, 1970).
Husserl, Edmund, *Philosophy of Arithmetic: Psychological and Logical Investigations, with supplementary texts from 1887-1901*, trans. Dallas Willard (Dordrecht: Kluwer, 2003).
Jakobson, Roman, *Language in Literature*, ed. Krystyna Pomorska and Stephen Rudy (Cambridge: Harvard University Press, 1987).
Kaiser, G. *Pietismus und Patriotismus im literarischen Deutschland*, 2nd. ed. (Frankfurt: Athenäum, 1973).
Kant, Immanuel, *Critique of Pure Reason*, trans. Werner Pluhar with an introduction by Patricia Kitcher (Hackett, 1996).
Kepes, Gyorgy, ed., *The Nature and Art of Motion* (New York: George Braziller, 1965).
Kierkegaard, Søren, *Stages on Life's Way*, ed. and trans. Howard V. Hong and Edna H. Hong (Princeton: Princeton University, 1988).
Kolakowski, Leszek, *Modernity on Endless Trial* (Chicago: University of Chicago Press, 1990).
Kolakowski, Leszek, *The Presence of Myth*, trans. Adam Czerniawski (Chicago: University of Chicago Press, 1989).
Koyré, Alexandre, *From the Closed World to the Infinite Universe* (Baltimore: Johns Hopkins, 1957).
Krieger, Murray, *Ekphrasis: The Illusion of the Natural Sign* (Baltimore: Johns Hopkins, 1992).
Kuhn, Thomas, "A Function for Thought Experiments," in *The Essential Tension: Selected Studies in Scientific Tradition and Change* (Chicago: University of Chicago, 1977), 240-65.
Kuhn, Thomas, *The Structure of Scientific Revolutions*, 2nd ed. (Chicago: University of Chicago Press, 1970).
Lakatos, Imre, *Mathematics, science and epistemology*, ed. John Worral and Gregory Currie (Cambridge, 1978).
Leibniz, G.W., *De quadratura circuli ellipseos et hyperbolae cujus corollarium est trigonometria sine tabulis*, ed. E. Knobloch (Vandenhoeck & Ruprecht, 1993).
Leibniz, G.W., *quadrature arithmétique du cercle, de l'ellipse et de l'hyperbole*, introduction, trans. and notes Marc Parmentier (Paris: Vrin, 2004).
Locke, John, *An essay concerning human understanding*, ed. Peter H. Nidditch

(Oxford: Clarendon Press, 1979).
Lucretius, *Lucretius on the Nature of Things*, trans. Cyril Bailey (Oxford: Clarendon Press, 1910).
Macksey, Richard, and Donato, Eugene, eds., *The Languages of Criticism and the Sciences of Man: The Structuralist Controversy* (Baltimore: Johns Hopkins, 1970).
Mailer, Norman, *harlot's ghost* (New York: Random House, 1991).
Mahnke, Dietrich, "Die Entstehung des Funktionsbegriffes," *Kantstudien* 31 (1926), 426-28.
Mancosu, Paolo. *Philosophy of Mathematics and Mathematical Practice in the Seventeenth Century* (New York: Oxford, 1996).
Musil, Robert, *The Man Without Qualities*, trans. Sophie Wilkins and Burton Pike (New York: Alfred A. Knopf, 1995).
Nietzsche, Friedrich, *The Gay Science*, trans. Walter Kaufmann (New York: Vintage, 1974).
Peirce, C. S., *Pragmatism as a Principle and Method of Right Thinking: the 1903 Havard Lectures on Pragmatism*, ed. Patricia Ann Turisi (Albany: State University of New York, 1997).
Penrose, Roger, *The Road to Reality* (London: Jonathan Cape, 2004).
Pérez-Ramos, Antonio, "Bacon's forms and the maker's knowledge tradition," in *The Cambridge Companion To Francis Bacon*, 99-120.
Pérez-Ramos, Antonio, *Francis Bacon's Idea of Science and the Maker's Knowledge Tradition* (Oxford: Oxford University Press, 1988).
Pierobon, Frank, *Kant et la fondation architectonique de la métaphysique* (Grenoble: Jérome Millon, 1990).
Plato, *Symposium*, trans. Michael Joyce, in Plato, *The Collected Dialogues*, ed. Edith Hamilton and Huntington Cairns (Princeton: Bollingen, 1961).
Poe, Edgar Allan, *Poetry, Tales, & Selected Essays* (New York: Library of America College Edition, 1996).
Pope-Hennessy, John, *The Portrait in the Renaissance* (New York, 1966).
Rivers, Larry, with Brightman, Carol, *Drawings and Digressions*, with a foreword by John Ashbery (New York: Clarkson N. Potter, 1979).
Robinson, Abraham, *Non-standard Analysis* 2nd ed. (Princeton: Princeton, 1996).
Rossi, Paolo, *Philosophy, Technology and the Arts in the Early Modern Era*, trans. Salvator Attanasio, ed. Benjamin Nelson (New York: Harper & Row, 1970).
Ryan, Lawrence J., *Hölderlins Lehre vom Wechsel der Töne* (Stuttgart: W. Kohlhammer, 1960).
Scanlon, John, "Forward," to Edmund Husserl, *Ideas Pertaining to a Pure Phenomenology and to a Phenomenological Philosophy*, second book, trans. R. Rojcewicz and A. Schuwer (Dordrecht: Kluwer, 1989).
Schumann, Karl, *Husserl-Chronik: Denk- und Lebensweg Edmund Husserls* (The

Hague: Nijhoff, 1977).
Shelley, Percy Bysshe, *Shelley's Poetry and Prose*, ed. Donald H. Reiman and Sharon B. Powers (New York: Norton, 1977).
Spitzer, Leo, *Classical and Christian Ideas of World Harmony: Prolegomena to an Interpretation of the Word "Stimmung"*, ed. Anna Granville Hatcher (Baltimore: Johns Hopkins, 1963), reprinted from *Traditio* **2** (1944): 409-64 and **3** (1945): 307-64.
Starobinski, Jean, *Action and Reaction: The Life and Adventures of a Couple*, trans. Sophie Hawkes (New York: Zone, 2003).
Starobinski, Jean, *Montaigne in Motion*, trans. Arthur Goldhammer (Chicago: Chicago, 1985).
Stern, David G., *Wittgenstein on Mind and Language* (New York: Oxford University Press, 1995).
Strand, Mark, *Selected Poems* (New York: Atheneum: 1980).
Toporov, Vladimir N., "Die Ursprünge der indoeuropäischen Poetik," trans. Peter L. W. Koch (from the original Russian), *Poetica* **13** 3-4 189-251.
Trimpi, Wesley, "Horace's 'Ut Pictura Poesis': The Argument for Stylistic Decorum," *Traditio* **34** (1978), 29-73.
Trimpi, Wesley, "The Meaning of Horace's Ut Pictura Poesis," JWCI **36** (1973), 1-34.
Trimpi, Wesley, *Muses of One Mind: The Literary Analysis of Experience and Its Continuity* (Princeton, 1983).
Valéry, Paul, « Mon Faust», in *Œuvres* (Paris: Gallimard, Bibliothéque de la Pléiade, 1960), II, 302).
Valéry, Paul, "My Faust," in Valéry, Paul, *Plays*, trans. David Paul and Robert Fitzgerald, Volume III of the *Collected Works of Paul Valéry* and Volume XLV in the Bollingen Series (New York: Bollingen, 1960).
Vendler, Helen, *Invisible Listeners: Lyric Intimacy in Herbert, Whitman, and Ashbery* (Princeton: Princeton University, 2005).
Venturi, Robert, *Complexity and Contradiction in Architecture*, 2nd ed., with an introduction by Vincent Scully (New York: The Museum of Modern Art, 1966, 1977).
Venturi, Robert; Brown, Denise Scott; Izenour, Steven, *Learning from Las Vegas*, revised edition (Cambridge: MIT, 1972, 1977).
Veyne, Paul, *René Char en ses Poèmes* (Paris: Gallimard, 1990).
Vico, Giambattista, *New Science*, trans. David Marsh (London: Penguin, 1999).
Walser, Jürg Peter, *Hölderlins Archipelagus* (Zürich: Atlantis, 1962).
Warren, Robert Penn, *Being Here: Poems 1977-1980* (New York: Random House, 1980).
Warren, Robert Penn, *The Collected Poems of Robert Penn Warren*, ed. John Burt, with a forward by Harold Bloom (Baton Rouge: LSU, 1998).
Warren, Robert Penn, *Democracy & Poetry* (Cambridge: Harvard, 1975).

Weinberger, Eliot, "James Jesus Angleton 1917-1987," in *Outside Stories: Essays by Eliot Weinberger* (New York: New Directions), 51-55.

Wittgenstein, Ludwig, *On Certainty*, ed. G.E.M. Anscombe and G.H. von Wright (New York: Harper Torchbooks, 1972).

Young-Bruehl, Elisabeth, *Hannah Arendt: For Love of the World* (New Haven: Yale, 1982).

Zilsel, Edgar, "The Genesis of the Concept of Scientific Progress," *Journal of the History of Ideas* (1945) VI 3.

Zukofsky, Louis, "Welcome to the Gas Age," in *Prepositions: The Collected Critical Essays of Louis Zukofsky*, expanded edition (Berkeley: University of California, 1981).

www.ingramcontent.com/pod-product-compliance
Lightning Source LLC
Chambersburg PA
CBHW030107170426
43198CB00009B/532